DISCLAIMER: This publication contains the opinions and ideas of its author. The advice contained herein is for informational purposes only. Please consult your medical professional before beginning any diet or exercise program. Every effort has been made to ensure the information contained in this book is complete and accurate.

ISBN: 978-0-578-51666-0
Printed in the United States of America

Photo Credits:
Cover photo from Creative Market
p. 4 Amy Shamblen
pp. 6, 9, 11, 14, 20, 30, 32, 33, 52, 72, 238, 254, 259, 270 Marie Maroun
p. 19 Ludmilla
p. 28 Carla Coulson
p. 43 and back cover Tim Mooney
p. 48 Marie Maroun and Patrick Onofre
All others by Kimberly Wilson

p. 36 illustration by Mary Catherine Starr

Layout design by Christy Jenkins • seewhydesignworks.com

Tranquility du Jour Daybook

A LIFE AND DAY PLANNER

Kimberly Wilson

THIS *DAYBOOK* IS DEDICATED TO THOSE OF YOU WHO HAVE SUPPORTED THIS PROJECT SINCE 2012 AND CONTINUE TO CHEER ON NEW EDITIONS.

THIS IS FOR YOU!

Tranquility du Jour Daybook

TABLE OF CONTENTS

PART I: LIFE PLANNING

PART II: DAY PLANNING

PART III: DREAMING

bonjour

"HOW WE SPEND OUR DAYS IS, OF COURSE, HOW WE SPEND OUR LIVES."
—ANNIE DILLARD

As a long-time lover of paper planning, I set out to blend function and style by releasing the first colorful Tranquility du Jour Daybook *in 2012. Chock-full of tips, tools, and checklists for living with productivity and tranquility, inside this edition you'll find four seasonal layouts, 12 monthly layouts, 60 weekly layouts, invitations to pause, lists to complete, plant-based recipes, and more.*

PLAN YOUR YEAR

Start anytime and use this dateless *Daybook* to guide you through a calendar year with weekly reminders to reflect and dream. Explore the tools and lists in Part I. Note what piques your curiosity. Begin by completing a Seasonal Life Review and capturing your Year's Dreams.

SEASONALLY

At the start of a new season, fill out the Seasonal Life Review and notice which areas need attention. List a few action steps to increase your level of satisfaction in them and honor yourself for those that feel satisfactory or better!

MONTHLY

Each month pen your Month's Dreams (what you want to manifest) and Month's Review (how it unfolded). Acknowledge all the dreams you completed, transfer any remaining dreams that still resonate but weren't completed, and let the others go. Follow the moon's four phases—new, waxing, full, waning—and use the prompts to stay in touch with them. Consider and check off the monthly Tranquility Tools to infuse into your weeks. Cheers to entertaining, volunteering, and reading two books.

WEEKLY

To stay connected to your intentions, set aside one hour each week to plan. Note all the completed to-dos and experiences from the week before. Kudos! Move over any important to-dos remaining. Fill in your projects by categorizing them (e.g., work, home, side hustle, community) and listing their associated needs (e.g., complete review, organize closet, create event page, volunteer at animal shelter). Review your schedule to account for energy and time management; adjust as needed. Set your week's intention and note one thing you're grateful for. Clarify your Most Important Tasks. Use the wellness planning to list your desired exercise and meal planning or to track your exercise and food intake. Engage in and check off the weekly Tranquility Tools. Let's clear clutter, pen a love note, and go on an Artist Date.

DAILY

Review your weekly layout at the start of the day, mid-day, and at the end of the day to prepare for tomorrow. When possible, set your days with restorative routines such as journaling, AM and PM rituals, and mindful movement. Review and check off the daily Tranquility Tools for more inspiration. Take a few minutes each day to savor and exhale.

#TDJDAYBOOK

KIMBERLYWILSON.COM

MAKE IT YOUR OWN

Or scrap the whole system and make it entirely your own. Pick it up when you crave a reset and wish to reflect and dream. Doodle. Chop off the binding at your local print shop and turn it into a pink or gold spiral bound book. Personalize it with ephemera, colored markers, washi tape, and your deepest desires.

My vision for this pink planner is for it to serve as a catch-all for your dreams, days' events, and deepest thoughts. Pen your plans, explore new tools, and check the boxes (so fulfilling!). Join the private *Tranquility du Jour Daybook* Facebook group to connect with like-hearted planners. Grab an assortment of bonuses at kimberlywilson.com/daybookbonus. May this be a year filled with tranquility!

bisous,
Kimberly

weekly guide

BRING PRODUCTIVITY AND TRANQUILITY INTO YOUR DAYS BY INCORPORATING THESE 10 SUGGESTED INGREDIENTS. MIX TOGETHER WITH AWARENESS AND SELF-COMPASSION FOR A NOURISHING WEEK.

1. INSERT DATE
2. SET YOUR WEEK'S INTENTION
3. WEEKLY TRANQUILITY TOOLS
4. LIST WEEK'S MOST IMPORTANT TASKS
5. TRACK EATING HABITS, PLAN MEALS, SCHEDULE EXERCISE
6. PEN YOUR GRATITUDE LIST
7. LIST YOUR DAY'S APPOINTMENTS
8. LIST YOUR DAY'S TO-DOS
9. LIST YOUR WEEK'S PROJECTS
10. DAILY TRANQUILITY TOOLS

2 INTENTION:

3 **weekly checklist**

- PLAN WEEK'S MITS
- SOAK IN THE TUB
- TAKE A DIGITAL DAY OFF
- CLEAR CLUTTER
- PEN A LOVE NOTE
- BUY/PICK FRESH FLOWERS
- TAKE AN ARTIST DATE
- SAVOR A GREEN JUICE
- ____

4 **MITs**

5 **wellness planning**

M ____
T ____
W ____
TH ____
F ____
S ____
S ____

6 GRATITUDE:

1 MONDAY ____ | TUESDAY ____ | WEDNESDAY ____

7 8 9 10 11 12 1 2 3 4 5 6 7 8 9 (7)

(8) (9)

daily checklist (10)

- MORNING RITUAL
- DAILY DRESS-UP
- MINDFUL MOVEMENT
- EAT YOUR VEGGIES
- JOURNAL
- GOAL REVIEW
- GRATITUDE
- EVENING RITUAL
- ____

everyday tranquility

SIP hot water with lemon.

Spend a few minutes in MEDITATION.

MOVE YOUR BODY through yoga, walks, dance, and more.

Enjoy a GREEN SMOOTHIE or juice plus plant-based whole foods.

Write in a JOURNAL to clarify your thoughts.

REVIEW YOUR *DAYBOOK* and note the week's intention and MITs plus month's and year's dreams.

Savor a pot of GREEN TEA and nibble a square of DARK CHOCOLATE.

Create a CAPSULE WARDROBE and layer in clothing that feels luxurious on your skin.

SPRITZ PERFUME and diffuse lavender.

Read books and LISTEN TO MUSIC and podcasts that inspire.

PRACTICE GRATITUDE.

MAKE SOMEONE'S DAY with a simple "I appreciate you" text or smile.

TRACK your energy, time, and money habits.

DECLUTTER your mind, home, and digital environments.

BATCH TASKS by categories and hats you wear.

ESTABLISH ROUTINES and healthy habits.

MAKE A DIFFERENCE as a volunteer, donor, and awareness-raiser.

Practice mindful SELF-COMPASSION and treat yourself as you would a dear friend.

Surround yourself with BEAUTIFUL THINGS such as flowers, art, plants, and twinkle lights.

Be a LIFELONG LEARNER and study what makes your heart sing.

FOREST BATHE and soak up the natural world.

Be a FLÂNEUR (A PASSIONATE WANDERER) to clear your mind and get those steps.

When triggered, take 10 DEEP BREATHS.

Make SLEEP a priority.

PRACTICE STOP: Stop, Take a breath, Observe what's happening, Proceed with awareness.

After a long day, put your LEGS UP THE WALL and exhale.

When in doubt, TAKE A NAP.

manifesto

I BELIEVE IN HANDWRITTEN NOTES. I BELIEVE IN EQUALITY FOR ALL. I BELIEVE IN USING CHINA AT EVERY MEAL. I BELIEVE ANIMALS ARE TO BE LOVED AND PROTECTED. I BELIEVE IN THE HEALING POWER OF BUBBLE BATHS, GREEN TEA, AND FRESH FLOWERS. I BELIEVE WE'RE NEVER TOO OLD TO BE BALLERINAS OR WEAR A TUTU. I BELIEVE PARIS IS A DELIGHT TO THE SENSES. I BELIEVE IN STARGAZING AND OBSERVING THE MOON'S PHASES. I BELIEVE THAT COMPASSION IS THE NEW BLACK. I BELIEVE IN EATING PLANTS. I BELIEVE IN LIVING LIFE FULL OUT. I BELIEVE NATURE HEALS. I BELIEVE THAT YOGA AND WRITING ARE TOOLS FOR DISCOVERY. I BELIEVE WOMEN CAN CHANGE THE WORLD. I BELIEVE IN DONNING NOIR AND LIVING PINK. I BELIEVE PILES OF BOOKS SPARK JOY. I BELIEVE IN THE EASE OF A CAPSULE WARDROBE. I BELIEVE IN LIGHTING CANDLES EVERY DAY. I BELIEVE IN USING PAINT, COLLAGE, AND WASHI TAPE TO AWAKEN OUR INNER ARTIST. I BELIEVE IN TWINKLE LIGHTS YEAR-ROUND. I BELIEVE IN SEEKING BALANCE BETWEEN DOING AND BEING. I BELIEVE WE HAVE A RESPONSIBILITY TO MAKE A DIFFERENCE. I BELIEVE IN HAPPINESS AND FREEDOM FOR ALL BEINGS.

tranquility du jour tenets

Tranquility du Jour *offers a space to explore living fully and intentionally. From the humble beginnings of a blog in 2004, we've grown into a sweet global community of like-hearted dreamers on a path to infuse more tranquility into our lives.* Below are the six principles of living the *Tranquility du Jour* lifestyle.

1 **COMPASSION:** Through our daily choices, we alleviate the suffering of all beings, including furry, scaled, and feathered ones. We treat others as we want to be treated. We honor the environment by reducing what we consume, reusing materials, and recycling.

2 **CREATIVITY:** We connect with our creative spark and let it shine through art, crafts, writing, brainstorming, or living out loud. We see most activities as a way to express our creativity and refuel our creative well regularly through reading, taking classes, and practicing. Our life is art.

3 **STYLE + BEAUTY:** We believe that how we present ourselves to and experience the world affects how we feel. We choose a signature style that is personal and reflects who we are. Our homes and offices are designed to nurture our spirits. We are moved by the arts, flowers, and simple pleasures.

4 **MINDFULNESS:** We bring awareness to our thoughts, feelings, and bodily sensations in a nurturing way. Through practices such as meditation and yoga, we connect with our minds and bodies. We value the present moment and encourage our mind to return to it when we find ourselves ruminating about a past situation or fretting about a future event.

5 **SELF-CARE:** The act of nourishing ourselves is akin to breathing. Reflecting through journaling, setting morning and evening rituals, eating plants, and moving our bodies help us stay in balance. We are lifelong learners and enjoy designing and following our dreams. We create meaningful community through healthy relationships, clear communication, and good boundaries.

6 **WELLNESS:** We intentionally choose how to spend our time, energy, and money to reflect our values. Since what we consume affects our mental health, we fuel ourselves with whole foods, inspiring multimedia, and enlightening events. We evaluate and adjust our thoughts and behaviors to align with our version of optimum health through regular Seasonal Life Reviews.

LADUREE

tranquility tools

32 TOOLS TO ENHANCE YOUR DAYS, WEEKS, MONTHS, AND SEASONS WITH TRANQUILITY

Tranquility Tools are daily, weekly, monthly, and seasonal practices to help align everyday activities with aspirations. Each is defined below. They serve as anchors to infuse the year with tranquility. These tools are listed throughout as reminders, along with a blank line for personalization.

8 DAILY TRANQUILITY TOOLS

1 MORNING RITUAL: Greet your day with a yoga sun salutation, cuppa tea, or brisk walk with your beloved four-legged friend. Begin each morning with an intentional, tranquil tone.

2 DAILY DRESS-UP: Let your daily dress reflect your personality, lifestyle, and signature style. Add a dose of flair and don't forget your smile, good attitude, and vintage accessory.

3 MINDFUL MOVEMENT: Take a moment each day to move your body through dance, walking, or any other activity that makes your skin glisten. Bookend the experience with a dose of meditation by sitting still and connecting to your breath. Inhale, exhale, ommmm.

4 EAT YOUR VEGGIES: Reduce animal products and processed foods. Increase plant-based consumption for a joyful effect on your health, the animals, and the planet.

5 JOURNAL: Spend a few moments penning your thoughts, noting highlights from your day, recurring dreams, what you consumed, how you're feeling, or anything else on your mind.

6 **GOAL REVIEW:** Read over your Month's Dreams each day. This helps those everyday decisions stay in alignment with your aspirations.

7 **GRATITUDE:** At the end of each day, note at least one thing for which you are grateful. It may be as simple as a warm bed or fresh water.

8 **EVENING RITUAL:** End your day with reflection. Write in your journal, shut down your computer and smartphone, take a warm bath with Epsom salts, or read in bed for 30 minutes before lights out.

8 WEEKLY TRANQUILITY TOOLS

1 **PLAN WEEK'S MITS:** These are your most important tasks. Choose three to five projects to focus on each week and align your daily actions with bringing them to fruition. They are your week's road map.

2 **SOAK IN THE TUB:** This grounding practice helps clear the mind after a long day. Light candles, play music, or bring in a flute of your favorite libation. Allow yourself to melt into this sensual renewal practice.

3 **TAKE A DIGITAL DAY OFF:** Grant yourself a sabbatical from being glued to technology. Get your hands dirty in the garden, bake a pie, read a book, connect with a loved one, or collage in your art journal. Our connection to technology needs the off switch from time to time.

4 **CLEAR CLUTTER:** Piles of paperwork become mountains when not handled regularly. Take time each week to reduce the clutter around you. Watch yourself breathe easier and feel lighter.

5 **PEN A LOVE NOTE:** Reach out to a friend, family member, pen pal, or even yourself (a letter to your past or future self) with a thoughtful note. Let someone know you're thinking of them and sending good thoughts. Insert a bag of tea,

article of interest, or token of love. This sweet gesture goes a long way in our fast-paced society.

6 **BUY OR PICK FRESH FLOWERS:** Surround yourself with a pop of living color through potted plants, cut flowers, herbs, or bamboo stalks. If you have a garden, pick flowers and bring them into your living space to spruce up a barren bedside table.

7 **TAKE AN ARTIST DATE:** Julia Cameron, author of *The Artist's Way*, encourages a solo excursion to nurture your inner artist for one hour each week. Try a trip to a flower market, café, museum, bookstore, or art gallery and watch your ideas flourish.

8 **SAVOR A GREEN JUICE:** Infuse your body with healing nutrients found in a green juice. Watch your energy and vitality soar as you get a "direct shot of vitamins, minerals, enzymes, protein, and oxygen" per Kris Carr, author of *Crazy Sexy Diet*.

8 MONTHLY TRANQUILITY TOOLS

1 **CRAFT MONTH'S DREAMS:** At the start of each month, write the big dreams you'd like to achieve. At the end of the month, review your list to give yourself a pat on the back for the items you accomplished, and carry over the ones that remain and still feel close to your heart.

2 **MANI/PEDI:** Nurture your nails by adding color, trimming your cuticles, and savoring an exfoliating footbath. Or, indulge in another form of well-deserved self-care.

3 **VOLUNTEER:** Give some of your resources—time, money, or energy—to a favorite cause and watch how you can have a ripple effect on others and your own well-being.

4. **ENTERTAIN:** Invite a friend over for tea or host an intimate dinner fête. Don an apron, set the table, light candles, and channel your inner Martha Stewart.

5. **REVIEW YOUR BUDGET:** Spend less than you make, save a little, and donate, too. Set up a system for regular review. It doesn't have to be fancy; pen and paper with a pile of receipts will work. Try the monthly budget review and the weekly spending chart (pp. 50-51). Or, go high tech with mint.com.

6. **READ TWO BOOKS:** To continually learn, grow, and expand your horizons, read and finish two books monthly. Watch your awareness grow.

7. **CREATE:** Bring something new into existence. Think intangible such as an idea or physical such as origami. Knit a scarf, make a banner, craft a meal, write blog posts, sew a dress, or paint a watercolor postcard.

8. **MASSAGE:** Massage has many benefits and is an antidote to stressed, achy muscles. If a spa isn't in the cards, consider a neck or foot rub at your neighborhood nail salon, or check out the local massage school for good deals from therapists-in-training. Or, ask your beloved for a complimentary rub down.

8 SEASONAL TRANQUILITY TOOLS

1. **DO THE SEASONAL LIFE REVIEW:** Seasonally reflect on areas of your life such as work, style, creativity, dreams, home, self-care, spirituality, health, relationships, finances, etc. Rate each one with your level of satisfaction (10=bliss, 5=so-so, 0=boo). Review the areas that ranked lower than you'd like and pen three action steps to increase your satisfaction in them (pp. 55, 105, 155, and 205).

2. **DEEP CLEAN:** Pull everything out of drawers, cupboards, closets, nooks, and crannies. Donate what no longer serves you, dust off what does, rotate seasonal wear, and put things back in their place with a renewed sense of order.

3 **PRACTICE ESSENTIALISM:** Review your life, personal and professional. Are you excited by what you see? Do plans make you feel drained? Have you signed up for that one thing too many? What small shifts can you make to bring your day back into balance? Surrender the glorification of busy. Carve out time to savor.

4 **TAKE A BED DAY:** Create a few hours to an entire day for a rejuvenating day in bed. Gather your tools: candles, eye pillow, tea, water, books, journal, rose water spray, comfy clothes, soft linens, a chunky knit blanket. Anything that soothes. Begin with a luxurious soak in the tub. Add a splash of sweet almond oil and a few drops of lavender oil. Then saunter into your quiet space to rest and reset.

5 **TRY SOMETHING NEW:** Take up a new hobby, make vegan cheese, study a new language, pick up the guitar, join a writing group, take a modern dance class. Studies show that lifelong learning is directly tied to health and longevity.

6 **TEND YOUR GARDEN:** Seasonally it's good to pull weeds, repot plants, rake leaves, plant bulbs, and trim trees, even if you don't have a garden. Metaphorically, what would you like to plant, trim, repot, and clean up in your life? Observe what needs tending and do so with care.

7 **REARRANGE:** An important principle of Feng Shui (a Chinese philosophical system of harmonizing the environment) is that if you're feeling stuck, do some rearranging. Switch furniture, books, lamps, or art to create a fresh feeling in your surroundings.

8 **GET CULTURED:** Travel, head out for live music, watch your nearest ballet ensemble, read the classics (hello Jane Austen), get to know the Impressionists, try new-to-you cuisine, watch a Broadway musical, check out an exhibit, listen to classical music, or visit a winery or tea salon for a tasting.

everyday activism

FOLLOW ISSUES YOU'RE PASSIONATE ABOUT. REDUCE. REUSE. RECYCLE. SIGN PETITIONS. ADOPT, DON'T SHOP. TREAT OTHERS WITH KINDNESS. SUPPORT SMALL BUSINESS AND SLOW FASHION. VISIT AN ANIMAL SANCTUARY OR SHELTER TO SPREAD LOVE. VOLUNTEER. DONATE. START A WOMEN'S GROUP. MARCH. BUY CRUELTY-FREE PRODUCTS. REACH OUT TO YOUR REPRESENTATIVES. BE AN ETHICAL CONSUMER AND BOYCOTT COMPANIES WHOSE PRACTICES DON'T ALIGN WITH YOUR VALUES. VOTE. SPONSOR AN ORANGUTAN, FARMED ANIMAL, COMPANION ANIMAL, OR OTHER VULNERABLE BEING THROUGH A SANCTUARY, SHELTER, OR RESCUE. SUPPORT NON-PROFITS DOING WORK YOU LOVE. BE AN ENGAGED COMMUNITY MEMBER. REFLECT ON YOUR ACTIONS. MAKE SMALL CHANGES. VISIT THE FARMERS' MARKET. TOTE YOUR REUSABLE BAG, FORK, TEA THERMOS, AND WATER BOTTLE. SKIP PLASTIC STRAWS. STAY INFORMED. SHOP SECONDHAND AND VINTAGE. HOST A CHARITEA EVENT. CONSUME LESS ANIMAL PRODUCTS. SMILE AT STRANGERS.

bucket list

DOODLE, LIST, COLLAGE, OR WRITE WHAT YOU'D LIKE TO MANIFEST IN YOUR LIFETIME.

write a letter to your future self

Picture yourself a year from today having accomplished or having taken steps toward accomplishing your Year's Dreams. How do you feel? Where are you? What are you doing? What are you eating? Who are you with? What are you wearing?

Pen yourself a letter to open a year from now and write it in the present tense. For example, "I'm so glad you made self-care a priority this year. You are now sleeping through the night, eating more whole foods, and doing yoga three times a week." Keep going. Bring those micromovements to life here and dream about how life will look once you make yourself and your goals a priority.

INSTRUCTIONS: Write your letter on favorite stationery and date it a year from today. Seal it in an envelope and stick it onto A Letter To My Future Self (p. 258) using decorative washi tape.

seasonal aspirations

AFTER COMPLETING YOUR SEASONAL LIFE REVIEW, ADD YOUR SEASONAL WISHES INSIDE EACH BOX.

WINTER

SPRING

SUMMER

FALL

year's layout

JANUARY

FEBRUARY

MARCH

APRIL

MAY

JUNE

DOODLE, LIST, COLLAGE, OR WRITE DATES TO REMEMBER SUCH AS BIRTHDAYS, PLANS, IDEAS, EVENTS, OR ANYTHING ELSE OF NOTE FOR YOUR YEAR.

JULY

AUGUST

SEPTEMBER

OCTOBER

NOVEMBER

DECEMBER

year's dreams

DOODLE, LIST, COLLAGE, OR WRITE WHAT YOU'D LIKE TO MANIFEST THIS YEAR.

MY WORD/THEME OF THE YEAR IS:

24 BOOKS TO READ THIS YEAR

1. ______
2. ______
3. ______
4. ______
5. ______
6. ______
7. ______
8. ______
9. ______
10. ______
11. ______
12. ______
13. ______
14. ______
15. ______
16. ______
17. ______
18. ______
19. ______
20. ______
21. ______
22. ______
23. ______
24. ______

10 PLACES TO VISIT THIS YEAR

1. ______________________
2. ______________________
3. ______________________
4. ______________________
5. ______________________
6. ______________________
7. ______________________
8. ______________________
9. ______________________
10. ______________________

30 THINGS TO EXPERIENCE THIS YEAR

1. ______________
2. ______________
3. ______________
4. ______________
5. ______________
6. ______________
7. ______________
8. ______________
9. ______________
10. ______________
11. ______________
12. ______________
13. ______________
14. ______________
15. ______________
16. ______________
17. ______________
18. ______________
19. ______________
20. ______________
21. ______________
22. ______________
23. ______________
24. ______________
25. ______________
26. ______________
27. ______________
28. ______________
29. ______________
30. ______________

STOP + START LIST

WHAT I WANT MORE OF AND LESS OF THIS YEAR.

START

1. ______________________
2. ______________________
3. ______________________
4. ______________________
5. ______________________
6. ______________________
7. ______________________
8. ______________________
9. ______________________
10. ______________________
11. ______________________
12. ______________________
13. ______________________
14. ______________________
15. ______________________

STOP

1. ______________________
2. ______________________
3. ______________________
4. ______________________
5. ______________________
6. ______________________
7. ______________________
8. ______________________
9. ______________________
10. ______________________
11. ______________________
12. ______________________
13. ______________________
14. ______________________
15. ______________________

GRATITUDE

ONE THING I'M GRATEFUL FOR EACH WEEK.

1. ______
2. ______
3. ______
4. ______
5. ______
6. ______
7. ______
8. ______
9. ______
10. ______
11. ______
12. ______
13. ______
14. ______
15. ______
16. ______
17. ______
18. ______
19. ______
20. ______
21. ______
22. ______
23. ______
24. ______
25. ______
26. ______
27. ______
28. ______
29. ______
30. ______
31. ______
32. ______
33. ______
34. ______
35. ______
36. ______
37. ______
38. ______
39. ______
40. ______
41. ______
42. ______
43. ______
44. ______
45. ______
46. ______
47. ______
48. ______
49. ______
50. ______
51. ______
52. ______

journaling

"JOURNAL WRITING IS A VOYAGE TO THE INTERIOR."
—CHRISTINA BALDWIN

WHAT IS JOURNALING?

The process of exploring thoughts and feelings on paper or the computer. It's a tool to help explore and better understand patterns, motivations, fears, and struggles. It's also a safe space to capture dreams, to celebrate, and to grow.

WHY IS IT BENEFICIAL?

Journaling can help strengthen immune cells, solve problems, clarify thoughts and feelings, better understand self and others, and reduce stress. It also serves as a safe space to brainstorm and muse.

HOW TO DO IT

Grab a pen and paper or pull out your computer. Let your thoughts flow.

PROMPTS

1. Turning to a journal entry from a year or more ago, what do I notice has changed and what has stayed the same?
2. I can experience a greater sense of meaning and love in my life by . . .
3. What is one thing I want to do, but haven't yet? What has prevented me from doing it?
4. If money wasn't an issue, how would I spend my time?
5. In sensory detail, my ideal day would be . . .
6. 10 things I want to do in my lifetime are . . .
7. What do I need to let go of to make space for something new?
8. If I write about a current challenge in first person ("I"), then in third person ("she/he"), what do I notice?
9. What excuses keep me stuck?
10. What can I do to increase balance in my life right now?
11. Make lists: strengths, favorite memories, worries, stories to write, today's accomplishments, wishes, books to read, DIY projects, habits to track, things I love.
12. At this moment I'm feeling and noticing . . .
13. What would I write in an unsent letter to someone who's hurt me, whom I've hurt, or who's no longer in my life?
14. Am I where I want to be in my life right now? If not, what can I change?
15. Thinking back on defining moments in my life—a phone call, a kiss, a job offer, a betrayal—what do those moments mean to me now?

mindfulness

"YOU ARE THE SKY. EVERYTHING ELSE—IT'S JUST THE WEATHER."
—PEMA CHÖDRÖN

WHAT IS MINDFULNESS?

Jon Kabat-Zinn defines mindfulness as "paying attention in a particular way: on purpose, in the present moment, and nonjudgmentally." Instead of going down the rabbit hole with our thoughts (usually about the past or future), we make a conscious effort to catch ourselves and bring awareness back to the present moment. Mindfulness is the process of deep awareness and accepting each experience, sensation, thought, or feeling, just as it is, without trying to change it.

WHY IS IT BENEFICIAL?

Benefits of mindfulness include an increase in acceptance, compassion, concentration, and self-control, along with a decrease in stress (to name a few). Neuroscientists have found that after just 11 hours of meditation, practitioners had structural changes in the part of the brain involved in monitoring focus and self-control.

10-MINUTE SEATED MEDITATION

Come to a comfortable seated position. Close your eyes and pay attention to your breath, body, thoughts, and emotions. As your mind wanders, bring it back to the breath to build concentration, observe your emotions, and notice physical sensations like clenching of the jaw. You will get distracted repeatedly and it doesn't mean you're doing it wrong. The act of noticing you're distracted and returning to your breath IS the practice of meditation.

WALKING MEDITATION

Instead of getting from point A to point B, the point of walking meditation is to arrive in the present moment of each step. Notice the movement of each foot as you lift it, move it forward, and place it back down with each step. Lift, shift, place. Walk back and forth in a line at home or wander on a large lawn. Practice for five to 10 minutes.

TAKE A BATH AND FEEL THE WATER ON YOUR SKIN. LISTEN TO MUSIC AND LET IT WASH OVER YOU (TRY BOLERO). WASH THE DISHES AND NOTICE THE SUDS. SIP YOUR MORNING TEA AND NOTICE THE SENSATION AS IT SLIDES DOWN YOUR THROAT. LET A PIECE OF DARK CHOCOLATE MELT IN YOUR MOUTH. LISTEN FULLY TO THE PERSON IN FRONT OF YOU. LAUGH AND FEEL YOUR BELLY MOVE. GO TO A MOVEMENT CLASS AND PAY ATTENTION TO THE SENSATIONS IN YOUR BODY. SLIP INTO YOUR CLOTHING AND NOTICE HOW IT FEELS AGAINST YOUR SKIN. EAT A MEAL IN SILENCE. CREATE A TO-DO LIST USING HAND LETTERING AND NOTICE THE MOVEMENTS OF THE PEN. VISIT A MUSEUM AND OBSERVE THE BRUSH STROKES IN A PAINTING. GO ON A WALK AND NOTICE THE FLORA AND FAUNA. BAKE SCONES AND FEEL YOUR HANDS KNEADING THE DOUGH. SAVOR THE SMELL OF FRESHLY-BAKED COOKIES STRAIGHT FROM THE OVEN. TEND TO YOUR PLANTS AND REMOVE DEAD LEAVES. WRITE IN YOUR JOURNAL AND FEEL THE PEN MOVE ACROSS THE PAGE AND THE EMOTIONS THAT ARISE. NOTICE AND NAME YOUR FEELINGS. SPEND TIME IN NATURE AND NOTICE THE SMELLS AND SOUNDS.

everyday mindfulness

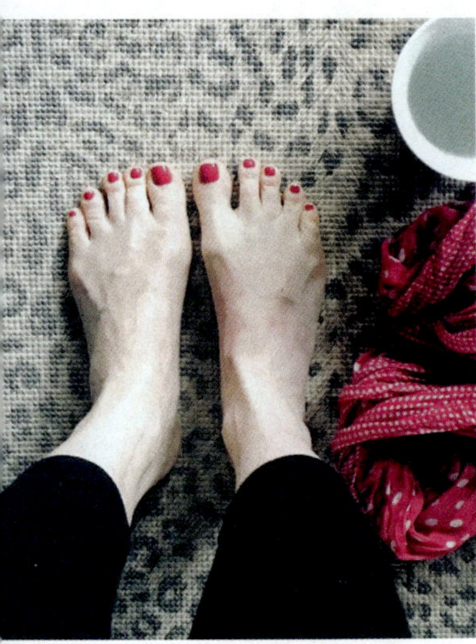

Yoga

"EACH MOMENT OF YOUR LIFE IS A MOMENT OF POTENTIAL PRACTICE."
—JUDITH LASATER

WHAT IS YOGA?

The word yoga comes from Sanskrit, an ancient Indian language. It is a derivation of the word *yuj*, which means to yoke. In contemporary practice, this is often interpreted as union of the mind, body, and spirit.

WHY IS IT BENEFICIAL?

Yoga is known to improve flexibility, build strength, quiet the mind, increase muscle tone, improve balance, support joint health, teach better breathing, increase self-confidence, and reduce stress.

HOW TO DO IT

Put on comfy clothing that stretches, light a candle, and roll out your yoga mat. Move slowly and intentionally. Listen to your body and avoid stretching beyond its limits. If something doesn't feel good, pause and modify.

Try this sun salutation:

1. Come to mountain pose at the top of the mat. Feel your feet grounded firmly. Set an intention. Inhale, reach your arms to the sky.

2. Exhale, trace the midline of your body through prayer position and into a forward fold.

3. Inhale, step back with your right leg to a lunge.

4. Exhale, step back with your left leg to downward-facing dog (an inverted "V").

5. Inhale, float forward to plank pose. Align your shoulders over your wrists and wiggle your feet back so your heels are over the balls of your feet. If this is too much on your wrists, drop your knees.

6. Exhale, drop your knees, bend your arms to a 90-degree angle, hug your elbows into your body, and lower down so that your shoulders and hips are in a straight line for half-chaturanga.

7. Inhale, uncurl your toes, drop your belly, lift your heart center, and slide into cobra. Relax your shoulders from your ears.

8. Exhale, curl your toes under, and lift your hips up and back into downward-facing dog.

9. Inhale, step forward with your right foot.

10. Exhale, step your left foot between both hands to a forward fold.

11. Inhale, trace your midline to the sky. Exhale, place your hands to prayer position in front of your heart. Repeat on the opposite side (step back with the left leg).

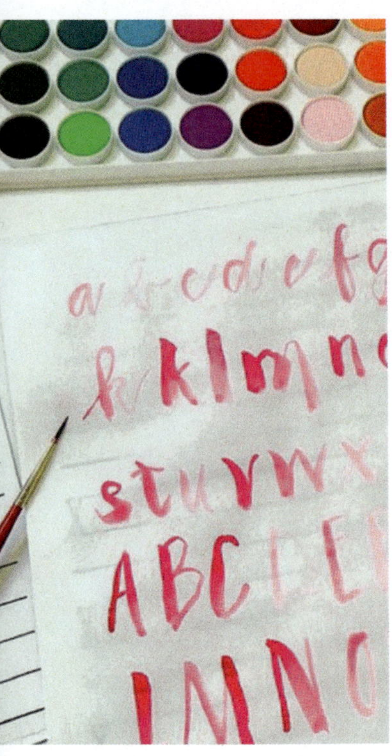

creativity

Julia Cameron, author of the life-changing book The Artist's Way, *coined Artist Dates—a one-hour weekly solo excursion to nurture your creative spark. It's about taking your inner artist out on a date to give the mind an opportunity to rest, play, and uncover ideas that may not show up in daily life.*

I've been an avid fan of the idea for nearly two decades and strive to include it in my weekly routine either spontaneously as I pass a bookstore, or planned by signing up for a calligraphy workshop. Here are some ideas on crafting your own:

- Sit at a café and pen your thoughts.
- Visit an art museum.
- Pick up supplies at a craft store.
- Browse in a bookstore.
- Wander the aisles of an art store.
- Take a hand lettering class.
- Visit an animal sanctuary or shelter.
- Plant herbs in terracotta pots.
- Picnic with a sketchbook.
- Try ice skating.
- People-watch in a park.
- Stroll with no intended destination.
- Enjoy a matinee.
- Take yourself out for tea.
- Pull out your creativity tools.
- Hit the library.
- Start a blog.
- Curate a care package.
- Write a letter to your future self.
- Lose yourself in a thrift store.
- Ride a subway train to the end.
- Read an old journal.
- Play tourist in your town.
- Pick up new-to-you produce at the farmers' market.
- Swing under the stars.
- Make your bucket list (see p. 19).

MORE IDEAS:

LOOK FOR BEAUTY ON YOUR DAILY WALK AND SNAP A PHOTO. TUCK A LOVE NOTE INSIDE YOUR PARTNER OR CHILD'S BAG. TRY A NEW RECIPE. PICK UP AN HERB, FRUIT, OR VEGETABLE THAT'S NEW TO YOU AND CREATE A DISH USING IT. DRIVE A NEW ROUTE TO WORK. START YOUR DAY DIFFERENTLY THAN USUAL—INCORPORATE MOVEMENT OR MEDITATION. WEAR A NEW SHADE OF LIPSTICK. ADD A SCARF IN A VIBRANT COLOR. WANDER DURING YOUR LUNCH BREAK. PICNIC IN THE PARK. TRY A NEW TYPE OF TEA. LISTEN TO A NEW PODCAST. ADD A NEW VOCABULARY WORD TO YOUR MIX. ADD A STRIPED PAPER STRAW TO YOUR FAVORITE LIBATION. TAKE NOTES WITH A CRAYOLA MARKER. BRING AN ARTSY NOTEBOOK OR PINK LEGAL PAD TO YOUR NEXT MEETING. ADD A FEW DROPS OF LAVENDER OIL TO YOUR BATH. TOTE YOUR MORNING SMOOTHIE TO WORK IN A MASON JAR. BRING FRESH-CUT FLOWERS TO YOUR HOME OR OFFICE. BROWSE A THRIFT STORE OR BOOKSTORE. TUCK A TEA BAG INSIDE AND SEAL YOUR NEXT THANK-YOU NOTE WITH WASHI TAPE. TRY A NEW YOGA, DANCE, OR MEDITATION TEACHER. LIGHT A CANDLE. PLUG IN TWINKLE LIGHTS. LISTEN TO A NEW GENRE OF MUSIC. LOOK FOR WAYS TO ADD MORE WHOLE FOODS. CREATE A MEAL PLAN. ADD A CHUNKY NECKLACE TO YOUR ENSEMBLE. SET YOUR WRITING TOOLS ON YOUR DESK IN A VINTAGE TEA CUP. MOVE YOUR FURNITURE AROUND, ADD A BRIGHTLY-COLORED THROW, AND TOSS YOUR MAGAZINES INTO A WICKER BASKET. TRY A NEW PERFUME. DISPLAY POSTCARDS FROM ART EXHIBITS IN FRAMES. WEED YOUR GARDEN (LITERALLY AND FIGURATIVELY). WEAR A FLOWER IN YOUR HAIR.

everyday creativity

current weekly schedule

TRACK HOW YOU CURRENTLY SPEND YOUR 168 HOURS:

	SUNDAY	MONDAY	TUESDAY	WEDNESDAY	THURSDAY	FRIDAY	SATURDAY
5 AM							
5:30							
6:00							
6:30							
7:00							
7:30							
8:00							
8:30							
9:00							
9:30							
10:00							
10:30							
11:00							
11:30							
12:00 PM							
12:30							
1:00							
1:30							
2:00							
2:30							
3:00							
3:30							
4:00							
4:30							
5:00							
5:30							
6:00							
6:30							
7:00							
7:30							
8:00							
8:30							
9:00							
9:30							
10:00							
10:30							
11:00							
11:30							
12:00 AM							

Download at kimberlywilson.com/daybookbonus.

ideal weekly schedule

NOTE HOW YOU'D LIKE TO SPEND YOUR 168 HOURS:

Tune into *Tranquility du Jour* podcasts #199, #263, #306, and #343 for ideas on optimizing your days with *168 Hours* author Laura Vanderkam.

	SUNDAY	MONDAY	TUESDAY	WEDNESDAY	THURSDAY	FRIDAY	SATURDAY
5 AM							
5:30							
6:00							
6:30							
7:00							
7:30							
8:00							
8:30							
9:00							
9:30							
10:00							
10:30							
11:00							
11:30							
12:00 PM							
12:30							
1:00							
1:30							
2:00							
2:30							
3:00							
3:30							
4:00							
4:30							
5:00							
5:30							
6:00							
6:30							
7:00							
7:30							
8:00							
8:30							
9:00							
9:30							
10:00							
10:30							
11:00							
11:30							
12:00 AM							

Download at kimberlywilson.com/daybookbonus.

wellness planning

	SUNDAY	MONDAY	TUESDAY	WEDNESDAY	THURSDAY	FRIDAY	SATURDAY
BREAKFAST							
LUNCH							
DINNER							
WATER	○○○○ ○○○○	○○○○ ○○○○	○○○○ ○○○○	○○○○ ○○○○	○○○○ ○○○○	○○○○ ○○○○	○○○○ ○○○○
EXERCISE							
SLEEP							
MOOD							

SHOPPING LIST

○ ______________________

○ ______________________

○ ______________________

○ ______________________

○ ______________________

○ ______________________

○ ______________________

○ ______________________

○ ______________________

○ ______________________

○ ______________________

○ ______________________

○ ______________________

○ ______________________

○ ______________________

○ ______________________

○ ______________________

○ ______________________

○ ______________________

○ ______________________

○ ______________________

○ ______________________

PLANT-BASED PROTEINS

1. NUTS: walnuts, almonds, cashews, peanuts
2. SEEDS: flax, chia, pumpkin
3. BEANS: black, lima, kidney, chickpeas, lentils, edamame
4. LEAFY GREENS: spinach, kale, collards
5. VEGGIES: broccoli, peas, cauliflower, asparagus, corn
6. OTHER: quinoa, tofu, tempeh, and more!

Download at kimberlywilson.com/daybookbonus.

meatless monday

I'm animal obsessed and on a mission to live my favorite mantra, Lokah Samastah Sukhino Bhavantu. *Translated by yoga teacher Sharon Gannon as,* May all beings everywhere be happy and free. May the thoughts, words, and actions of my own life contribute in some way to that happiness and to that freedom for all. *Ommmm. What a beautiful life message!*

Going meatless, even once a week, lessens the risk of chronic conditions such as cancer, cardiovascular disease, diabetes, and obesity. It also reduces our carbon footprint and saves 28 land animals and 175 aquatic animals per year. Oh, and saves money, too!

Yes, by just one day a week. Good for us, the animals, and the environment! Tune into *Tranquility du Jour* podcasts #111, #186, #236, #303, #335, #349, #354, #365, #377, #391, #394, and #452. Learn more at kimberlywilson.com/animals.

MINDFUL EATING TIPS

1. Make eating an experience: light candles, set the table, and sit down.
2. Pack your plate with colorful veggies, chew slowly, and savor each bite.
3. When eating, single task and only eat. Try dining in silence, sans TV, phone, or other distractions.
4. Pause between bites, put your fork down, and notice sensations.

detox

Feeling lethargic, overindulgent, or in need of a reset? Try this seven-day cleanse by combining self-care with clean food to release toxins, feel lighter, and rejuvenate.

BASIC PLAN

		DAY 1	DAY 2	DAY 3	DAY 4	DAY 5	DAY 6	DAY 7
A.M.	8OZ WARM WATER WITH LEMON AND 1-2 TBSP GROUND FLAXSEED							
	GREEN SMOOTHIE OR CHIA SEED PUDDING							
	TONGUE SCRAPE							
	DRY SKIN BRUSH							
LUNCH	LUNCH MEAL*							
	EXERCISE							
P.M.	DINNER MEAL*							
	JOURNAL							
	BATH							
	HERBAL TEA							
	EXERCISE							

*MEAL IDEAS: MIXED GREENS SALAD, STEAMED VEGGIES OVER BROWN RICE, VEGGIE SOUP, SWEET POTATO NOODLES, SPICY HUMMUS, STUFFED AVOCADO OR RED PEPPER, LETTUCE WRAP BLACK BEAN TACOS, OR ROASTED VEGGIES WITH QUINOA.

ELIMINATE

- Gluten (wheat, rye, barley)
- Animal products (fish, eggs, meat)
- Caffeine, alcohol, soda
- Added sugar
- Dairy
- Processed or fried foods

INCLUDE

- Veggies (lots of dark leafy greens)
- Quinoa, brown rice, millet
- Beans, legumes, lentils
- Unsalted/unroasted nuts and seeds
- Fruits
- Fresh herbs
- Water
- Herbal tea
- Unsweetened non-dairy milks
- Extra virgin olive oil

Download at kimberlywilson.com/daybookbonus.

detox tips

1. Remove temptations from your home. Bye, bye sugar-coated cereals.
2. Review the basic food plan and pick up these staples: brown rice, fresh and/or frozen veggies (especially kale, spinach, avocados, cauliflower—for cauliflower wings), frozen fruit (for green smoothies or smoothie bowls), chia seeds, ground flaxseed, lemon, herbal tea, raw nuts, veggie stock for soups, apples, nut butters, gluten-free whole grains, hummus.
3. Start weaning off the sugar, alcohol, and caffeine. I know, I know, it may sound impossible, but it's worth the effort. Promise!
4. Upgrade your eating to include five servings of fruit and veggies each day.
5. Gather your tools and schedule your self-care: journal, tongue scraper, bath supplies, dry skin brush, exercise, massage.
6. Schedule time for food shopping and prep.
7. Eat an abundance of healthy fats like nuts, seeds, avocados, and edamame to help curb cravings.
8. Drink plenty of water to help release toxins. Add lemon, mint, and cucumber slices to spice it up.
9. Believe you can do this and enlist the support of others. Better yet, have them join you!
10. Track your journey and strive for progress, not perfection. You've got this!

BREATHE
IN.
BREATHE
OUT.
REPEAT.

plant-based treats

PROTEIN BALLS

These no-bake balls offer a protein punch and are great on-the-go. Enjoy as a snack, dessert, or breakfast.

INGREDIENTS:
1 cup dates, pitted
½ cup rolled oats
¼ cup chia seeds
⅓ cup vegan chocolate chips
¼ cup vegan protein powder
¼ cup unsweetened shredded coconut
3 tablespoons almond butter

DIRECTIONS:
Place all ingredients in a food processor or blender. Mix until it forms a dough. Roll into balls. Store in the fridge or freezer.

AVOCADO TOAST

Avocado has protein and healthy fat plus is high in fiber, potassium, vitamins B, C, E, and K.

INGREDIENTS:
bread
avocado
extra virgin olive oil

DIRECTIONS:
Slice and toast bread, drizzle with olive oil, and mash half an avocado on top with a fork. Top with Montreal steak seasoning, arugula, peaches, tomatoes, pine nuts, chili flakes, or chia seeds.

CHIA SEED PUDDING

Chia seeds are a source of antioxidants and rich in fiber, omega-3 fats, protein, vitamins, minerals, and essential fatty acids.

INGREDIENTS:
3 cups unsweetened almond milk
½ cup chia seeds

DIRECTIONS:
Whisk the almond milk and chia seeds.Let sit for 5–10 minutes and then whisk again. Cover and chill in the fridge for 2.5–3 hours, or overnight. Stir well before serving. Add toppings such as granola, diced fruit, nuts, or seeds.

KALE CHIPS

Kale is nutrient dense with protein and iron, a great source of fiber, and full of vitamins A, C, and K.

INGREDIENTS:
a large bag of kale
extra virgin olive oil
nutritional yeast

DIRECTIONS:
Preheat the oven to 350 degrees. Remove leaves from the stalks, wash and dry in a salad spinner, and massage ½ tablespoon of extra virgin olive oil into the leaves. Spread them out on a baking sheet. Add Montreal steak seasoning or nutritional yeast. Bake 15 minutes or until crisp.

GREEN SMOOTHIE

This smoothie is high in fiber, low in sugar, and rich in vitamins and healthy fats.

INGREDIENTS:
½ cup vegan protein powder
2 handfuls spinach
1 tablespoon chia seeds
1 cup almond milk or water
½ avocado
1 tablespoon coconut oil
assorted frozen fruit
1 tablespoon ground flaxseed
½ banana

DIRECTIONS:
Combine all ingredients in a blender.

CRISPY CAULIFLOWER

Cauliflower is full of nutrients, high in fiber, and has anti-inflammatory benefits.

INGREDIENTS:
1 head of cauliflower cut into florets
1 tablespoon of extra virgin olive oil
¼ teaspoon black pepper
¼ teaspoon paprika
¼ teaspoon turmeric

DIRECTIONS:
Preheat the oven to 450 degrees. Toss cauliflower in oil and other ingredients. Spread the florets out evenly on a metal baking sheet. Bake for 20–30 minutes until a crispy golden brown. Enjoy with buffalo wing sauce.

capsule dressing

Make daily dress-up tranquil with a few timeless essentials that mix and match. **TIPS:** *Going monochromatic offers a chic look, ensures everything matches, and can be easily dressed up or down. Top with a colorful scarf, strands of faux pearls, vintage earrings, red lips, and a dab of parfum.*

Tune into *Tranquility du Jour* podcasts #259 and #310 for more on capsule dressing. Learn more at TranquiliT.com/capsule.

6 + 11

3 + 10

2 + 9

MY 11 STAPLES ARE:

tranquil travel

"TRAVEL BRINGS POWER AND LOVE BACK INTO YOUR LIFE."
—RUMI

TIPS:

1. Wear your bulkiest items when you travel.
2. Roll your clothing.
3. Pack products that serve multiple purposes such as Dr. Bronner's, shampoo/soap, and body/face moisturizer.
4. Pack versatile pieces that can be worn in multiple ways such as a skirt that can also be a dress.

TWO-WEEK PACKING LIST:

- ❍ Swimsuit
- ❍ Five pairs undies
- ❍ Two bras
- ❍ Three pairs of versatile shoes
- ❍ Five neutral-colored pants and/or shorts
- ❍ Three neutral-colored dresses and/or skirts
- ❍ Five neutral-colored tops
- ❍ Sun hat or beanie
- ❍ One–two colorful scarves
- ❍ One coat/jacket
- ❍ Socks and/or tights

TOOLS:

- ❍ Travel yoga mat
- ❍ Scented candle and lighter
- ❍ Earplugs and eye mask
- ❍ Lavender oil and parfum
- ❍ Assortment of teas and treats
- ❍ Reusable water bottle
- ❍ Medication
- ❍ Journal and pens
- ❍ Camera and/or smartphone
- ❍ Chargers
- ❍ Travel-size toiletries: soap, shampoo, conditioner, deodorant, moisturizer
- ❍ Razor and tweezers
- ❍ Band-aids
- ❍ Face oil, mascara, lipstick
- ❍ Slippers
- ❍ Travel-size detergent
- ❍ Headphones
- ❍ Passport
- ❍ Books
- ❍ Travel guides

MY TRAVEL MUST-HAVES:

weekly spending

WEEK OF: ____________ INCOME: ____________ BUDGET: ____________

	SUNDAY	MONDAY	TUESDAY	WEDNESDAY	THURSDAY	FRIDAY	SATURDAY
RENT/MORTGAGE							
ELECTRICITY							
WATER							
GAS							
CABLE/INTERNET							
PHONE							
CAR FUEL							
CAR INSURANCE							
CAR LOAN							
CAR MAINTENANCE							
GROCERIES							
DINING OUT							
MEDICAL INSURANCE							
CO-PAYS							
PHARMACY							
CLOTHING							
ENTERTAINMENT							
DEBT/LOAN PAYMENTS							
CHARITABLE GIVING							
TOTAL							

OBSERVATIONS:

Download at kimberlywilson.com/daybookbonus.

monthly budget

FINANCIAL GOALS:

EXPENSES

HOUSING

Rent/Mortgage $ ______________

{ } $ ______________

{ } $ ______________

UTILITIES

Electricity $ ______________

Water $ ______________

Gas $ ______________

Cable/Internet $ ______________

Phone $ ______________

{ } $ ______________

{ } $ ______________

{ } $ ______________

TRANSPORTATION

Fuel $ ______________

Insurance $ ______________

Car Payment $ ______________

Maintenance $ ______________

{ } $ ______________

{ } $ ______________

FOOD

Groceries $ ______________

Dining Out $ ______________

MEDICAL

Premiums $ ______________

Co-pays $ ______________

Pharmacy $ ______________

{ } $ ______________

{ } $ ______________

PERSONAL

Clothing $ ______________

Entertainment $ ______________

{ } $ ______________

{ } $ ______________

{ } $ ______________

{ } $ ______________

{ } $ ______________

{ } $ ______________

DEBT/LOANS

{ } $ ______________

{ } $ ______________

{ } $ ______________

{ } $ ______________

{ } $ ______________

TOTAL $ ______________

INCOME

Income #1 $ ______________

Income #2 $ ______________

{ } $ ______________

TOTAL $ ______________

GIVING

{ } $ ______________

{ } $ ______________

{ } $ ______________

TOTAL $ ______________

SAVINGS

Emergency $ ______________

Retirement $ ______________

{ } $ ______________

TOTAL $ ______________

Download at kimberlywilson.com/daybookbonus.

savvy sources

ENJOY THESE *TRANQUILITY DU JOUR* PODCAST RESOURCES TO DIVE DEEPER INTO A POTPOURRI OF TRANQUILITY-INFUSED TOPICS.

DREAMS

#95 Scheduling and Time Management

#117 The Power of Writing Things Down

#211 Dreams to Reality

#313 Procrastination to Creative Genius

#396 Start Right Where You Are

LOVE

#22 Mindful Relationships

#62 Refined Relations

#156 Musings on Self-Love

#230 Friendship Fix

#270 Relationships + Tiny Living

#362 Succulent Wild Love

#408 Big Love

STYLE + BEAUTY

#42 Outer Beauty

#179 Signature Style

#259 Project 333

#289 Finding Your Ooh la la

#310 Style Secrets

#338 All About the Pretty

#351 At Home with Madame Chic

#354 The Good Karma Diet

#366 Polish Your Poise

#414 Parisian Charm School

CREATIVITY

#78 Creativity Cravings

#122 Being Succulent with SARK

#152 Musings on Creativity

#154 Guide to Creativity

#184 Creative Awakenings

#238 Abundant Wild Life

#242 Brave Intuitive Painting

#273 Making Your Creative Mark

#307 Yoga + Creativity

#373 Creative Practice

MINIMALISM

#149 Secrets of Simplicity

#207 Simplification

#253 You Can Buy Happiness

#259 Simplicity

#389 Less = More

#426 Breaking Up With Busy

#438 Living The Simply Luxurious Life

WELLNESS

#181 Living The Not So Big Life

#240 Main Street Vegan

#335 Walk On the Healthy Side

#370 Sipping Tea

#397 Nourish 360

#398 Make Peace with Your Mind

#421 From Anxiety to Love

YOGA

#126 Living Your Yoga

#194 A Life Worth Breathing

#246 Yoga Philosophy

#307 Yoga + Creativity

#315 Picking Your Practice

#355 Restorative Yoga Therapy

#425 The Magic Ten

SELF-CARE

#61 Self-Nurturing Survival

#348 Mindful Self-Care

#370 Sipping Tea

#397 Nourish 360

#426 Breaking Up with Busy

MINDFULNESS

#171 Musings on Mindfulness

#267 Mindfulness with Elisha Goldstein

#317 Mindfulness Diaries

#320 Mindfulness

#341 Everyday Mindfulness

#356 Uncovering Happiness

#357 Mindful Eating

#416 All Our Waves Are Water

WRITING

#20 Journal Writing 101

#33 Book Writing 101

#96 The Writing Life

#142 Musing on Journal Writing

#222 Idea Mapping

#337 Writing + Yoga

#363 The Writing Habit

#369 The Writing Practice

#407 The Writing Process

ENTREPRENEURSHIP

#132 Hot Mommas Project

#160 Unfold Your Life Vision

#199 168 Hours

#209 Right Brain Business Plan

#211 Dreams to Reality

#306 What Most Successful People Do at Work

#314 Building Your Biz the Right-Brain Way

#343 I Know How She Does It

#396 Start Right Where You Are

#404 Transitions

MEANING

#116 Spiritual Activism

#328 Life Purpose Bootcamp

#336 Women Entrepreneur Revolution

#359 Artistic Activism

#428 Transitions

MY LIFE IS MY ART.

seasonal life review

DATE: ____________

SEASONALLY REFLECT ON AREAS OF YOUR LIFE. RATE EACH ONE WITH YOUR LEVEL OF SATISFACTION 10 = BLISS, 5 = SO-SO, 0 = BOO.

Here are some additional areas to consider: social life, romance, family, education, health, fitness, meaning, activism. Next, take a moment to note the areas that ranked low and create three action steps to increase your tranquility in these areas. Be gentle. Plant seeds. Watch dreams take root.

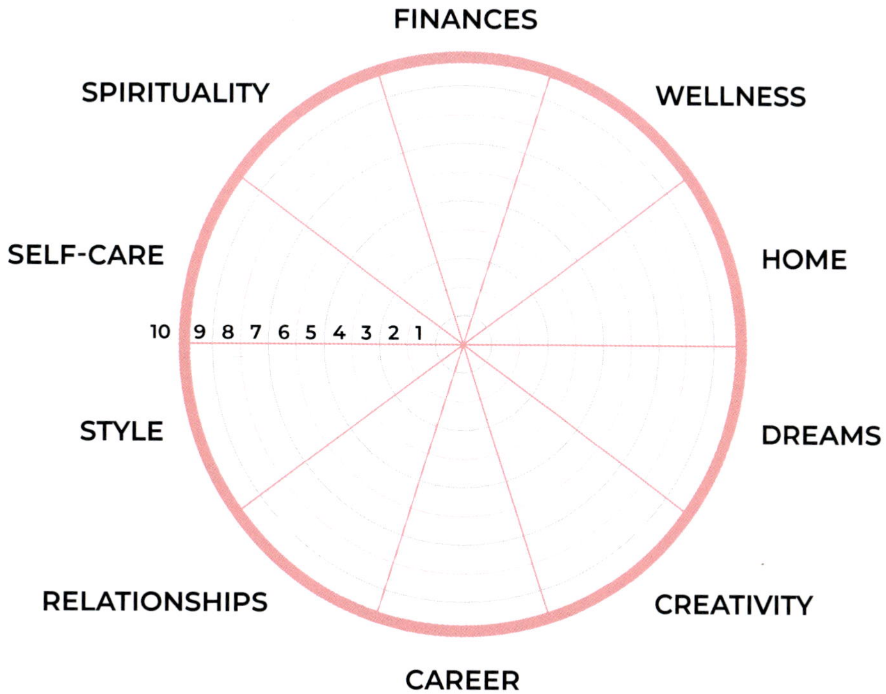

ACTION STEPS TO INCREASE AREAS THAT ARE LOWER THAN I'D LIKE:

month's dreams

DOODLE, LIST, COLLAGE, OR WRITE WHAT YOU'D LIKE TO MANIFEST THIS MONTH.

month's review

REVISIT YOUR MONTH'S DREAMS AND NOTE HOW THEY UNFOLDED FOR YOU.

30 days of tranquility

TRY THIS 30-DAY CHALLENGE TO INFUSE YOUR MONTH WITH SIMPLE PLEASURES.

1 SIT STILL FOR FIVE MINUTES	2 DO SIX SUN SALUTATIONS	3 WRITE A LOVE LETTER	4 APOLOGIZE	5 TELL THE TRUTH
6 CONSUME A GREEN DRINK	7 GO MEAT-FREE	8 WALK FOR 20 MINUTES	9 DO LEGS UP THE WALL	10 GIVE $10 TO CHARITY
11 PEN TWO JOURNAL PAGES	12 REVIEW YOUR YEAR'S DREAMS	13 CLEAR CLUTTER	14 GO ON AN ARTIST DATE	15 COLLAGE TWO PAGES
16 TREAT YOURSELF TO TEA	17 READ FOR 20 MINUTES	18 BUY YOURSELF FLOWERS	19 DANCE TO A FAVORITE TUNE	20 EXPRESS GRATITUDE
21 EAT ONLY UNPROCESSED FOODS	22 SOAK IN A BUBBLE BATH	23 MINDFULLY SIP A LIBATION	24 GET OUT IN NATURE	25 FORGO COMPLAINING
26 TAKE A DIGITAL DAY OFF	27 SNAP PHOTOS FROM YOUR DAY	28 MAKE A FAVORITE MEAL	29 HUG	30 BE FULLY PRESENT

habit tracking

NOTE HABITS YOU'RE TRYING TO ADD OR SUBTRACT AND TRACK THEM DAILY TO HELP WITH ACCOUNTABILITY. CELEBRATE YOUR SUCCESSES AND OBSERVE AREAS FOR GROWTH.

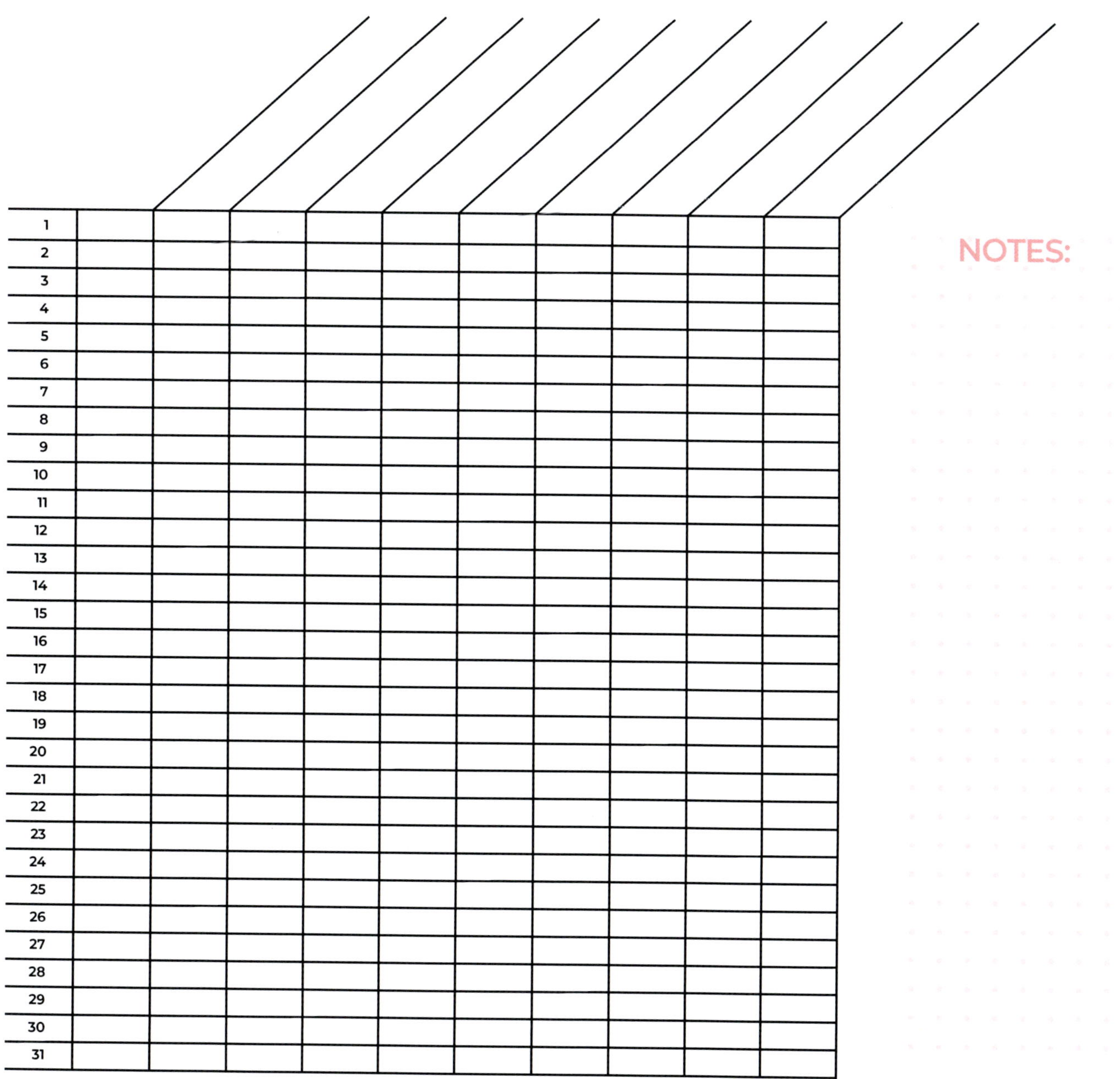

1										
2										
3										
4										
5										
6										
7										
8										
9										
10										
11										
12										
13										
14										
15										
16										
17										
18										
19										
20										
21										
22										
23										
24										
25										
26										
27										
28										
29										
30										
31										

NOTES:

moon phases

Notice your connection to the moon's cycles in these four phases: new, waxing, full, waning. Consider the prompts below as a way to tie into your Month's Dreams and provide space for monthly reflection. Tune into Tranquility du Jour *podcast #424 Moon Wisdom.*

new moon

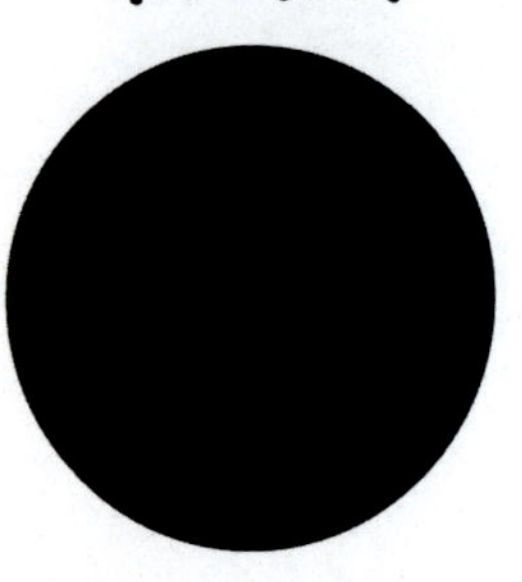

A TIME FOR SETTING INTENTIONS.
I WANT . . .

waxing moon

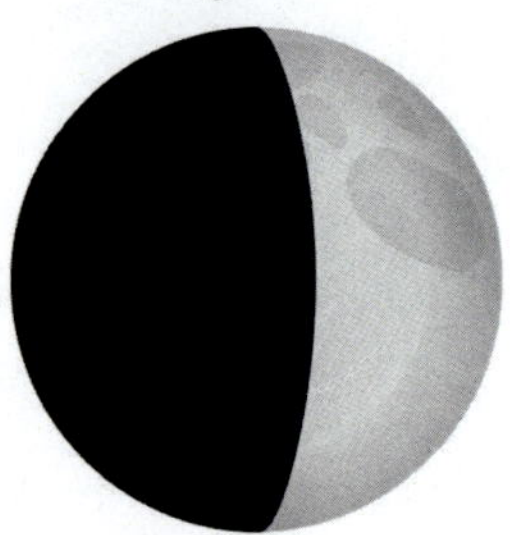

A TIME FOR ACTION. I WILL . . .

full moon

A TIME FOR HARVEST AND CLOSURE.
I RELEASE . . .

waning moon

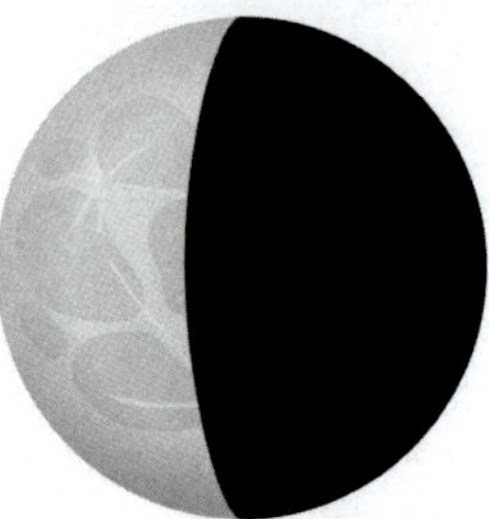

A TIME FOR SOFTENING. I FEEL . . .

monthly planner

MONTH: ______________________ INTENTION: ______________________

SUNDAY	MONDAY	TUESDAY	WEDNESDAY	THURSDAY	FRIDAY	SATURDAY

MONTHLY TRANQUILITY TOOLS

- ❍ CRAFT MONTH'S DREAMS
- ❍ REVIEW BUDGET
- ❍ CREATE SOMETHING
- ❍ READ TWO BOOKS
- ❍ VOLUNTEER
- ❍ MANI/PEDI
- ❍ ENTERTAIN
- ❍ MASSAGE

INTENTION:

weekly checklist

- PLAN WEEK'S MITS
- SOAK IN THE TUB
- TAKE A DIGITAL DAY OFF
- CLEAR CLUTTER
- PEN A LOVE NOTE
- BUY/PICK FRESH FLOWERS
- TAKE AN ARTIST DATE
- SAVOR A GREEN JUICE
- ______

MITs

- ______
- ______
- ______
- ______
- ______

wellness planning

M ______
T ______
W ______
TH ______
F ______
S ______
S ______

GRATITUDE:

MONDAY ______

7 ______
8 ______
9 ______
10 ______
11 ______
12 ______
1 ______
2 ______
3 ______
4 ______
5 ______
6 ______
7 ______
8 ______
9 ______

daily checklist

- MORNING RITUAL
- DAILY DRESS-UP
- MINDFUL MOVEMENT
- EAT YOUR VEGGIES
- JOURNAL
- GOAL REVIEW
- GRATITUDE
- EVENING RITUAL
- ______

TUESDAY ______

7 ______
8 ______
9 ______
10 ______
11 ______
12 ______
1 ______
2 ______
3 ______
4 ______
5 ______
6 ______
7 ______
8 ______
9 ______

daily checklist

- MORNING RITUAL
- DAILY DRESS-UP
- MINDFUL MOVEMENT
- EAT YOUR VEGGIES
- JOURNAL
- GOAL REVIEW
- GRATITUDE
- EVENING RITUAL
- ______

WEDNESDAY ______

7 ______
8 ______
9 ______
10 ______
11 ______
12 ______
1 ______
2 ______
3 ______
4 ______
5 ______
6 ______
7 ______
8 ______
9 ______

daily checklist

- MORNING RITUAL
- DAILY DRESS-UP
- MINDFUL MOVEMENT
- EAT YOUR VEGGIES
- JOURNAL
- GOAL REVIEW
- GRATITUDE
- EVENING RITUAL
- ______

THURSDAY

7
8
9
10
11
12
1
2
3
4
5
6
7
8
9

daily checklist

- MORNING RITUAL
- DAILY DRESS-UP
- MINDFUL MOVEMENT
- EAT YOUR VEGGIES
- JOURNAL
- GOAL REVIEW
- GRATITUDE
- EVENING RITUAL

FRIDAY

7
8
9
10
11
12
1
2
3
4
5
6
7
8
9

daily checklist

- MORNING RITUAL
- DAILY DRESS-UP
- MINDFUL MOVEMENT
- EAT YOUR VEGGIES
- JOURNAL
- GOAL REVIEW
- GRATITUDE
- EVENING RITUAL

SATURDAY

7
8
9
10
11
12
1
2
3
4
5
6
7
8
9

daily checklist

- MORNING RITUAL
- DAILY DRESS-UP
- MINDFUL MOVEMENT
- EAT YOUR VEGGIES
- JOURNAL
- GOAL REVIEW
- GRATITUDE
- EVENING RITUAL

SUNDAY

7
8
9
10
11
12
1
2
3
4
5
6
7
8
9

daily checklist

- MORNING RITUAL
- DAILY DRESS-UP
- MINDFUL MOVEMENT
- EAT YOUR VEGGIES
- JOURNAL
- GOAL REVIEW
- GRATITUDE
- EVENING RITUAL

INTENTION:

weekly checklist

- PLAN WEEK'S MITS
- SOAK IN THE TUB
- TAKE A DIGITAL DAY OFF
- CLEAR CLUTTER
- PEN A LOVE NOTE
- BUY/PICK FRESH FLOWERS
- TAKE AN ARTIST DATE
- SAVOR A GREEN JUICE
- ______

MITs

- ______
- ______
- ______
- ______
- ______

wellness planning

M ______
T ______
W ______
TH ______
F ______
S ______
S ______

GRATITUDE:

MONDAY ______

7 ______
8 ______
9 ______
10 ______
11 ______
12 ______
1 ______
2 ______
3 ______
4 ______
5 ______
6 ______
7 ______
8 ______
9 ______

daily checklist

- MORNING RITUAL
- DAILY DRESS-UP
- MINDFUL MOVEMENT
- EAT YOUR VEGGIES
- JOURNAL
- GOAL REVIEW
- GRATITUDE
- EVENING RITUAL
- ______

TUESDAY ______

7 ______
8 ______
9 ______
10 ______
11 ______
12 ______
1 ______
2 ______
3 ______
4 ______
5 ______
6 ______
7 ______
8 ______
9 ______

daily checklist

- MORNING RITUAL
- DAILY DRESS-UP
- MINDFUL MOVEMENT
- EAT YOUR VEGGIES
- JOURNAL
- GOAL REVIEW
- GRATITUDE
- EVENING RITUAL
- ______

WEDNESDAY ______

7 ______
8 ______
9 ______
10 ______
11 ______
12 ______
1 ______
2 ______
3 ______
4 ______
5 ______
6 ______
7 ______
8 ______
9 ______

daily checklist

- MORNING RITUAL
- DAILY DRESS-UP
- MINDFUL MOVEMENT
- EAT YOUR VEGGIES
- JOURNAL
- GOAL REVIEW
- GRATITUDE
- EVENING RITUAL
- ______

THURSDAY

7
8
9
10
11
12
1
2
3
4
5
6
7
8
9

daily checklist

- MORNING RITUAL
- DAILY DRESS-UP
- MINDFUL MOVEMENT
- EAT YOUR VEGGIES
- JOURNAL
- GOAL REVIEW
- GRATITUDE
- EVENING RITUAL

FRIDAY

7
8
9
10
11
12
1
2
3
4
5
6
7
8
9

daily checklist

- MORNING RITUAL
- DAILY DRESS-UP
- MINDFUL MOVEMENT
- EAT YOUR VEGGIES
- JOURNAL
- GOAL REVIEW
- GRATITUDE
- EVENING RITUAL

SATURDAY

7
8
9
10
11
12
1
2
3
4
5
6
7
8
9

daily checklist

- MORNING RITUAL
- DAILY DRESS-UP
- MINDFUL MOVEMENT
- EAT YOUR VEGGIES
- JOURNAL
- GOAL REVIEW
- GRATITUDE
- EVENING RITUAL

SUNDAY

7
8
9
10
11
12
1
2
3
4
5
6
7
8
9

daily checklist

- MORNING RITUAL
- DAILY DRESS-UP
- MINDFUL MOVEMENT
- EAT YOUR VEGGIES
- JOURNAL
- GOAL REVIEW
- GRATITUDE
- EVENING RITUAL

INTENTION:

weekly checklist

- PLAN WEEK'S MITS
- SOAK IN THE TUB
- TAKE A DIGITAL DAY OFF
- CLEAR CLUTTER
- PEN A LOVE NOTE
- BUY/PICK FRESH FLOWERS
- TAKE AN ARTIST DATE
- SAVOR A GREEN JUICE
- ______

MITs

- ______
- ______
- ______
- ______
- ______

wellness planning

M ______
T ______
W ______
TH ______
F ______
S ______
S ______

GRATITUDE:

MONDAY ______

7 ______
8 ______
9 ______
10 ______
11 ______
12 ______
1 ______
2 ______
3 ______
4 ______
5 ______
6 ______
7 ______
8 ______
9 ______

daily checklist

- MORNING RITUAL
- DAILY DRESS-UP
- MINDFUL MOVEMENT
- EAT YOUR VEGGIES
- JOURNAL
- GOAL REVIEW
- GRATITUDE
- EVENING RITUAL
- ______

TUESDAY ______

7 ______
8 ______
9 ______
10 ______
11 ______
12 ______
1 ______
2 ______
3 ______
4 ______
5 ______
6 ______
7 ______
8 ______
9 ______

daily checklist

- MORNING RITUAL
- DAILY DRESS-UP
- MINDFUL MOVEMENT
- EAT YOUR VEGGIES
- JOURNAL
- GOAL REVIEW
- GRATITUDE
- EVENING RITUAL
- ______

WEDNESDAY ______

7 ______
8 ______
9 ______
10 ______
11 ______
12 ______
1 ______
2 ______
3 ______
4 ______
5 ______
6 ______
7 ______
8 ______
9 ______

daily checklist

- MORNING RITUAL
- DAILY DRESS-UP
- MINDFUL MOVEMENT
- EAT YOUR VEGGIES
- JOURNAL
- GOAL REVIEW
- GRATITUDE
- EVENING RITUAL
- ______

THURSDAY

7
8
9
10
11
12
1
2
3
4
5
6
7
8
9

daily checklist

- MORNING RITUAL
- DAILY DRESS-UP
- MINDFUL MOVEMENT
- EAT YOUR VEGGIES
- JOURNAL
- GOAL REVIEW
- GRATITUDE
- EVENING RITUAL

FRIDAY

7
8
9
10
11
12
1
2
3
4
5
6
7
8
9

daily checklist

- MORNING RITUAL
- DAILY DRESS-UP
- MINDFUL MOVEMENT
- EAT YOUR VEGGIES
- JOURNAL
- GOAL REVIEW
- GRATITUDE
- EVENING RITUAL

SATURDAY

7
8
9
10
11
12
1
2
3
4
5
6
7
8
9

daily checklist

- MORNING RITUAL
- DAILY DRESS-UP
- MINDFUL MOVEMENT
- EAT YOUR VEGGIES
- JOURNAL
- GOAL REVIEW
- GRATITUDE
- EVENING RITUAL

SUNDAY

7
8
9
10
11
12
1
2
3
4
5
6
7
8
9

daily checklist

- MORNING RITUAL
- DAILY DRESS-UP
- MINDFUL MOVEMENT
- EAT YOUR VEGGIES
- JOURNAL
- GOAL REVIEW
- GRATITUDE
- EVENING RITUAL

INTENTION:

weekly checklist

- PLAN WEEK'S MITS
- SOAK IN THE TUB
- TAKE A DIGITAL DAY OFF
- CLEAR CLUTTER
- PEN A LOVE NOTE
- BUY/PICK FRESH FLOWERS
- TAKE AN ARTIST DATE
- SAVOR A GREEN JUICE
- ____

MITs

- ____
- ____
- ____
- ____
- ____

wellness planning

M ____
T ____
W ____
TH ____
F ____
S ____
S ____

GRATITUDE:

MONDAY ____

7 ____
8 ____
9 ____
10 ____
11 ____
12 ____
1 ____
2 ____
3 ____
4 ____
5 ____
6 ____
7 ____
8 ____
9 ____

daily checklist

- MORNING RITUAL
- DAILY DRESS-UP
- MINDFUL MOVEMENT
- EAT YOUR VEGGIES
- JOURNAL
- GOAL REVIEW
- GRATITUDE
- EVENING RITUAL
- ____

TUESDAY ____

7 ____
8 ____
9 ____
10 ____
11 ____
12 ____
1 ____
2 ____
3 ____
4 ____
5 ____
6 ____
7 ____
8 ____
9 ____

daily checklist

- MORNING RITUAL
- DAILY DRESS-UP
- MINDFUL MOVEMENT
- EAT YOUR VEGGIES
- JOURNAL
- GOAL REVIEW
- GRATITUDE
- EVENING RITUAL
- ____

WEDNESDAY ____

7 ____
8 ____
9 ____
10 ____
11 ____
12 ____
1 ____
2 ____
3 ____
4 ____
5 ____
6 ____
7 ____
8 ____
9 ____

daily checklist

- MORNING RITUAL
- DAILY DRESS-UP
- MINDFUL MOVEMENT
- EAT YOUR VEGGIES
- JOURNAL
- GOAL REVIEW
- GRATITUDE
- EVENING RITUAL
- ____

THURSDAY

7
8
9
10
11
12
1
2
3
4
5
6
7
8
9

daily checklist

- MORNING RITUAL
- DAILY DRESS-UP
- MINDFUL MOVEMENT
- EAT YOUR VEGGIES
- JOURNAL
- GOAL REVIEW
- GRATITUDE
- EVENING RITUAL

FRIDAY

7
8
9
10
11
12
1
2
3
4
5
6
7
8
9

daily checklist

- MORNING RITUAL
- DAILY DRESS-UP
- MINDFUL MOVEMENT
- EAT YOUR VEGGIES
- JOURNAL
- GOAL REVIEW
- GRATITUDE
- EVENING RITUAL

SATURDAY

7
8
9
10
11
12
1
2
3
4
5
6
7
8
9

daily checklist

- MORNING RITUAL
- DAILY DRESS-UP
- MINDFUL MOVEMENT
- EAT YOUR VEGGIES
- JOURNAL
- GOAL REVIEW
- GRATITUDE
- EVENING RITUAL

SUNDAY

7
8
9
10
11
12
1
2
3
4
5
6
7
8
9

daily checklist

- MORNING RITUAL
- DAILY DRESS-UP
- MINDFUL MOVEMENT
- EAT YOUR VEGGIES
- JOURNAL
- GOAL REVIEW
- GRATITUDE
- EVENING RITUAL

INTENTION:

weekly checklist

- ○ PLAN WEEK'S MITS
- ○ SOAK IN THE TUB
- ○ TAKE A DIGITAL DAY OFF
- ○ CLEAR CLUTTER
- ○ PEN A LOVE NOTE
- ○ BUY/PICK FRESH FLOWERS
- ○ TAKE AN ARTIST DATE
- ○ SAVOR A GREEN JUICE
- ○ ______

MITs

- ○ ______
- ○ ______
- ○ ______
- ○ ______
- ○ ______

wellness planning

M ______
T ______
W ______
TH ______
F ______
S ______
S ______

GRATITUDE:

MONDAY ______

7 ______
8 ______
9 ______
10 ______
11 ______
12 ______
1 ______
2 ______
3 ______
4 ______
5 ______
6 ______
7 ______
8 ______
9 ______

- ○ ______
- ○ ______
- ○ ______
- ○ ______
- ○ ______
- ○ ______
- ○ ______
- ○ ______
- ○ ______
- ○ ______

- ○ ______
- ○ ______
- ○ ______
- ○ ______
- ○ ______
- ○ ______

daily checklist

- ○ MORNING RITUAL
- ○ DAILY DRESS-UP
- ○ MINDFUL MOVEMENT
- ○ EAT YOUR VEGGIES
- ○ JOURNAL
- ○ GOAL REVIEW
- ○ GRATITUDE
- ○ EVENING RITUAL
- ○ ______

TUESDAY ______

7 ______
8 ______
9 ______
10 ______
11 ______
12 ______
1 ______
2 ______
3 ______
4 ______
5 ______
6 ______
7 ______
8 ______
9 ______

- ○ ______
- ○ ______
- ○ ______
- ○ ______
- ○ ______
- ○ ______
- ○ ______
- ○ ______
- ○ ______
- ○ ______

- ○ ______
- ○ ______
- ○ ______
- ○ ______
- ○ ______
- ○ ______

daily checklist

- ○ MORNING RITUAL
- ○ DAILY DRESS-UP
- ○ MINDFUL MOVEMENT
- ○ EAT YOUR VEGGIES
- ○ JOURNAL
- ○ GOAL REVIEW
- ○ GRATITUDE
- ○ EVENING RITUAL
- ○ ______

WEDNESDAY ______

7 ______
8 ______
9 ______
10 ______
11 ______
12 ______
1 ______
2 ______
3 ______
4 ______
5 ______
6 ______
7 ______
8 ______
9 ______

- ○ ______
- ○ ______
- ○ ______
- ○ ______
- ○ ______
- ○ ______
- ○ ______
- ○ ______
- ○ ______
- ○ ______

- ○ ______
- ○ ______
- ○ ______
- ○ ______
- ○ ______
- ○ ______

daily checklist

- ○ MORNING RITUAL
- ○ DAILY DRESS-UP
- ○ MINDFUL MOVEMENT
- ○ EAT YOUR VEGGIES
- ○ JOURNAL
- ○ GOAL REVIEW
- ○ GRATITUDE
- ○ EVENING RITUAL
- ○ ______

THURSDAY ____

7 ____
8 ____
9 ____
10 ____
11 ____
12 ____
1 ____
2 ____
3 ____
4 ____
5 ____
6 ____
7 ____
8 ____
9 ____

daily checklist

- MORNING RITUAL
- DAILY DRESS-UP
- MINDFUL MOVEMENT
- EAT YOUR VEGGIES
- JOURNAL
- GOAL REVIEW
- GRATITUDE
- EVENING RITUAL

FRIDAY ____

7 ____
8 ____
9 ____
10 ____
11 ____
12 ____
1 ____
2 ____
3 ____
4 ____
5 ____
6 ____
7 ____
8 ____
9 ____

daily checklist

- MORNING RITUAL
- DAILY DRESS-UP
- MINDFUL MOVEMENT
- EAT YOUR VEGGIES
- JOURNAL
- GOAL REVIEW
- GRATITUDE
- EVENING RITUAL

SATURDAY ____

7 ____
8 ____
9 ____
10 ____
11 ____
12 ____
1 ____
2 ____
3 ____
4 ____
5 ____
6 ____
7 ____
8 ____
9 ____

daily checklist

- MORNING RITUAL
- DAILY DRESS-UP
- MINDFUL MOVEMENT
- EAT YOUR VEGGIES
- JOURNAL
- GOAL REVIEW
- GRATITUDE
- EVENING RITUAL

SUNDAY ____

7 ____
8 ____
9 ____
10 ____
11 ____
12 ____
1 ____
2 ____
3 ____
4 ____
5 ____
6 ____
7 ____
8 ____
9 ____

daily checklist

- MORNING RITUAL
- DAILY DRESS-UP
- MINDFUL MOVEMENT
- EAT YOUR VEGGIES
- JOURNAL
- GOAL REVIEW
- GRATITUDE
- EVENING RITUAL

LOVE
WHO
YOU
ARE

month's dreams

DOODLE, LIST, COLLAGE, OR WRITE WHAT YOU'D LIKE TO MANIFEST THIS MONTH.

month's review

REVISIT YOUR MONTH'S DREAMS AND NOTE HOW THEY UNFOLDED FOR YOU.

30 days of tranquility

TRY THIS 30-DAY CHALLENGE TO INFUSE YOUR MONTH WITH SIMPLE PLEASURES.

1 SIT STILL FOR FIVE MINUTES

2 DO SIX SUN SALUTATIONS

3 WRITE A LOVE LETTER

4 APOLOGIZE

5 TELL THE TRUTH

6 CONSUME A GREEN DRINK

7 GO MEAT-FREE

8 WALK FOR 20 MINUTES

9 DO LEGS UP THE WALL

10 GIVE $10 TO CHARITY

11 PEN TWO JOURNAL PAGES

12 REVIEW YOUR YEAR'S DREAMS

13 CLEAR CLUTTER

14 GO ON AN ARTIST DATE

15 COLLAGE TWO PAGES

16 TREAT YOURSELF TO TEA

17 READ FOR 20 MINUTES

18 BUY YOURSELF FLOWERS

19 DANCE TO A FAVORITE TUNE

20 EXPRESS GRATITUDE

21 EAT ONLY UNPROCESSED FOODS

22 SOAK IN A BUBBLE BATH

23 MINDFULLY SIP A LIBATION

24 GET OUT IN NATURE

25 FORGO COMPLAINING

26 TAKE A DIGITAL DAY OFF

27 SNAP PHOTOS FROM YOUR DAY

28 MAKE A FAVORITE MEAL

29 HUG

30 BE FULLY PRESENT

habit tracking

NOTE HABITS YOU'RE TRYING TO ADD OR SUBTRACT AND TRACK THEM DAILY TO HELP WITH ACCOUNTABILITY. CELEBRATE YOUR SUCCESSES AND OBSERVE AREAS FOR GROWTH.

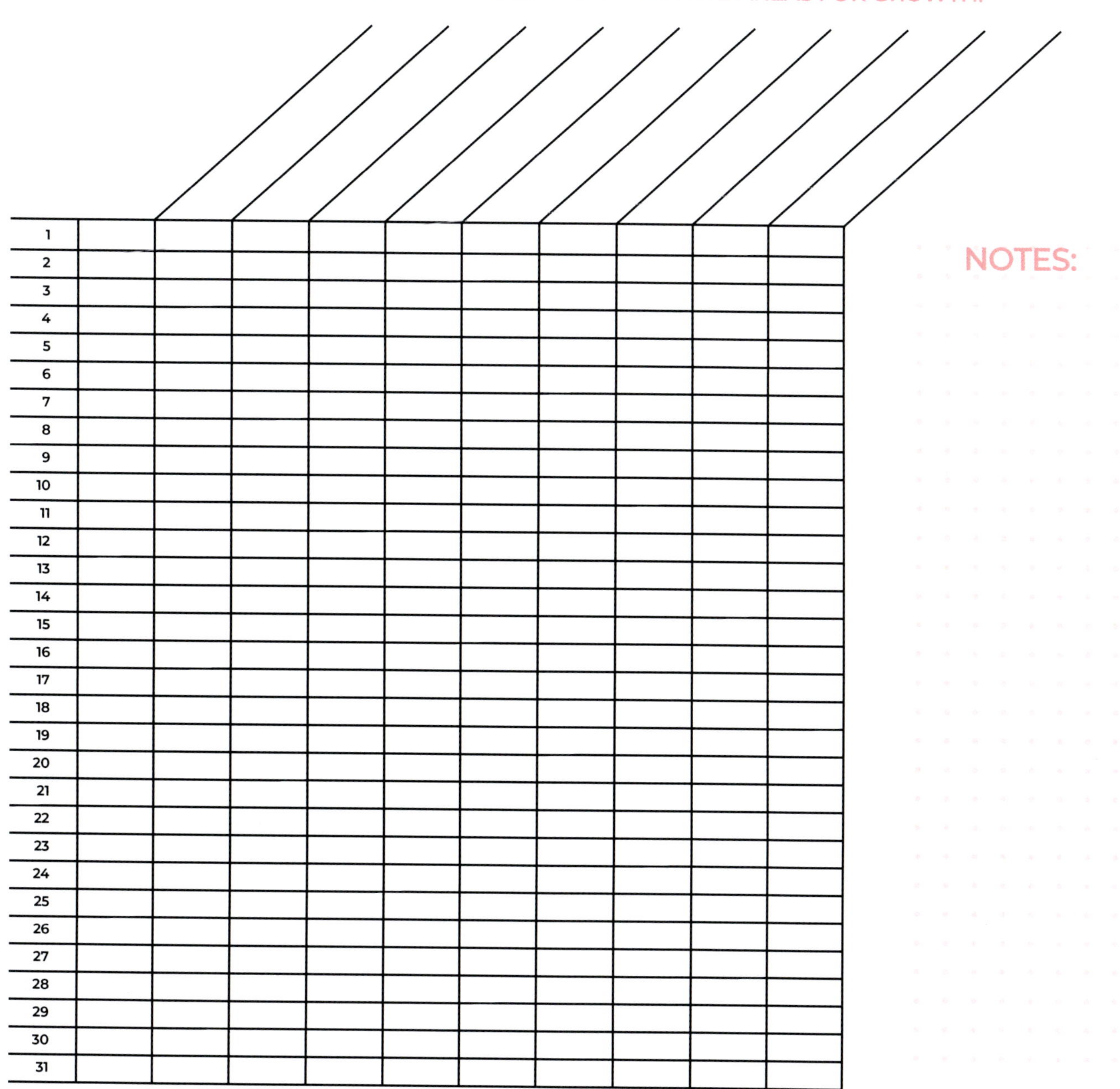

1										
2										
3										
4										
5										
6										
7										
8										
9										
10										
11										
12										
13										
14										
15										
16										
17										
18										
19										
20										
21										
22										
23										
24										
25										
26										
27										
28										
29										
30										
31										

NOTES:

moon phases

Notice your connection to the moon's cycles in these four phases: new, waxing, full, waning. Consider the prompts below as a way to tie into your Month's Dreams and provide space for monthly reflection.*

new moon

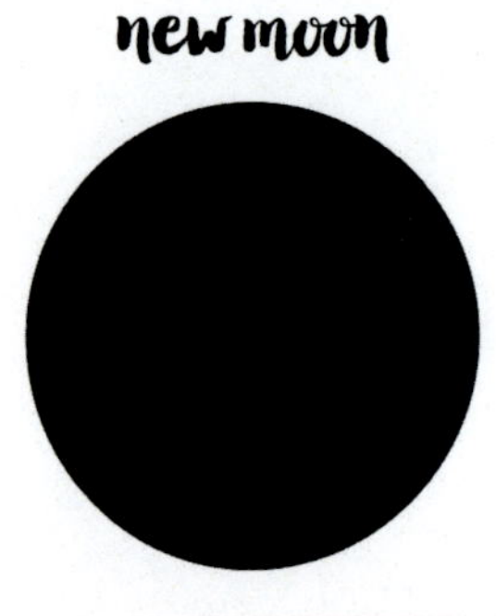

A TIME FOR SETTING INTENTIONS.
I WANT . . .

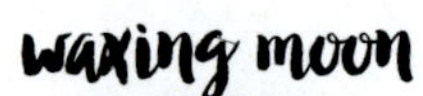

A TIME FOR ACTION. I WILL . . .

full moon

A TIME FOR HARVEST AND CLOSURE.
I RELEASE . . .

waning moon

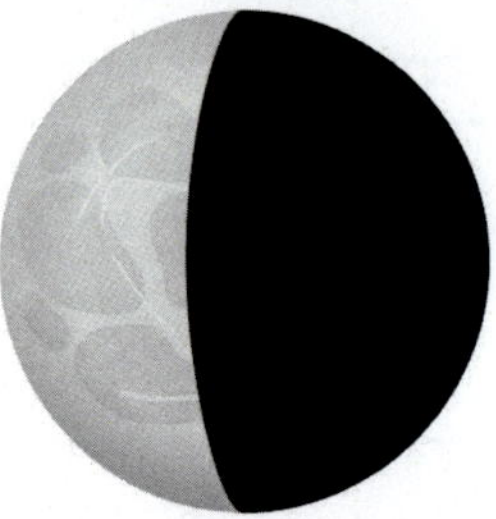

A TIME FOR SOFTENING. I FEEL . . .

monthly planner

MONTH: ______________________ INTENTION: ______________________

SUNDAY	MONDAY	TUESDAY	WEDNESDAY	THURSDAY	FRIDAY	SATURDAY

MONTHLY TRANQUILITY TOOLS

- ❍ CRAFT MONTH'S DREAMS
- ❍ REVIEW BUDGET
- ❍ CREATE SOMETHING
- ❍ READ TWO BOOKS
- ❍ VOLUNTEER
- ❍ MANI/PEDI
- ❍ ENTERTAIN
- ❍ MASSAGE

INTENTION:

weekly checklist

- ❍ PLAN WEEK'S MITS
- ❍ SOAK IN THE TUB
- ❍ TAKE A DIGITAL DAY OFF
- ❍ CLEAR CLUTTER
- ❍ PEN A LOVE NOTE
- ❍ BUY/PICK FRESH FLOWERS
- ❍ TAKE AN ARTIST DATE
- ❍ SAVOR A GREEN JUICE
- ❍ ____

MITs

- ❍ ____
- ❍ ____
- ❍ ____
- ❍ ____
- ❍ ____

wellness planning

M ____
T ____
W ____
TH ____
F ____
S ____
S ____

GRATITUDE:

MONDAY ____

7 ____
8 ____
9 ____
10 ____
11 ____
12 ____
1 ____
2 ____
3 ____
4 ____
5 ____
6 ____
7 ____
8 ____
9 ____

- ❍ ____
- ❍ ____
- ❍ ____
- ❍ ____
- ❍ ____
- ❍ ____
- ❍ ____
- ❍ ____
- ❍ ____
- ❍ ____

- ❍ ____
- ❍ ____
- ❍ ____
- ❍ ____
- ❍ ____
- ❍ ____

daily checklist

- ❍ MORNING RITUAL
- ❍ DAILY DRESS-UP
- ❍ MINDFUL MOVEMENT
- ❍ EAT YOUR VEGGIES
- ❍ JOURNAL
- ❍ GOAL REVIEW
- ❍ GRATITUDE
- ❍ EVENING RITUAL
- ❍ ____

TUESDAY ____

7 ____
8 ____
9 ____
10 ____
11 ____
12 ____
1 ____
2 ____
3 ____
4 ____
5 ____
6 ____
7 ____
8 ____
9 ____

- ❍ ____
- ❍ ____
- ❍ ____
- ❍ ____
- ❍ ____
- ❍ ____
- ❍ ____
- ❍ ____
- ❍ ____
- ❍ ____

- ❍ ____
- ❍ ____
- ❍ ____
- ❍ ____
- ❍ ____
- ❍ ____

daily checklist

- ❍ MORNING RITUAL
- ❍ DAILY DRESS-UP
- ❍ MINDFUL MOVEMENT
- ❍ EAT YOUR VEGGIES
- ❍ JOURNAL
- ❍ GOAL REVIEW
- ❍ GRATITUDE
- ❍ EVENING RITUAL
- ❍ ____

WEDNESDAY ____

7 ____
8 ____
9 ____
10 ____
11 ____
12 ____
1 ____
2 ____
3 ____
4 ____
5 ____
6 ____
7 ____
8 ____
9 ____

- ❍ ____
- ❍ ____
- ❍ ____
- ❍ ____
- ❍ ____
- ❍ ____
- ❍ ____
- ❍ ____
- ❍ ____
- ❍ ____

- ❍ ____
- ❍ ____
- ❍ ____
- ❍ ____
- ❍ ____
- ❍ ____

daily checklist

- ❍ MORNING RITUAL
- ❍ DAILY DRESS-UP
- ❍ MINDFUL MOVEMENT
- ❍ EAT YOUR VEGGIES
- ❍ JOURNAL
- ❍ GOAL REVIEW
- ❍ GRATITUDE
- ❍ EVENING RITUAL
- ❍ ____

THURSDAY

7
8
9
10
11
12
1
2
3
4
5
6
7
8
9

daily checklist

- MORNING RITUAL
- DAILY DRESS-UP
- MINDFUL MOVEMENT
- EAT YOUR VEGGIES
- JOURNAL
- GOAL REVIEW
- GRATITUDE
- EVENING RITUAL

FRIDAY

7
8
9
10
11
12
1
2
3
4
5
6
7
8
9

daily checklist

- MORNING RITUAL
- DAILY DRESS-UP
- MINDFUL MOVEMENT
- EAT YOUR VEGGIES
- JOURNAL
- GOAL REVIEW
- GRATITUDE
- EVENING RITUAL

SATURDAY

7
8
9
10
11
12
1
2
3
4
5
6
7
8
9

daily checklist

- MORNING RITUAL
- DAILY DRESS-UP
- MINDFUL MOVEMENT
- EAT YOUR VEGGIES
- JOURNAL
- GOAL REVIEW
- GRATITUDE
- EVENING RITUAL

SUNDAY

7
8
9
10
11
12
1
2
3
4
5
6
7
8
9

daily checklist

- MORNING RITUAL
- DAILY DRESS-UP
- MINDFUL MOVEMENT
- EAT YOUR VEGGIES
- JOURNAL
- GOAL REVIEW
- GRATITUDE
- EVENING RITUAL

INTENTION:

weekly checklist

- PLAN WEEK'S MITS
- SOAK IN THE TUB
- TAKE A DIGITAL DAY OFF
- CLEAR CLUTTER
- PEN A LOVE NOTE
- BUY/PICK FRESH FLOWERS
- TAKE AN ARTIST DATE
- SAVOR A GREEN JUICE
- __________

MITs

wellness planning

M

T

W

TH

F

S

S

GRATITUDE:

MONDAY

7
8
9
10
11
12
1
2
3
4
5
6
7
8
9

daily checklist

- MORNING RITUAL
- DAILY DRESS-UP
- MINDFUL MOVEMENT
- EAT YOUR VEGGIES
- JOURNAL
- GOAL REVIEW
- GRATITUDE
- EVENING RITUAL

TUESDAY

7
8
9
10
11
12
1
2
3
4
5
6
7
8
9

daily checklist

- MORNING RITUAL
- DAILY DRESS-UP
- MINDFUL MOVEMENT
- EAT YOUR VEGGIES
- JOURNAL
- GOAL REVIEW
- GRATITUDE
- EVENING RITUAL

WEDNESDAY

7
8
9
10
11
12
1
2
3
4
5
6
7
8
9

daily checklist

- MORNING RITUAL
- DAILY DRESS-UP
- MINDFUL MOVEMENT
- EAT YOUR VEGGIES
- JOURNAL
- GOAL REVIEW
- GRATITUDE
- EVENING RITUAL

THURSDAY ____________

7 ____________
8 ____________
9 ____________
10 ____________
11 ____________
12 ____________
1 ____________
2 ____________
3 ____________
4 ____________
5 ____________
6 ____________
7 ____________
8 ____________
9 ____________

daily checklist

- MORNING RITUAL
- DAILY DRESS-UP
- MINDFUL MOVEMENT
- EAT YOUR VEGGIES
- JOURNAL
- GOAL REVIEW
- GRATITUDE
- EVENING RITUAL

FRIDAY ____________

7 ____________
8 ____________
9 ____________
10 ____________
11 ____________
12 ____________
1 ____________
2 ____________
3 ____________
4 ____________
5 ____________
6 ____________
7 ____________
8 ____________
9 ____________

daily checklist

- MORNING RITUAL
- DAILY DRESS-UP
- MINDFUL MOVEMENT
- EAT YOUR VEGGIES
- JOURNAL
- GOAL REVIEW
- GRATITUDE
- EVENING RITUAL

SATURDAY ____________

7 ____________
8 ____________
9 ____________
10 ____________
11 ____________
12 ____________
1 ____________
2 ____________
3 ____________
4 ____________
5 ____________
6 ____________
7 ____________
8 ____________
9 ____________

daily checklist

- MORNING RITUAL
- DAILY DRESS-UP
- MINDFUL MOVEMENT
- EAT YOUR VEGGIES
- JOURNAL
- GOAL REVIEW
- GRATITUDE
- EVENING RITUAL

SUNDAY ____________

7 ____________
8 ____________
9 ____________
10 ____________
11 ____________
12 ____________
1 ____________
2 ____________
3 ____________
4 ____________
5 ____________
6 ____________
7 ____________
8 ____________
9 ____________

daily checklist

- MORNING RITUAL
- DAILY DRESS-UP
- MINDFUL MOVEMENT
- EAT YOUR VEGGIES
- JOURNAL
- GOAL REVIEW
- GRATITUDE
- EVENING RITUAL

INTENTION:

weekly checklist

- ❍ PLAN WEEK'S MITS
- ❍ SOAK IN THE TUB
- ❍ TAKE A DIGITAL DAY OFF
- ❍ CLEAR CLUTTER
- ❍ PEN A LOVE NOTE
- ❍ BUY/PICK FRESH FLOWERS
- ❍ TAKE AN ARTIST DATE
- ❍ SAVOR A GREEN JUICE
- ❍ ____________

MITs

- ❍ ____________
- ❍ ____________
- ❍ ____________
- ❍ ____________
- ❍ ____________

wellness planning

M ____________
T ____________
W ____________
TH ____________
F ____________
S ____________
S ____________

GRATITUDE:

MONDAY ____________

7 ____________
8 ____________
9 ____________
10 ____________
11 ____________
12 ____________
1 ____________
2 ____________
3 ____________
4 ____________
5 ____________
6 ____________
7 ____________
8 ____________
9 ____________

daily checklist

- ❍ MORNING RITUAL
- ❍ DAILY DRESS-UP
- ❍ MINDFUL MOVEMENT
- ❍ EAT YOUR VEGGIES
- ❍ JOURNAL
- ❍ GOAL REVIEW
- ❍ GRATITUDE
- ❍ EVENING RITUAL
- ❍ ____________

TUESDAY ____________

7 ____________
8 ____________
9 ____________
10 ____________
11 ____________
12 ____________
1 ____________
2 ____________
3 ____________
4 ____________
5 ____________
6 ____________
7 ____________
8 ____________
9 ____________

daily checklist

- ❍ MORNING RITUAL
- ❍ DAILY DRESS-UP
- ❍ MINDFUL MOVEMENT
- ❍ EAT YOUR VEGGIES
- ❍ JOURNAL
- ❍ GOAL REVIEW
- ❍ GRATITUDE
- ❍ EVENING RITUAL
- ❍ ____________

WEDNESDAY ____________

7 ____________
8 ____________
9 ____________
10 ____________
11 ____________
12 ____________
1 ____________
2 ____________
3 ____________
4 ____________
5 ____________
6 ____________
7 ____________
8 ____________
9 ____________

daily checklist

- ❍ MORNING RITUAL
- ❍ DAILY DRESS-UP
- ❍ MINDFUL MOVEMENT
- ❍ EAT YOUR VEGGIES
- ❍ JOURNAL
- ❍ GOAL REVIEW
- ❍ GRATITUDE
- ❍ EVENING RITUAL
- ❍ ____________

THURSDAY

7
8
9
10
11
12
1
2
3
4
5
6
7
8
9

daily checklist

- MORNING RITUAL
- DAILY DRESS-UP
- MINDFUL MOVEMENT
- EAT YOUR VEGGIES
- JOURNAL
- GOAL REVIEW
- GRATITUDE
- EVENING RITUAL

FRIDAY

7
8
9
10
11
12
1
2
3
4
5
6
7
8
9

daily checklist

- MORNING RITUAL
- DAILY DRESS-UP
- MINDFUL MOVEMENT
- EAT YOUR VEGGIES
- JOURNAL
- GOAL REVIEW
- GRATITUDE
- EVENING RITUAL

SATURDAY

7
8
9
10
11
12
1
2
3
4
5
6
7
8
9

daily checklist

- MORNING RITUAL
- DAILY DRESS-UP
- MINDFUL MOVEMENT
- EAT YOUR VEGGIES
- JOURNAL
- GOAL REVIEW
- GRATITUDE
- EVENING RITUAL

SUNDAY

7
8
9
10
11
12
1
2
3
4
5
6
7
8
9

daily checklist

- MORNING RITUAL
- DAILY DRESS-UP
- MINDFUL MOVEMENT
- EAT YOUR VEGGIES
- JOURNAL
- GOAL REVIEW
- GRATITUDE
- EVENING RITUAL

INTENTION:

weekly checklist

- PLAN WEEK'S MITS
- SOAK IN THE TUB
- TAKE A DIGITAL DAY OFF
- CLEAR CLUTTER
- PEN A LOVE NOTE
- BUY/PICK FRESH FLOWERS
- TAKE AN ARTIST DATE
- SAVOR A GREEN JUICE
- ______

MITs

- ______
- ______
- ______
- ______
- ______

wellness planning

M ______
T ______
W ______
TH ______
F ______
S ______
S ______

GRATITUDE:

MONDAY ______

7 ______
8 ______
9 ______
10 ______
11 ______
12 ______
1 ______
2 ______
3 ______
4 ______
5 ______
6 ______
7 ______
8 ______
9 ______

daily checklist

- MORNING RITUAL
- DAILY DRESS-UP
- MINDFUL MOVEMENT
- EAT YOUR VEGGIES
- JOURNAL
- GOAL REVIEW
- GRATITUDE
- EVENING RITUAL
- ______

TUESDAY ______

7 ______
8 ______
9 ______
10 ______
11 ______
12 ______
1 ______
2 ______
3 ______
4 ______
5 ______
6 ______
7 ______
8 ______
9 ______

daily checklist

- MORNING RITUAL
- DAILY DRESS-UP
- MINDFUL MOVEMENT
- EAT YOUR VEGGIES
- JOURNAL
- GOAL REVIEW
- GRATITUDE
- EVENING RITUAL
- ______

WEDNESDAY ______

7 ______
8 ______
9 ______
10 ______
11 ______
12 ______
1 ______
2 ______
3 ______
4 ______
5 ______
6 ______
7 ______
8 ______
9 ______

daily checklist

- MORNING RITUAL
- DAILY DRESS-UP
- MINDFUL MOVEMENT
- EAT YOUR VEGGIES
- JOURNAL
- GOAL REVIEW
- GRATITUDE
- EVENING RITUAL
- ______

THURSDAY
7
8
9
10
11
12
1
2
3
4
5
6
7
8
9

daily checklist
- MORNING RITUAL
- DAILY DRESS-UP
- MINDFUL MOVEMENT
- EAT YOUR VEGGIES
- JOURNAL
- GOAL REVIEW
- GRATITUDE
- EVENING RITUAL

FRIDAY
7
8
9
10
11
12
1
2
3
4
5
6
7
8
9

daily checklist
- MORNING RITUAL
- DAILY DRESS-UP
- MINDFUL MOVEMENT
- EAT YOUR VEGGIES
- JOURNAL
- GOAL REVIEW
- GRATITUDE
- EVENING RITUAL

SATURDAY
7
8
9
10
11
12
1
2
3
4
5
6
7
8
9

daily checklist
- MORNING RITUAL
- DAILY DRESS-UP
- MINDFUL MOVEMENT
- EAT YOUR VEGGIES
- JOURNAL
- GOAL REVIEW
- GRATITUDE
- EVENING RITUAL

SUNDAY
7
8
9
10
11
12
1
2
3
4
5
6
7
8
9

daily checklist
- MORNING RITUAL
- DAILY DRESS-UP
- MINDFUL MOVEMENT
- EAT YOUR VEGGIES
- JOURNAL
- GOAL REVIEW
- GRATITUDE
- EVENING RITUAL

INTENTION:

MONDAY ______

7 ______
8 ______
9 ______
10 ______
11 ______
12 ______
1 ______
2 ______
3 ______
4 ______
5 ______
6 ______
7 ______
8 ______
9 ______

TUESDAY ______

7 ______
8 ______
9 ______
10 ______
11 ______
12 ______
1 ______
2 ______
3 ______
4 ______
5 ______
6 ______
7 ______
8 ______
9 ______

WEDNESDAY ______

7 ______
8 ______
9 ______
10 ______
11 ______
12 ______
1 ______
2 ______
3 ______
4 ______
5 ______
6 ______
7 ______
8 ______
9 ______

weekly checklist

- ❍ PLAN WEEK'S MITS
- ❍ SOAK IN THE TUB
- ❍ TAKE A DIGITAL DAY OFF
- ❍ CLEAR CLUTTER
- ❍ PEN A LOVE NOTE
- ❍ BUY/PICK FRESH FLOWERS
- ❍ TAKE AN ARTIST DATE
- ❍ SAVOR A GREEN JUICE
- ❍ ______

MITs

- ❍ ______
- ❍ ______
- ❍ ______
- ❍ ______
- ❍ ______

wellness planning

M ______
T ______
W ______
TH ______
F ______
S ______
S ______

GRATITUDE:

daily checklist

- ❍ MORNING RITUAL
- ❍ DAILY DRESS-UP
- ❍ MINDFUL MOVEMENT
- ❍ EAT YOUR VEGGIES
- ❍ JOURNAL
- ❍ GOAL REVIEW
- ❍ GRATITUDE
- ❍ EVENING RITUAL
- ❍ ______

daily checklist

- ❍ MORNING RITUAL
- ❍ DAILY DRESS-UP
- ❍ MINDFUL MOVEMENT
- ❍ EAT YOUR VEGGIES
- ❍ JOURNAL
- ❍ GOAL REVIEW
- ❍ GRATITUDE
- ❍ EVENING RITUAL
- ❍ ______

daily checklist

- ❍ MORNING RITUAL
- ❍ DAILY DRESS-UP
- ❍ MINDFUL MOVEMENT
- ❍ EAT YOUR VEGGIES
- ❍ JOURNAL
- ❍ GOAL REVIEW
- ❍ GRATITUDE
- ❍ EVENING RITUAL
- ❍ ______

THURSDAY

7
8
9
10
11
12
1
2
3
4
5
6
7
8
9

daily checklist

- MORNING RITUAL
- DAILY DRESS-UP
- MINDFUL MOVEMENT
- EAT YOUR VEGGIES
- JOURNAL
- GOAL REVIEW
- GRATITUDE
- EVENING RITUAL

FRIDAY

7
8
9
10
11
12
1
2
3
4
5
6
7
8
9

daily checklist

- MORNING RITUAL
- DAILY DRESS-UP
- MINDFUL MOVEMENT
- EAT YOUR VEGGIES
- JOURNAL
- GOAL REVIEW
- GRATITUDE
- EVENING RITUAL

SATURDAY

7
8
9
10
11
12
1
2
3
4
5
6
7
8
9

daily checklist

- MORNING RITUAL
- DAILY DRESS-UP
- MINDFUL MOVEMENT
- EAT YOUR VEGGIES
- JOURNAL
- GOAL REVIEW
- GRATITUDE
- EVENING RITUAL

SUNDAY

7
8
9
10
11
12
1
2
3
4
5
6
7
8
9

daily checklist

- MORNING RITUAL
- DAILY DRESS-UP
- MINDFUL MOVEMENT
- EAT YOUR VEGGIES
- JOURNAL
- GOAL REVIEW
- GRATITUDE
- EVENING RITUAL

Hortensia
20 €
pot.

month's dreams

DOODLE, LIST, COLLAGE, OR WRITE WHAT YOU'D LIKE TO MANIFEST THIS MONTH.

month's review

REVISIT YOUR MONTH'S DREAMS AND NOTE HOW THEY UNFOLDED FOR YOU.

30 days of tranquility

TRY THIS 30-DAY CHALLENGE TO INFUSE YOUR MONTH WITH SIMPLE PLEASURES.

1 SIT STILL FOR FIVE MINUTES	2 DO SIX SUN SALUTATIONS	3 WRITE A LOVE LETTER	4 APOLOGIZE	5 TELL THE TRUTH
6 CONSUME A GREEN DRINK	7 GO MEAT-FREE	8 WALK FOR 20 MINUTES	9 DO LEGS UP THE WALL	10 GIVE $10 TO CHARITY
11 PEN TWO JOURNAL PAGES	12 REVIEW YOUR YEAR'S DREAMS	13 CLEAR CLUTTER	14 GO ON AN ARTIST DATE	15 COLLAGE TWO PAGES
16 TREAT YOURSELF TO TEA	17 READ FOR 20 MINUTES	18 BUY YOURSELF FLOWERS	19 DANCE TO A FAVORITE TUNE	20 EXPRESS GRATITUDE
21 EAT ONLY UNPROCESSED FOODS	22 SOAK IN A BUBBLE BATH	23 MINDFULLY SIP A LIBATION	24 GET OUT IN NATURE	25 FORGO COMPLAINING
26 TAKE A DIGITAL DAY OFF	27 SNAP PHOTOS FROM YOUR DAY	28 MAKE A FAVORITE MEAL	29 HUG	30 BE FULLY PRESENT

habit tracking

NOTE HABITS YOU'RE TRYING TO ADD OR SUBTRACT AND TRACK THEM DAILY TO HELP WITH ACCOUNTABILITY. CELEBRATE YOUR SUCCESSES AND OBSERVE AREAS FOR GROWTH.

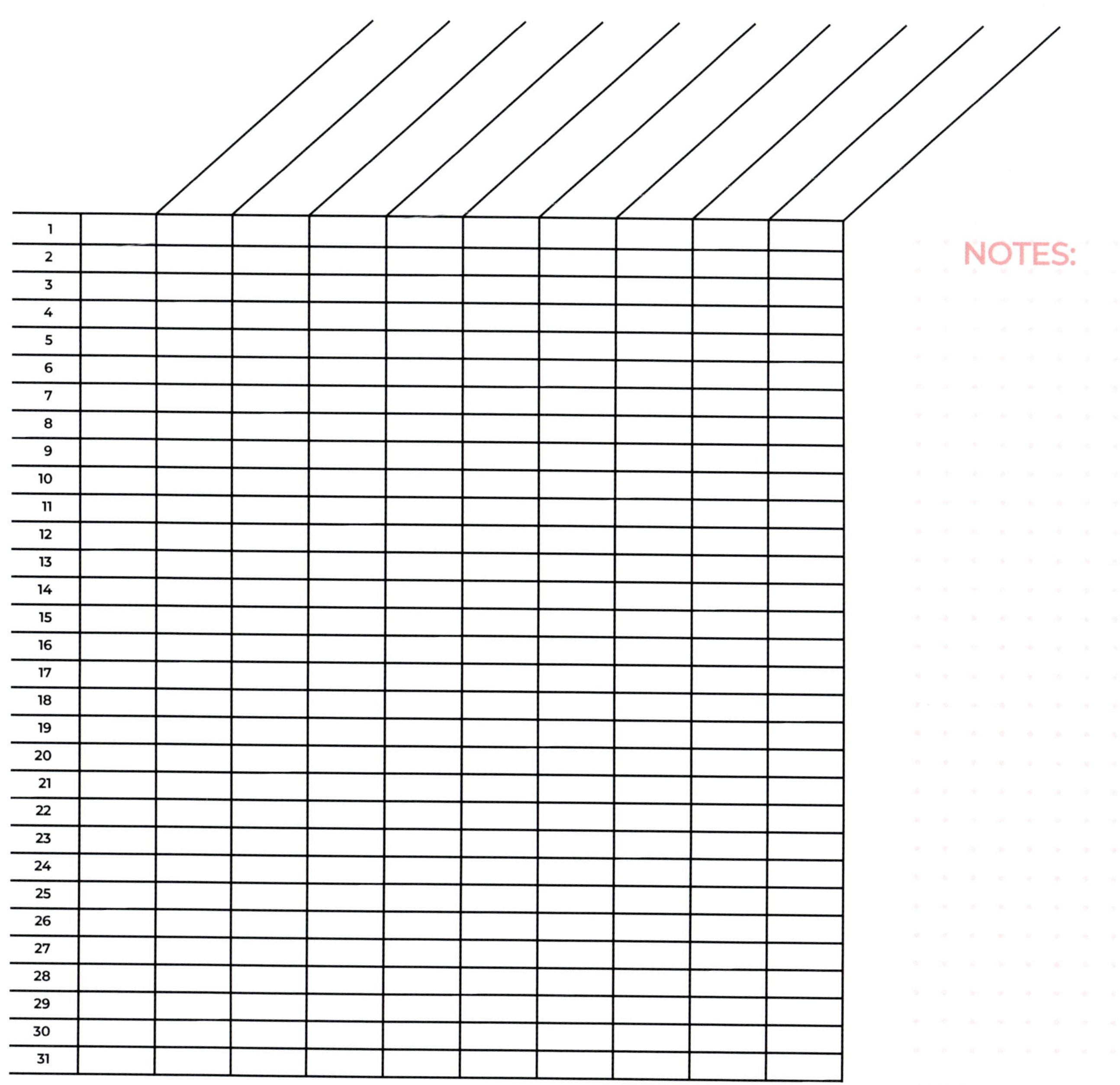

moon phases

Notice your connection to the moon's cycles in these four phases: new, waxing, full, waning. Consider the prompts below as a way to tie into your Month's Dreams and provide space for monthly reflection.

new moon

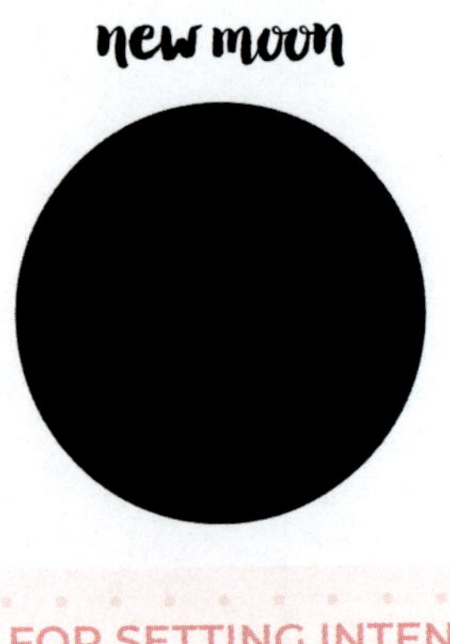

A TIME FOR SETTING INTENTIONS.
I WANT . . .

waxing moon

A TIME FOR ACTION. I WILL . . .

full moon

A TIME FOR HARVEST AND CLOSURE.
I RELEASE . . .

waning moon

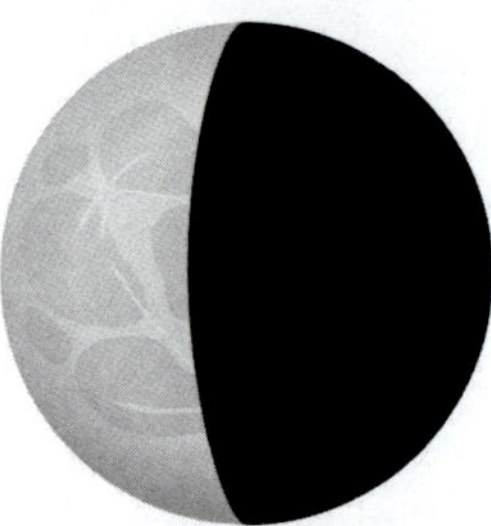

A TIME FOR SOFTENING. I FEEL . . .

monthly planner

MONTH: ______________________ INTENTION: ______________________

SUNDAY	MONDAY	TUESDAY	WEDNESDAY	THURSDAY	FRIDAY	SATURDAY

MONTHLY TRANQUILITY TOOLS

- ❍ CRAFT MONTH'S DREAMS
- ❍ REVIEW BUDGET
- ❍ CREATE SOMETHING
- ❍ READ TWO BOOKS
- ❍ VOLUNTEER
- ❍ MANI/PEDI
- ❍ ENTERTAIN
- ❍ MASSAGE

INTENTION:

weekly checklist

- ❍ PLAN WEEK'S MITS
- ❍ SOAK IN THE TUB
- ❍ TAKE A DIGITAL DAY OFF
- ❍ CLEAR CLUTTER
- ❍ PEN A LOVE NOTE
- ❍ BUY/PICK FRESH FLOWERS
- ❍ TAKE AN ARTIST DATE
- ❍ SAVOR A GREEN JUICE
- ❍ ______

MITs

- ❍ ______
- ❍ ______
- ❍ ______
- ❍ ______
- ❍ ______

wellness planning

M ______
T ______
W ______
TH ______
F ______
S ______
S ______

GRATITUDE:

MONDAY ______

7 ______
8 ______
9 ______
10 ______
11 ______
12 ______
1 ______
2 ______
3 ______
4 ______
5 ______
6 ______
7 ______
8 ______
9 ______

daily checklist

- ❍ MORNING RITUAL
- ❍ DAILY DRESS-UP
- ❍ MINDFUL MOVEMENT
- ❍ EAT YOUR VEGGIES
- ❍ JOURNAL
- ❍ GOAL REVIEW
- ❍ GRATITUDE
- ❍ EVENING RITUAL
- ❍ ______

TUESDAY ______

7 ______
8 ______
9 ______
10 ______
11 ______
12 ______
1 ______
2 ______
3 ______
4 ______
5 ______
6 ______
7 ______
8 ______
9 ______

daily checklist

- ❍ MORNING RITUAL
- ❍ DAILY DRESS-UP
- ❍ MINDFUL MOVEMENT
- ❍ EAT YOUR VEGGIES
- ❍ JOURNAL
- ❍ GOAL REVIEW
- ❍ GRATITUDE
- ❍ EVENING RITUAL
- ❍ ______

WEDNESDAY ______

7 ______
8 ______
9 ______
10 ______
11 ______
12 ______
1 ______
2 ______
3 ______
4 ______
5 ______
6 ______
7 ______
8 ______
9 ______

daily checklist

- ❍ MORNING RITUAL
- ❍ DAILY DRESS-UP
- ❍ MINDFUL MOVEMENT
- ❍ EAT YOUR VEGGIES
- ❍ JOURNAL
- ❍ GOAL REVIEW
- ❍ GRATITUDE
- ❍ EVENING RITUAL
- ❍ ______

THURSDAY

7
8
9
10
11
12
1
2
3
4
5
6
7
8
9

daily checklist

- MORNING RITUAL
- DAILY DRESS-UP
- MINDFUL MOVEMENT
- EAT YOUR VEGGIES
- JOURNAL
- GOAL REVIEW
- GRATITUDE
- EVENING RITUAL

FRIDAY

7
8
9
10
11
12
1
2
3
4
5
6
7
8
9

daily checklist

- MORNING RITUAL
- DAILY DRESS-UP
- MINDFUL MOVEMENT
- EAT YOUR VEGGIES
- JOURNAL
- GOAL REVIEW
- GRATITUDE
- EVENING RITUAL

SATURDAY

7
8
9
10
11
12
1
2
3
4
5
6
7
8
9

daily checklist

- MORNING RITUAL
- DAILY DRESS-UP
- MINDFUL MOVEMENT
- EAT YOUR VEGGIES
- JOURNAL
- GOAL REVIEW
- GRATITUDE
- EVENING RITUAL

SUNDAY

7
8
9
10
11
12
1
2
3
4
5
6
7
8
9

daily checklist

- MORNING RITUAL
- DAILY DRESS-UP
- MINDFUL MOVEMENT
- EAT YOUR VEGGIES
- JOURNAL
- GOAL REVIEW
- GRATITUDE
- EVENING RITUAL

INTENTION:

weekly checklist

- PLAN WEEK'S MITS
- SOAK IN THE TUB
- TAKE A DIGITAL DAY OFF
- CLEAR CLUTTER
- PEN A LOVE NOTE
- BUY/PICK FRESH FLOWERS
- TAKE AN ARTIST DATE
- SAVOR A GREEN JUICE
- ______

MITs

- ______
- ______
- ______
- ______
- ______

wellness planning

M ______
T ______
W ______
TH ______
F ______
S ______
S ______

GRATITUDE:

MONDAY ______

7 ______
8 ______
9 ______
10 ______
11 ______
12 ______
1 ______
2 ______
3 ______
4 ______
5 ______
6 ______
7 ______
8 ______
9 ______

daily checklist

- MORNING RITUAL
- DAILY DRESS-UP
- MINDFUL MOVEMENT
- EAT YOUR VEGGIES
- JOURNAL
- GOAL REVIEW
- GRATITUDE
- EVENING RITUAL
- ______

TUESDAY ______

7 ______
8 ______
9 ______
10 ______
11 ______
12 ______
1 ______
2 ______
3 ______
4 ______
5 ______
6 ______
7 ______
8 ______
9 ______

daily checklist

- MORNING RITUAL
- DAILY DRESS-UP
- MINDFUL MOVEMENT
- EAT YOUR VEGGIES
- JOURNAL
- GOAL REVIEW
- GRATITUDE
- EVENING RITUAL
- ______

WEDNESDAY ______

7 ______
8 ______
9 ______
10 ______
11 ______
12 ______
1 ______
2 ______
3 ______
4 ______
5 ______
6 ______
7 ______
8 ______
9 ______

daily checklist

- MORNING RITUAL
- DAILY DRESS-UP
- MINDFUL MOVEMENT
- EAT YOUR VEGGIES
- JOURNAL
- GOAL REVIEW
- GRATITUDE
- EVENING RITUAL
- ______

THURSDAY	FRIDAY	SATURDAY	SUNDAY
7	7	7	7
8	8	8	8
9	9	9	9
10	10	10	10
11	11	11	11
12	12	12	12
1	1	1	1
2	2	2	2
3	3	3	3
4	4	4	4
5	5	5	5
6	6	6	6
7	7	7	7
8	8	8	8
9	9	9	9

daily checklist

- MORNING RITUAL
- DAILY DRESS-UP
- MINDFUL MOVEMENT
- EAT YOUR VEGGIES
- JOURNAL
- GOAL REVIEW
- GRATITUDE
- EVENING RITUAL

daily checklist

- MORNING RITUAL
- DAILY DRESS-UP
- MINDFUL MOVEMENT
- EAT YOUR VEGGIES
- JOURNAL
- GOAL REVIEW
- GRATITUDE
- EVENING RITUAL

daily checklist

- MORNING RITUAL
- DAILY DRESS-UP
- MINDFUL MOVEMENT
- EAT YOUR VEGGIES
- JOURNAL
- GOAL REVIEW
- GRATITUDE
- EVENING RITUAL

daily checklist

- MORNING RITUAL
- DAILY DRESS-UP
- MINDFUL MOVEMENT
- EAT YOUR VEGGIES
- JOURNAL
- GOAL REVIEW
- GRATITUDE
- EVENING RITUAL

INTENTION:

weekly checklist

- ❍ PLAN WEEK'S MITS
- ❍ SOAK IN THE TUB
- ❍ TAKE A DIGITAL DAY OFF
- ❍ CLEAR CLUTTER
- ❍ PEN A LOVE NOTE
- ❍ BUY/PICK FRESH FLOWERS
- ❍ TAKE AN ARTIST DATE
- ❍ SAVOR A GREEN JUICE
- ❍ ______

MITs

- ❍ ______
- ❍ ______
- ❍ ______
- ❍ ______
- ❍ ______

wellness planning

M ______
T ______
W ______
TH ______
F ______
S ______
S ______

GRATITUDE:

MONDAY ______

7 ______
8 ______
9 ______
10 ______
11 ______
12 ______
1 ______
2 ______
3 ______
4 ______
5 ______
6 ______
7 ______
8 ______
9 ______

daily checklist

- ❍ MORNING RITUAL
- ❍ DAILY DRESS-UP
- ❍ MINDFUL MOVEMENT
- ❍ EAT YOUR VEGGIES
- ❍ JOURNAL
- ❍ GOAL REVIEW
- ❍ GRATITUDE
- ❍ EVENING RITUAL
- ❍ ______

TUESDAY ______

7 ______
8 ______
9 ______
10 ______
11 ______
12 ______
1 ______
2 ______
3 ______
4 ______
5 ______
6 ______
7 ______
8 ______
9 ______

daily checklist

- ❍ MORNING RITUAL
- ❍ DAILY DRESS-UP
- ❍ MINDFUL MOVEMENT
- ❍ EAT YOUR VEGGIES
- ❍ JOURNAL
- ❍ GOAL REVIEW
- ❍ GRATITUDE
- ❍ EVENING RITUAL
- ❍ ______

WEDNESDAY ______

7 ______
8 ______
9 ______
10 ______
11 ______
12 ______
1 ______
2 ______
3 ______
4 ______
5 ______
6 ______
7 ______
8 ______
9 ______

daily checklist

- ❍ MORNING RITUAL
- ❍ DAILY DRESS-UP
- ❍ MINDFUL MOVEMENT
- ❍ EAT YOUR VEGGIES
- ❍ JOURNAL
- ❍ GOAL REVIEW
- ❍ GRATITUDE
- ❍ EVENING RITUAL
- ❍ ______

THURSDAY

7
8
9
10
11
12
1
2
3
4
5
6
7
8
9

daily checklist

- MORNING RITUAL
- DAILY DRESS-UP
- MINDFUL MOVEMENT
- EAT YOUR VEGGIES
- JOURNAL
- GOAL REVIEW
- GRATITUDE
- EVENING RITUAL

FRIDAY

7
8
9
10
11
12
1
2
3
4
5
6
7
8
9

daily checklist

- MORNING RITUAL
- DAILY DRESS-UP
- MINDFUL MOVEMENT
- EAT YOUR VEGGIES
- JOURNAL
- GOAL REVIEW
- GRATITUDE
- EVENING RITUAL

SATURDAY

7
8
9
10
11
12
1
2
3
4
5
6
7
8
9

daily checklist

- MORNING RITUAL
- DAILY DRESS-UP
- MINDFUL MOVEMENT
- EAT YOUR VEGGIES
- JOURNAL
- GOAL REVIEW
- GRATITUDE
- EVENING RITUAL

SUNDAY

7
8
9
10
11
12
1
2
3
4
5
6
7
8
9

daily checklist

- MORNING RITUAL
- DAILY DRESS-UP
- MINDFUL MOVEMENT
- EAT YOUR VEGGIES
- JOURNAL
- GOAL REVIEW
- GRATITUDE
- EVENING RITUAL

INTENTION:

weekly checklist

- PLAN WEEK'S MITS
- SOAK IN THE TUB
- TAKE A DIGITAL DAY OFF
- CLEAR CLUTTER
- PEN A LOVE NOTE
- BUY/PICK FRESH FLOWERS
- TAKE AN ARTIST DATE
- SAVOR A GREEN JUICE
- ______

MITs

- ______
- ______
- ______
- ______
- ______

wellness planning

M ______
T ______
W ______
TH ______
F ______
S ______
S ______

GRATITUDE:

MONDAY ______

7 ______
8 ______
9 ______
10 ______
11 ______
12 ______
1 ______
2 ______
3 ______
4 ______
5 ______
6 ______
7 ______
8 ______
9 ______

daily checklist

- MORNING RITUAL
- DAILY DRESS-UP
- MINDFUL MOVEMENT
- EAT YOUR VEGGIES
- JOURNAL
- GOAL REVIEW
- GRATITUDE
- EVENING RITUAL
- ______

TUESDAY ______

7 ______
8 ______
9 ______
10 ______
11 ______
12 ______
1 ______
2 ______
3 ______
4 ______
5 ______
6 ______
7 ______
8 ______
9 ______

daily checklist

- MORNING RITUAL
- DAILY DRESS-UP
- MINDFUL MOVEMENT
- EAT YOUR VEGGIES
- JOURNAL
- GOAL REVIEW
- GRATITUDE
- EVENING RITUAL
- ______

WEDNESDAY ______

7 ______
8 ______
9 ______
10 ______
11 ______
12 ______
1 ______
2 ______
3 ______
4 ______
5 ______
6 ______
7 ______
8 ______
9 ______

daily checklist

- MORNING RITUAL
- DAILY DRESS-UP
- MINDFUL MOVEMENT
- EAT YOUR VEGGIES
- JOURNAL
- GOAL REVIEW
- GRATITUDE
- EVENING RITUAL
- ______

THURSDAY

7
8
9
10
11
12
1
2
3
4
5
6
7
8
9

daily checklist

- MORNING RITUAL
- DAILY DRESS-UP
- MINDFUL MOVEMENT
- EAT YOUR VEGGIES
- JOURNAL
- GOAL REVIEW
- GRATITUDE
- EVENING RITUAL

FRIDAY

7
8
9
10
11
12
1
2
3
4
5
6
7
8
9

daily checklist

- MORNING RITUAL
- DAILY DRESS-UP
- MINDFUL MOVEMENT
- EAT YOUR VEGGIES
- JOURNAL
- GOAL REVIEW
- GRATITUDE
- EVENING RITUAL

SATURDAY

7
8
9
10
11
12
1
2
3
4
5
6
7
8
9

daily checklist

- MORNING RITUAL
- DAILY DRESS-UP
- MINDFUL MOVEMENT
- EAT YOUR VEGGIES
- JOURNAL
- GOAL REVIEW
- GRATITUDE
- EVENING RITUAL

SUNDAY

7
8
9
10
11
12
1
2
3
4
5
6
7
8
9

daily checklist

- MORNING RITUAL
- DAILY DRESS-UP
- MINDFUL MOVEMENT
- EAT YOUR VEGGIES
- JOURNAL
- GOAL REVIEW
- GRATITUDE
- EVENING RITUAL

INTENTION:

weekly checklist

- PLAN WEEK'S MITS
- SOAK IN THE TUB
- TAKE A DIGITAL DAY OFF
- CLEAR CLUTTER
- PEN A LOVE NOTE
- BUY/PICK FRESH FLOWERS
- TAKE AN ARTIST DATE
- SAVOR A GREEN JUICE
- ____

MITs

- ____
- ____
- ____
- ____
- ____

wellness planning

M ____
T ____
W ____
TH ____
F ____
S ____
S ____

GRATITUDE:

MONDAY ____

7 ____
8 ____
9 ____
10 ____
11 ____
12 ____
1 ____
2 ____
3 ____
4 ____
5 ____
6 ____
7 ____
8 ____
9 ____

daily checklist

- MORNING RITUAL
- DAILY DRESS-UP
- MINDFUL MOVEMENT
- EAT YOUR VEGGIES
- JOURNAL
- GOAL REVIEW
- GRATITUDE
- EVENING RITUAL
- ____

TUESDAY ____

7 ____
8 ____
9 ____
10 ____
11 ____
12 ____
1 ____
2 ____
3 ____
4 ____
5 ____
6 ____
7 ____
8 ____
9 ____

daily checklist

- MORNING RITUAL
- DAILY DRESS-UP
- MINDFUL MOVEMENT
- EAT YOUR VEGGIES
- JOURNAL
- GOAL REVIEW
- GRATITUDE
- EVENING RITUAL
- ____

WEDNESDAY ____

7 ____
8 ____
9 ____
10 ____
11 ____
12 ____
1 ____
2 ____
3 ____
4 ____
5 ____
6 ____
7 ____
8 ____
9 ____

daily checklist

- MORNING RITUAL
- DAILY DRESS-UP
- MINDFUL MOVEMENT
- EAT YOUR VEGGIES
- JOURNAL
- GOAL REVIEW
- GRATITUDE
- EVENING RITUAL
- ____

THURSDAY

7
8
9
10
11
12
1
2
3
4
5
6
7
8
9

daily checklist

- MORNING RITUAL
- DAILY DRESS-UP
- MINDFUL MOVEMENT
- EAT YOUR VEGGIES
- JOURNAL
- GOAL REVIEW
- GRATITUDE
- EVENING RITUAL

FRIDAY

7
8
9
10
11
12
1
2
3
4
5
6
7
8
9

daily checklist

- MORNING RITUAL
- DAILY DRESS-UP
- MINDFUL MOVEMENT
- EAT YOUR VEGGIES
- JOURNAL
- GOAL REVIEW
- GRATITUDE
- EVENING RITUAL

SATURDAY

7
8
9
10
11
12
1
2
3
4
5
6
7
8
9

daily checklist

- MORNING RITUAL
- DAILY DRESS-UP
- MINDFUL MOVEMENT
- EAT YOUR VEGGIES
- JOURNAL
- GOAL REVIEW
- GRATITUDE
- EVENING RITUAL

SUNDAY

7
8
9
10
11
12
1
2
3
4
5
6
7
8
9

daily checklist

- MORNING RITUAL
- DAILY DRESS-UP
- MINDFUL MOVEMENT
- EAT YOUR VEGGIES
- JOURNAL
- GOAL REVIEW
- GRATITUDE
- EVENING RITUAL

COMPASSION
IS THE NEW
BLACK.

seasonal life review

DATE: ______________

SEASONALLY REFLECT ON AREAS OF YOUR LIFE. RATE EACH ONE WITH YOUR LEVEL OF SATISFACTION 10 = BLISS, 5 = SO-SO, 0 = BOO.

Here are some additional areas to consider: social life, romance, family, education, health, fitness, meaning, activism. Next, take a moment to note the areas that ranked low and create three action steps to increase your tranquility in these areas. Be gentle. Plant seeds. Watch dreams take root.

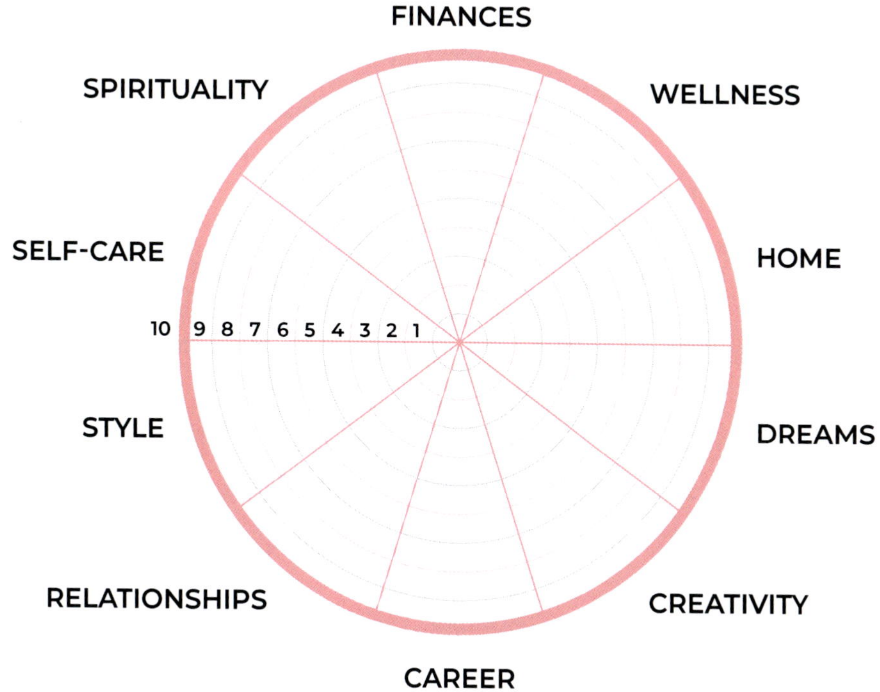

ACTION STEPS TO INCREASE AREAS THAT ARE LOWER THAN I'D LIKE:

month's dreams

DOODLE, LIST, COLLAGE, OR WRITE WHAT YOU'D LIKE TO MANIFEST THIS MONTH.

month's review

REVISIT YOUR MONTH'S DREAMS AND NOTE HOW THEY UNFOLDED FOR YOU.

30 days of tranquility

TRY THIS 30-DAY CHALLENGE TO INFUSE YOUR MONTH WITH SIMPLE PLEASURES.

1 SIT STILL FOR FIVE MINUTES	2 DO SIX SUN SALUTATIONS	3 WRITE A LOVE LETTER	4 APOLOGIZE	5 TELL THE TRUTH
6 CONSUME A GREEN DRINK	7 GO MEAT-FREE	8 WALK FOR 20 MINUTES	9 DO LEGS UP THE WALL	10 GIVE $10 TO CHARITY
11 PEN TWO JOURNAL PAGES	12 REVIEW YOUR YEAR'S DREAMS	13 CLEAR CLUTTER	14 GO ON AN ARTIST DATE	15 COLLAGE TWO PAGES
16 TREAT YOURSELF TO TEA	17 READ FOR 20 MINUTES	18 BUY YOURSELF FLOWERS	19 DANCE TO A FAVORITE TUNE	20 EXPRESS GRATITUDE
21 EAT ONLY UNPROCESSED FOODS	22 SOAK IN A BUBBLE BATH	23 MINDFULLY SIP A LIBATION	24 GET OUT IN NATURE	25 FORGO COMPLAINING
26 TAKE A DIGITAL DAY OFF	27 SNAP PHOTOS FROM YOUR DAY	28 MAKE A FAVORITE MEAL	29 HUG	30 BE FULLY PRESENT

habit tracking

NOTE HABITS YOU'RE TRYING TO ADD OR SUBTRACT AND TRACK THEM DAILY TO HELP WITH ACCOUNTABILITY. CELEBRATE YOUR SUCCESSES AND OBSERVE AREAS FOR GROWTH.

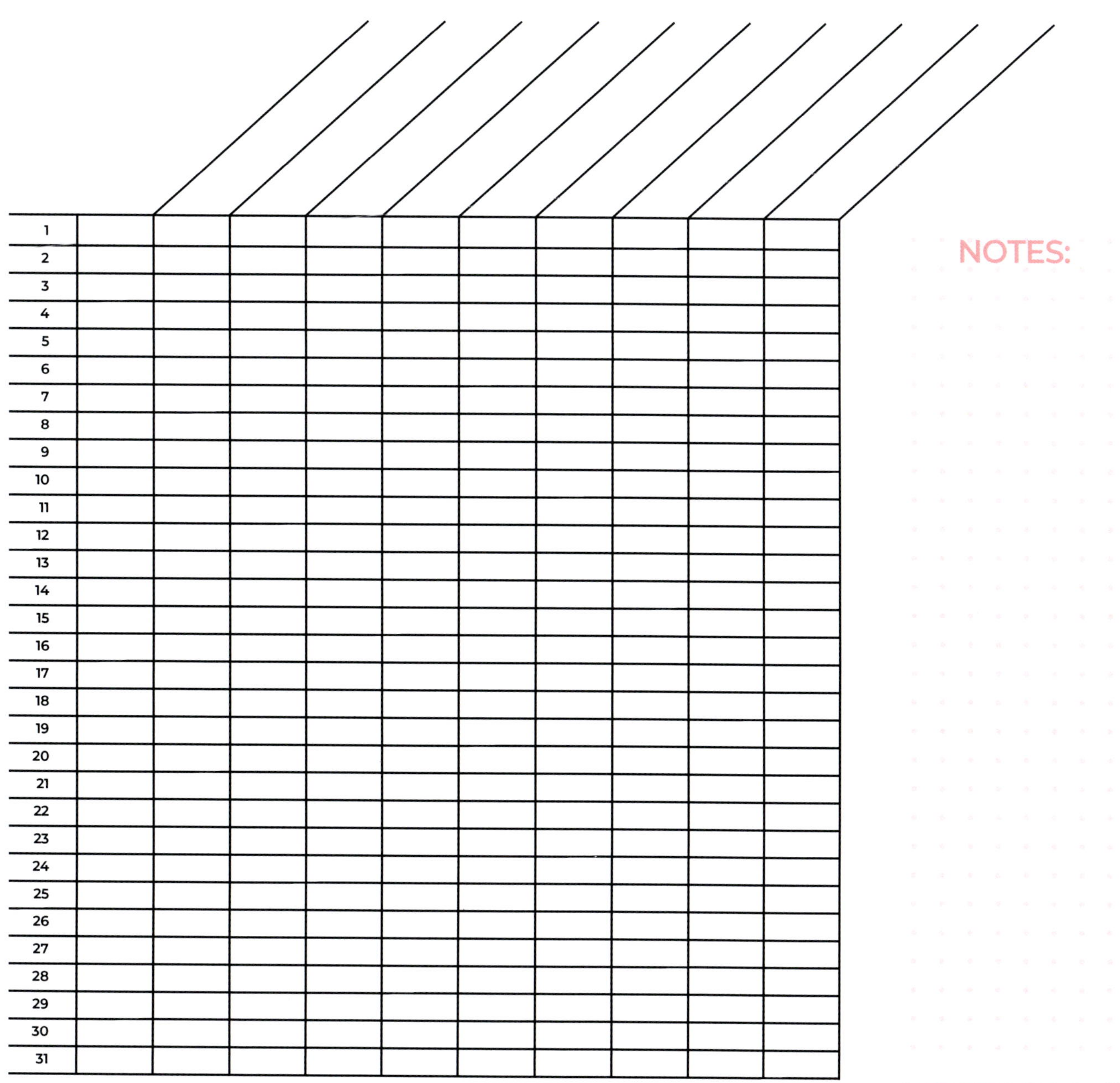

moon phases

Notice your connection to the moon's cycles in these four phases: new, waxing, full, waning. Consider the prompts below as a way to tie into your Month's Dreams and provide space for monthly reflection.

new moon

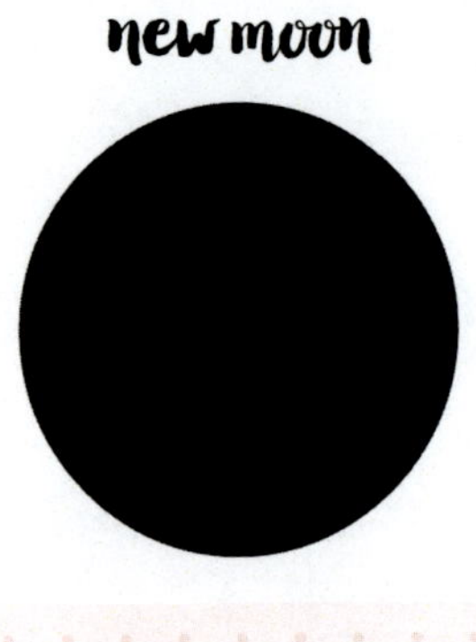

A TIME FOR SETTING INTENTIONS.
I WANT . . .

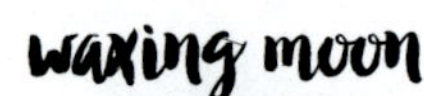

A TIME FOR ACTION. I WILL . . .

full moon

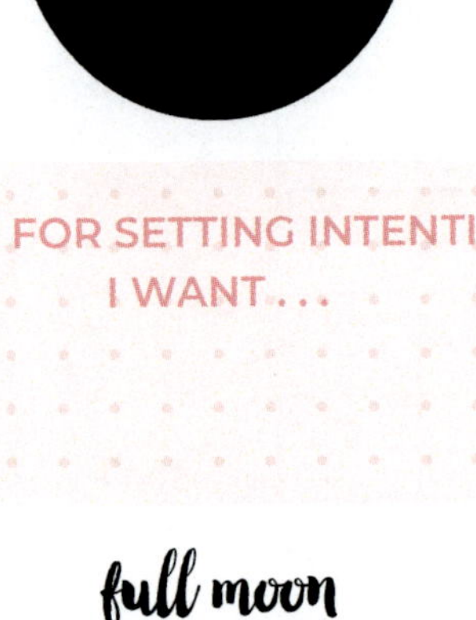

A TIME FOR HARVEST AND CLOSURE.
I RELEASE . . .

waning moon

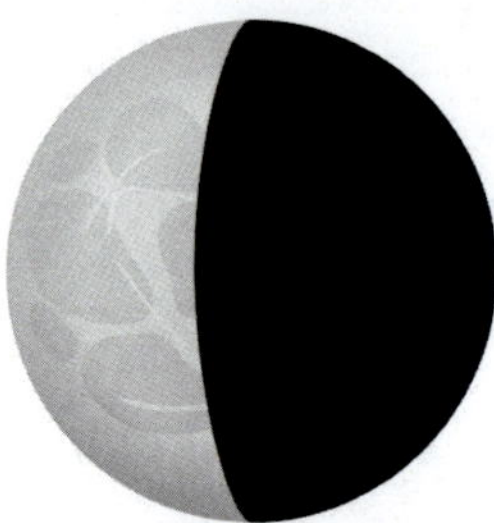

A TIME FOR SOFTENING. I FEEL . . .

monthly planner

MONTH: ______________________ INTENTION: ______________________

SUNDAY	MONDAY	TUESDAY	WEDNESDAY	THURSDAY	FRIDAY	SATURDAY

MONTHLY TRANQUILITY TOOLS

- ❍ CRAFT MONTH'S DREAMS
- ❍ REVIEW BUDGET
- ❍ CREATE SOMETHING
- ❍ READ TWO BOOKS
- ❍ VOLUNTEER
- ❍ MANI/PEDI
- ❍ ENTERTAIN
- ❍ MASSAGE

INTENTION:

weekly checklist

- ❍ PLAN WEEK'S MITS
- ❍ SOAK IN THE TUB
- ❍ TAKE A DIGITAL DAY OFF
- ❍ CLEAR CLUTTER
- ❍ PEN A LOVE NOTE
- ❍ BUY/PICK FRESH FLOWERS
- ❍ TAKE AN ARTIST DATE
- ❍ SAVOR A GREEN JUICE
- ❍ ____

MITs

- ❍ ____
- ❍ ____
- ❍ ____
- ❍ ____
- ❍ ____

wellness planning

M ____
T ____
W ____
TH ____
F ____
S ____
S ____

GRATITUDE:

MONDAY ____

7 ____
8 ____
9 ____
10 ____
11 ____
12 ____
1 ____
2 ____
3 ____
4 ____
5 ____
6 ____
7 ____
8 ____
9 ____

daily checklist

- ❍ MORNING RITUAL
- ❍ DAILY DRESS-UP
- ❍ MINDFUL MOVEMENT
- ❍ EAT YOUR VEGGIES
- ❍ JOURNAL
- ❍ GOAL REVIEW
- ❍ GRATITUDE
- ❍ EVENING RITUAL
- ❍ ____

TUESDAY ____

7 ____
8 ____
9 ____
10 ____
11 ____
12 ____
1 ____
2 ____
3 ____
4 ____
5 ____
6 ____
7 ____
8 ____
9 ____

daily checklist

- ❍ MORNING RITUAL
- ❍ DAILY DRESS-UP
- ❍ MINDFUL MOVEMENT
- ❍ EAT YOUR VEGGIES
- ❍ JOURNAL
- ❍ GOAL REVIEW
- ❍ GRATITUDE
- ❍ EVENING RITUAL
- ❍ ____

WEDNESDAY ____

7 ____
8 ____
9 ____
10 ____
11 ____
12 ____
1 ____
2 ____
3 ____
4 ____
5 ____
6 ____
7 ____
8 ____
9 ____

daily checklist

- ❍ MORNING RITUAL
- ❍ DAILY DRESS-UP
- ❍ MINDFUL MOVEMENT
- ❍ EAT YOUR VEGGIES
- ❍ JOURNAL
- ❍ GOAL REVIEW
- ❍ GRATITUDE
- ❍ EVENING RITUAL
- ❍ ____

THURSDAY

7
8
9
10
11
12
1
2
3
4
5
6
7
8
9

daily checklist

- MORNING RITUAL
- DAILY DRESS-UP
- MINDFUL MOVEMENT
- EAT YOUR VEGGIES
- JOURNAL
- GOAL REVIEW
- GRATITUDE
- EVENING RITUAL

FRIDAY

7
8
9
10
11
12
1
2
3
4
5
6
7
8
9

daily checklist

- MORNING RITUAL
- DAILY DRESS-UP
- MINDFUL MOVEMENT
- EAT YOUR VEGGIES
- JOURNAL
- GOAL REVIEW
- GRATITUDE
- EVENING RITUAL

SATURDAY

7
8
9
10
11
12
1
2
3
4
5
6
7
8
9

daily checklist

- MORNING RITUAL
- DAILY DRESS-UP
- MINDFUL MOVEMENT
- EAT YOUR VEGGIES
- JOURNAL
- GOAL REVIEW
- GRATITUDE
- EVENING RITUAL

SUNDAY

7
8
9
10
11
12
1
2
3
4
5
6
7
8
9

daily checklist

- MORNING RITUAL
- DAILY DRESS-UP
- MINDFUL MOVEMENT
- EAT YOUR VEGGIES
- JOURNAL
- GOAL REVIEW
- GRATITUDE
- EVENING RITUAL

INTENTION:

weekly checklist

- PLAN WEEK'S MITS
- SOAK IN THE TUB
- TAKE A DIGITAL DAY OFF
- CLEAR CLUTTER
- PEN A LOVE NOTE
- BUY/PICK FRESH FLOWERS
- TAKE AN ARTIST DATE
- SAVOR A GREEN JUICE
- ______

MITs

- ______
- ______
- ______
- ______
- ______

wellness planning

M ______
T ______
W ______
TH ______
F ______
S ______
S ______

GRATITUDE:

MONDAY ______

7 ______
8 ______
9 ______
10 ______
11 ______
12 ______
1 ______
2 ______
3 ______
4 ______
5 ______
6 ______
7 ______
8 ______
9 ______

daily checklist

- MORNING RITUAL
- DAILY DRESS-UP
- MINDFUL MOVEMENT
- EAT YOUR VEGGIES
- JOURNAL
- GOAL REVIEW
- GRATITUDE
- EVENING RITUAL
- ______

TUESDAY ______

7 ______
8 ______
9 ______
10 ______
11 ______
12 ______
1 ______
2 ______
3 ______
4 ______
5 ______
6 ______
7 ______
8 ______
9 ______

daily checklist

- MORNING RITUAL
- DAILY DRESS-UP
- MINDFUL MOVEMENT
- EAT YOUR VEGGIES
- JOURNAL
- GOAL REVIEW
- GRATITUDE
- EVENING RITUAL
- ______

WEDNESDAY ______

7 ______
8 ______
9 ______
10 ______
11 ______
12 ______
1 ______
2 ______
3 ______
4 ______
5 ______
6 ______
7 ______
8 ______
9 ______

daily checklist

- MORNING RITUAL
- DAILY DRESS-UP
- MINDFUL MOVEMENT
- EAT YOUR VEGGIES
- JOURNAL
- GOAL REVIEW
- GRATITUDE
- EVENING RITUAL
- ______

THURSDAY

7
8
9
10
11
12
1
2
3
4
5
6
7
8
9

daily checklist

- MORNING RITUAL
- DAILY DRESS-UP
- MINDFUL MOVEMENT
- EAT YOUR VEGGIES
- JOURNAL
- GOAL REVIEW
- GRATITUDE
- EVENING RITUAL

FRIDAY

7
8
9
10
11
12
1
2
3
4
5
6
7
8
9

daily checklist

- MORNING RITUAL
- DAILY DRESS-UP
- MINDFUL MOVEMENT
- EAT YOUR VEGGIES
- JOURNAL
- GOAL REVIEW
- GRATITUDE
- EVENING RITUAL

SATURDAY

7
8
9
10
11
12
1
2
3
4
5
6
7
8
9

daily checklist

- MORNING RITUAL
- DAILY DRESS-UP
- MINDFUL MOVEMENT
- EAT YOUR VEGGIES
- JOURNAL
- GOAL REVIEW
- GRATITUDE
- EVENING RITUAL

SUNDAY

7
8
9
10
11
12
1
2
3
4
5
6
7
8
9

daily checklist

- MORNING RITUAL
- DAILY DRESS-UP
- MINDFUL MOVEMENT
- EAT YOUR VEGGIES
- JOURNAL
- GOAL REVIEW
- GRATITUDE
- EVENING RITUAL

INTENTION:

weekly checklist

- ❍ PLAN WEEK'S MITS
- ❍ SOAK IN THE TUB
- ❍ TAKE A DIGITAL DAY OFF
- ❍ CLEAR CLUTTER
- ❍ PEN A LOVE NOTE
- ❍ BUY/PICK FRESH FLOWERS
- ❍ TAKE AN ARTIST DATE
- ❍ SAVOR A GREEN JUICE
- ❍ ____________

MITs

- ❍ ____________
- ❍ ____________
- ❍ ____________
- ❍ ____________
- ❍ ____________

wellness planning

M ____________
T ____________
W ____________
TH ____________
F ____________
S ____________
S ____________

GRATITUDE:

MONDAY ____________

7 ____________
8 ____________
9 ____________
10 ____________
11 ____________
12 ____________
1 ____________
2 ____________
3 ____________
4 ____________
5 ____________
6 ____________
7 ____________
8 ____________
9 ____________

daily checklist

- ❍ MORNING RITUAL
- ❍ DAILY DRESS-UP
- ❍ MINDFUL MOVEMENT
- ❍ EAT YOUR VEGGIES
- ❍ JOURNAL
- ❍ GOAL REVIEW
- ❍ GRATITUDE
- ❍ EVENING RITUAL
- ❍ ____________

TUESDAY ____________

7 ____________
8 ____________
9 ____________
10 ____________
11 ____________
12 ____________
1 ____________
2 ____________
3 ____________
4 ____________
5 ____________
6 ____________
7 ____________
8 ____________
9 ____________

daily checklist

- ❍ MORNING RITUAL
- ❍ DAILY DRESS-UP
- ❍ MINDFUL MOVEMENT
- ❍ EAT YOUR VEGGIES
- ❍ JOURNAL
- ❍ GOAL REVIEW
- ❍ GRATITUDE
- ❍ EVENING RITUAL
- ❍ ____________

WEDNESDAY ____________

7 ____________
8 ____________
9 ____________
10 ____________
11 ____________
12 ____________
1 ____________
2 ____________
3 ____________
4 ____________
5 ____________
6 ____________
7 ____________
8 ____________
9 ____________

daily checklist

- ❍ MORNING RITUAL
- ❍ DAILY DRESS-UP
- ❍ MINDFUL MOVEMENT
- ❍ EAT YOUR VEGGIES
- ❍ JOURNAL
- ❍ GOAL REVIEW
- ❍ GRATITUDE
- ❍ EVENING RITUAL
- ❍ ____________

THURSDAY

7
8
9
10
11
12
1
2
3
4
5
6
7
8
9

daily checklist

- MORNING RITUAL
- DAILY DRESS-UP
- MINDFUL MOVEMENT
- EAT YOUR VEGGIES
- JOURNAL
- GOAL REVIEW
- GRATITUDE
- EVENING RITUAL

FRIDAY

7
8
9
10
11
12
1
2
3
4
5
6
7
8
9

daily checklist

- MORNING RITUAL
- DAILY DRESS-UP
- MINDFUL MOVEMENT
- EAT YOUR VEGGIES
- JOURNAL
- GOAL REVIEW
- GRATITUDE
- EVENING RITUAL

SATURDAY

7
8
9
10
11
12
1
2
3
4
5
6
7
8
9

daily checklist

- MORNING RITUAL
- DAILY DRESS-UP
- MINDFUL MOVEMENT
- EAT YOUR VEGGIES
- JOURNAL
- GOAL REVIEW
- GRATITUDE
- EVENING RITUAL

SUNDAY

7
8
9
10
11
12
1
2
3
4
5
6
7
8
9

daily checklist

- MORNING RITUAL
- DAILY DRESS-UP
- MINDFUL MOVEMENT
- EAT YOUR VEGGIES
- JOURNAL
- GOAL REVIEW
- GRATITUDE
- EVENING RITUAL

INTENTION:

weekly checklist

- PLAN WEEK'S MITS
- SOAK IN THE TUB
- TAKE A DIGITAL DAY OFF
- CLEAR CLUTTER
- PEN A LOVE NOTE
- BUY/PICK FRESH FLOWERS
- TAKE AN ARTIST DATE
- SAVOR A GREEN JUICE
- ____

MITs

- ____
- ____
- ____
- ____
- ____

wellness planning

M ____
T ____
W ____
TH ____
F ____
S ____
S ____

GRATITUDE:

MONDAY ____

7 ____
8 ____
9 ____
10 ____
11 ____
12 ____
1 ____
2 ____
3 ____
4 ____
5 ____
6 ____
7 ____
8 ____
9 ____

daily checklist

- MORNING RITUAL
- DAILY DRESS-UP
- MINDFUL MOVEMENT
- EAT YOUR VEGGIES
- JOURNAL
- GOAL REVIEW
- GRATITUDE
- EVENING RITUAL
- ____

TUESDAY ____

7 ____
8 ____
9 ____
10 ____
11 ____
12 ____
1 ____
2 ____
3 ____
4 ____
5 ____
6 ____
7 ____
8 ____
9 ____

daily checklist

- MORNING RITUAL
- DAILY DRESS-UP
- MINDFUL MOVEMENT
- EAT YOUR VEGGIES
- JOURNAL
- GOAL REVIEW
- GRATITUDE
- EVENING RITUAL
- ____

WEDNESDAY ____

7 ____
8 ____
9 ____
10 ____
11 ____
12 ____
1 ____
2 ____
3 ____
4 ____
5 ____
6 ____
7 ____
8 ____
9 ____

daily checklist

- MORNING RITUAL
- DAILY DRESS-UP
- MINDFUL MOVEMENT
- EAT YOUR VEGGIES
- JOURNAL
- GOAL REVIEW
- GRATITUDE
- EVENING RITUAL
- ____

THURSDAY

7
8
9
10
11
12
1
2
3
4
5
6
7
8
9

daily checklist

- MORNING RITUAL
- DAILY DRESS-UP
- MINDFUL MOVEMENT
- EAT YOUR VEGGIES
- JOURNAL
- GOAL REVIEW
- GRATITUDE
- EVENING RITUAL

FRIDAY

7
8
9
10
11
12
1
2
3
4
5
6
7
8
9

daily checklist

- MORNING RITUAL
- DAILY DRESS-UP
- MINDFUL MOVEMENT
- EAT YOUR VEGGIES
- JOURNAL
- GOAL REVIEW
- GRATITUDE
- EVENING RITUAL

SATURDAY

7
8
9
10
11
12
1
2
3
4
5
6
7
8
9

daily checklist

- MORNING RITUAL
- DAILY DRESS-UP
- MINDFUL MOVEMENT
- EAT YOUR VEGGIES
- JOURNAL
- GOAL REVIEW
- GRATITUDE
- EVENING RITUAL

SUNDAY

7
8
9
10
11
12
1
2
3
4
5
6
7
8
9

daily checklist

- MORNING RITUAL
- DAILY DRESS-UP
- MINDFUL MOVEMENT
- EAT YOUR VEGGIES
- JOURNAL
- GOAL REVIEW
- GRATITUDE
- EVENING RITUAL

INTENTION:

weekly checklist

- PLAN WEEK'S MITS
- SOAK IN THE TUB
- TAKE A DIGITAL DAY OFF
- CLEAR CLUTTER
- PEN A LOVE NOTE
- BUY/PICK FRESH FLOWERS
- TAKE AN ARTIST DATE
- SAVOR A GREEN JUICE
- ______

MITs

- ______
- ______
- ______
- ______
- ______

wellness planning

M ______
T ______
W ______
TH ______
F ______
S ______
S ______

GRATITUDE:

MONDAY ______
7 ______
8 ______
9 ______
10 ______
11 ______
12 ______
1 ______
2 ______
3 ______
4 ______
5 ______
6 ______
7 ______
8 ______
9 ______

daily checklist

- MORNING RITUAL
- DAILY DRESS-UP
- MINDFUL MOVEMENT
- EAT YOUR VEGGIES
- JOURNAL
- GOAL REVIEW
- GRATITUDE
- EVENING RITUAL
- ______

TUESDAY ______
7 ______
8 ______
9 ______
10 ______
11 ______
12 ______
1 ______
2 ______
3 ______
4 ______
5 ______
6 ______
7 ______
8 ______
9 ______

daily checklist

- MORNING RITUAL
- DAILY DRESS-UP
- MINDFUL MOVEMENT
- EAT YOUR VEGGIES
- JOURNAL
- GOAL REVIEW
- GRATITUDE
- EVENING RITUAL
- ______

WEDNESDAY ______
7 ______
8 ______
9 ______
10 ______
11 ______
12 ______
1 ______
2 ______
3 ______
4 ______
5 ______
6 ______
7 ______
8 ______
9 ______

daily checklist

- MORNING RITUAL
- DAILY DRESS-UP
- MINDFUL MOVEMENT
- EAT YOUR VEGGIES
- JOURNAL
- GOAL REVIEW
- GRATITUDE
- EVENING RITUAL
- ______

THURSDAY

7
8
9
10
11
12
1
2
3
4
5
6
7
8
9

daily checklist

- MORNING RITUAL
- DAILY DRESS-UP
- MINDFUL MOVEMENT
- EAT YOUR VEGGIES
- JOURNAL
- GOAL REVIEW
- GRATITUDE
- EVENING RITUAL

FRIDAY

7
8
9
10
11
12
1
2
3
4
5
6
7
8
9

daily checklist

- MORNING RITUAL
- DAILY DRESS-UP
- MINDFUL MOVEMENT
- EAT YOUR VEGGIES
- JOURNAL
- GOAL REVIEW
- GRATITUDE
- EVENING RITUAL

SATURDAY

7
8
9
10
11
12
1
2
3
4
5
6
7
8
9

daily checklist

- MORNING RITUAL
- DAILY DRESS-UP
- MINDFUL MOVEMENT
- EAT YOUR VEGGIES
- JOURNAL
- GOAL REVIEW
- GRATITUDE
- EVENING RITUAL

SUNDAY

7
8
9
10
11
12
1
2
3
4
5
6
7
8
9

daily checklist

- MORNING RITUAL
- DAILY DRESS-UP
- MINDFUL MOVEMENT
- EAT YOUR VEGGIES
- JOURNAL
- GOAL REVIEW
- GRATITUDE
- EVENING RITUAL

month's dreams

DOODLE, LIST, COLLAGE, OR WRITE WHAT YOU'D LIKE TO MANIFEST THIS MONTH.

month's review

REVISIT YOUR MONTH'S DREAMS AND NOTE HOW THEY UNFOLDED FOR YOU.

30 days of tranquility

TRY THIS 30-DAY CHALLENGE TO INFUSE YOUR MONTH WITH SIMPLE PLEASURES.

1 SIT STILL FOR FIVE MINUTES	2 DO SIX SUN SALUTATIONS	3 WRITE A LOVE LETTER	4 APOLOGIZE	5 TELL THE TRUTH
6 CONSUME A GREEN DRINK	7 GO MEAT-FREE	8 WALK FOR 20 MINUTES	9 DO LEGS UP THE WALL	10 GIVE $10 TO CHARITY
11 PEN TWO JOURNAL PAGES	12 REVIEW YOUR YEAR'S DREAMS	13 CLEAR CLUTTER	14 GO ON AN ARTIST DATE	15 COLLAGE TWO PAGES
16 TREAT YOURSELF TO TEA	17 READ FOR 20 MINUTES	18 BUY YOURSELF FLOWERS	19 DANCE TO A FAVORITE TUNE	20 EXPRESS GRATITUDE
21 EAT ONLY UNPROCESSED FOODS	22 SOAK IN A BUBBLE BATH	23 MINDFULLY SIP A LIBATION	24 GET OUT IN NATURE	25 FORGO COMPLAINING
26 TAKE A DIGITAL DAY OFF	27 SNAP PHOTOS FROM YOUR DAY	28 MAKE A FAVORITE MEAL	29 HUG	30 BE FULLY PRESENT

habit tracking

NOTE HABITS YOU'RE TRYING TO ADD OR SUBTRACT AND TRACK THEM DAILY TO HELP WITH ACCOUNTABILITY. CELEBRATE YOUR SUCCESSES AND OBSERVE AREAS FOR GROWTH.

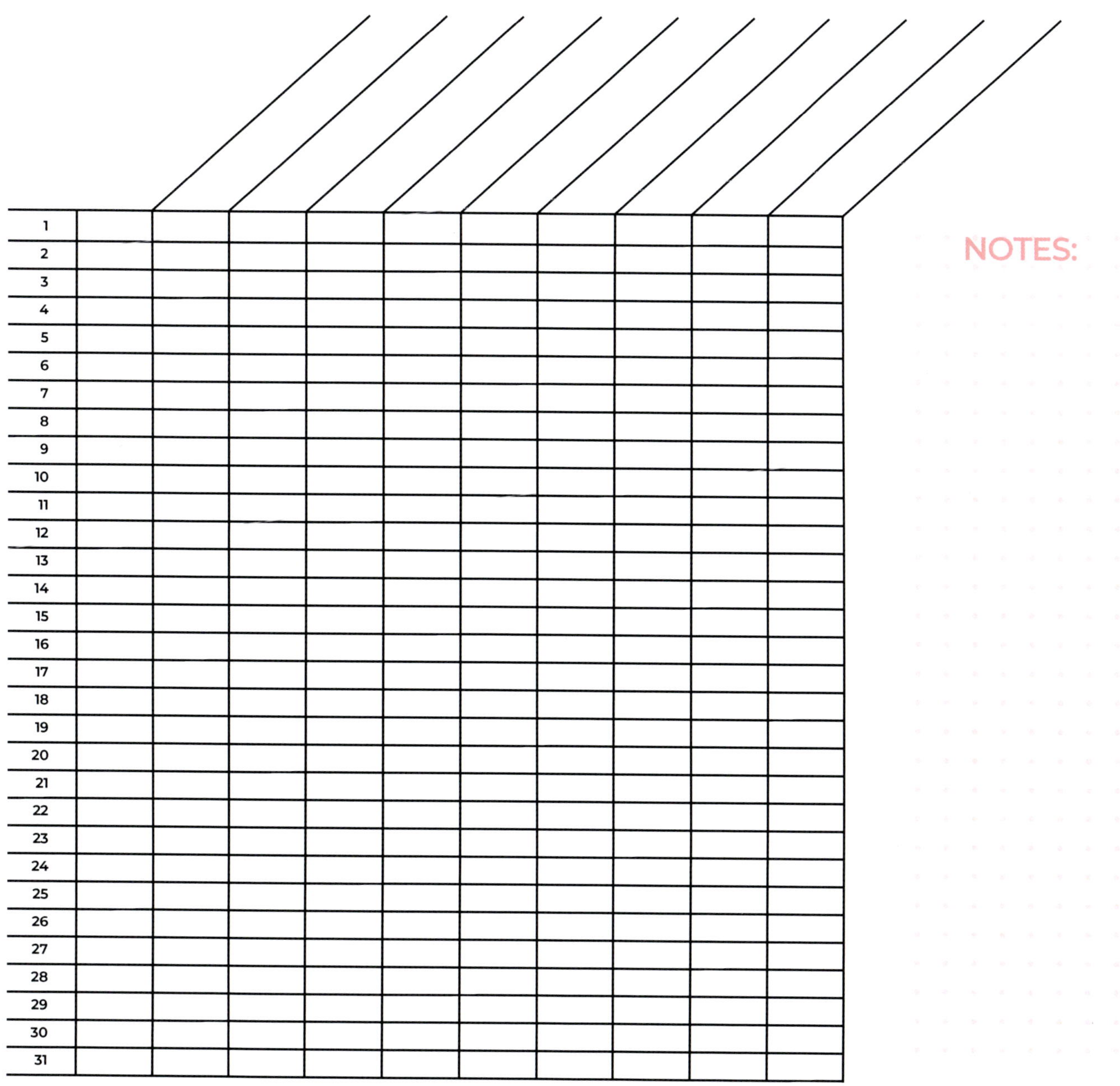

1										
2										
3										
4										
5										
6										
7										
8										
9										
10										
11										
12										
13										
14										
15										
16										
17										
18										
19										
20										
21										
22										
23										
24										
25										
26										
27										
28										
29										
30										
31										

NOTES:

moon phases

N*otice your connection to the moon's cycles in these four phases: new, waxing, full, waning. Consider the prompts below as a way to tie into your Month's Dreams and provide space for monthly reflection.*

new moon

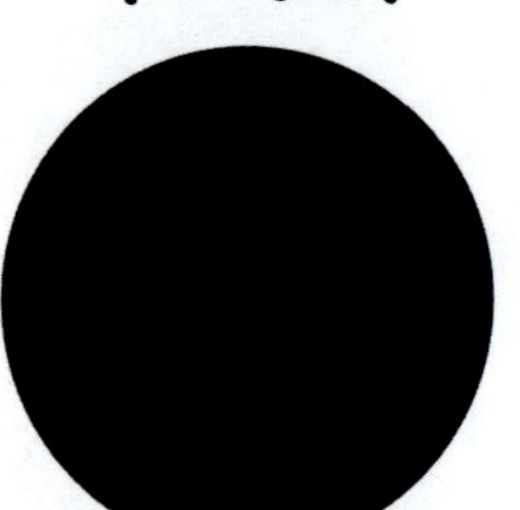

A TIME FOR SETTING INTENTIONS.
I WANT . . .

waxing moon

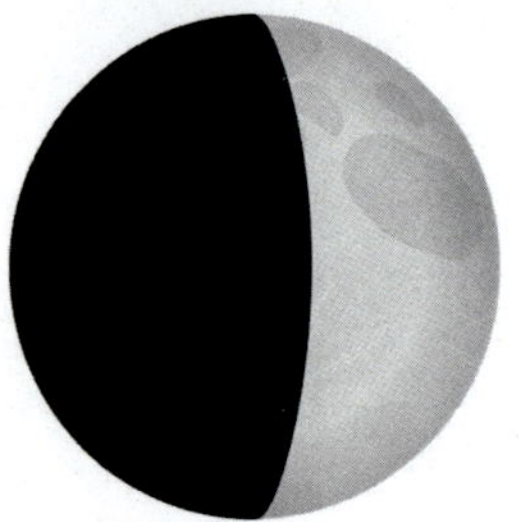

A TIME FOR ACTION. I WILL . . .

full moon

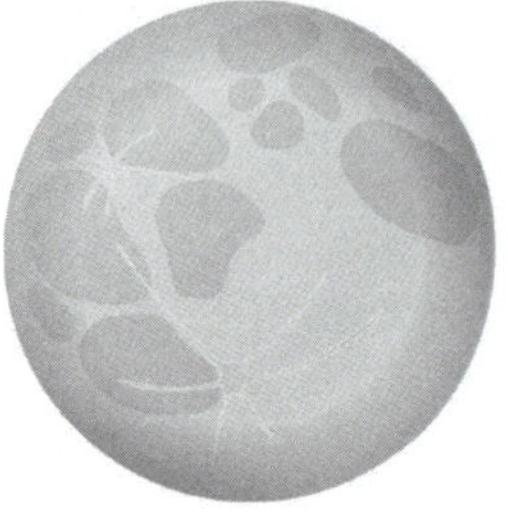

A TIME FOR HARVEST AND CLOSURE.
I RELEASE . . .

waning moon

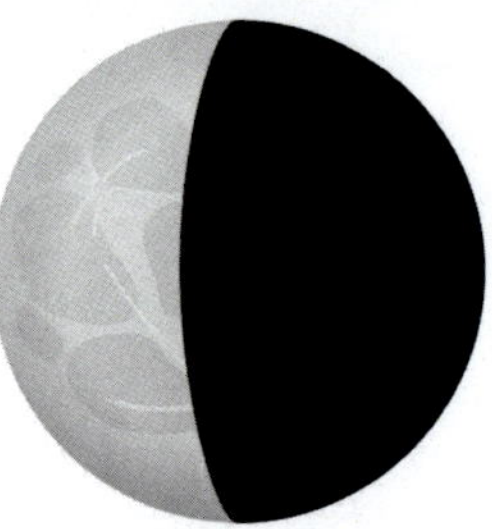

A TIME FOR SOFTENING. I FEEL . . .

monthly planner

MONTH: ______________________ INTENTION: ______________________

SUNDAY	MONDAY	TUESDAY	WEDNESDAY	THURSDAY	FRIDAY	SATURDAY

MONTHLY TRANQUILITY TOOLS

- ❍ CRAFT MONTH'S DREAMS
- ❍ REVIEW BUDGET
- ❍ CREATE SOMETHING
- ❍ READ TWO BOOKS
- ❍ VOLUNTEER
- ❍ MANI/PEDI
- ❍ ENTERTAIN
- ❍ MASSAGE

INTENTION:

weekly checklist

- ❍ PLAN WEEK'S MITS
- ❍ SOAK IN THE TUB
- ❍ TAKE A DIGITAL DAY OFF
- ❍ CLEAR CLUTTER
- ❍ PEN A LOVE NOTE
- ❍ BUY/PICK FRESH FLOWERS
- ❍ TAKE AN ARTIST DATE
- ❍ SAVOR A GREEN JUICE
- ❍ ____________

MITs

- ❍ ____________
- ❍ ____________
- ❍ ____________
- ❍ ____________
- ❍ ____________

wellness planning

M ____________

T ____________

W ____________

TH ____________

F ____________

S ____________

S ____________

GRATITUDE:

MONDAY ____________

7 ____________
8 ____________
9 ____________
10 ____________
11 ____________
12 ____________
1 ____________
2 ____________
3 ____________
4 ____________
5 ____________
6 ____________
7 ____________
8 ____________
9 ____________

daily checklist

- ❍ MORNING RITUAL
- ❍ DAILY DRESS-UP
- ❍ MINDFUL MOVEMENT
- ❍ EAT YOUR VEGGIES
- ❍ JOURNAL
- ❍ GOAL REVIEW
- ❍ GRATITUDE
- ❍ EVENING RITUAL
- ❍ ____________

TUESDAY ____________

7 ____________
8 ____________
9 ____________
10 ____________
11 ____________
12 ____________
1 ____________
2 ____________
3 ____________
4 ____________
5 ____________
6 ____________
7 ____________
8 ____________
9 ____________

daily checklist

- ❍ MORNING RITUAL
- ❍ DAILY DRESS-UP
- ❍ MINDFUL MOVEMENT
- ❍ EAT YOUR VEGGIES
- ❍ JOURNAL
- ❍ GOAL REVIEW
- ❍ GRATITUDE
- ❍ EVENING RITUAL
- ❍ ____________

WEDNESDAY ____________

7 ____________
8 ____________
9 ____________
10 ____________
11 ____________
12 ____________
1 ____________
2 ____________
3 ____________
4 ____________
5 ____________
6 ____________
7 ____________
8 ____________
9 ____________

daily checklist

- ❍ MORNING RITUAL
- ❍ DAILY DRESS-UP
- ❍ MINDFUL MOVEMENT
- ❍ EAT YOUR VEGGIES
- ❍ JOURNAL
- ❍ GOAL REVIEW
- ❍ GRATITUDE
- ❍ EVENING RITUAL
- ❍ ____________

THURSDAY ______

7
8
9
10
11
12
1
2
3
4
5
6
7
8
9

daily checklist

- MORNING RITUAL
- DAILY DRESS-UP
- MINDFUL MOVEMENT
- EAT YOUR VEGGIES
- JOURNAL
- GOAL REVIEW
- GRATITUDE
- EVENING RITUAL

FRIDAY ______

7
8
9
10
11
12
1
2
3
4
5
6
7
8
9

daily checklist

- MORNING RITUAL
- DAILY DRESS-UP
- MINDFUL MOVEMENT
- EAT YOUR VEGGIES
- JOURNAL
- GOAL REVIEW
- GRATITUDE
- EVENING RITUAL

SATURDAY ______

7
8
9
10
11
12
1
2
3
4
5
6
7
8
9

daily checklist

- MORNING RITUAL
- DAILY DRESS-UP
- MINDFUL MOVEMENT
- EAT YOUR VEGGIES
- JOURNAL
- GOAL REVIEW
- GRATITUDE
- EVENING RITUAL

SUNDAY ______

7
8
9
10
11
12
1
2
3
4
5
6
7
8
9

daily checklist

- MORNING RITUAL
- DAILY DRESS-UP
- MINDFUL MOVEMENT
- EAT YOUR VEGGIES
- JOURNAL
- GOAL REVIEW
- GRATITUDE
- EVENING RITUAL

INTENTION:

weekly checklist

- PLAN WEEK'S MITS
- SOAK IN THE TUB
- TAKE A DIGITAL DAY OFF
- CLEAR CLUTTER
- PEN A LOVE NOTE
- BUY/PICK FRESH FLOWERS
- TAKE AN ARTIST DATE
- SAVOR A GREEN JUICE
- ____________________

MITs

- ____________________
- ____________________
- ____________________
- ____________________
- ____________________

wellness planning

M ____________________
T ____________________
W ____________________
TH ____________________
F ____________________
S ____________________
S ____________________

GRATITUDE:

MONDAY ____________________

7 ____________________
8 ____________________
9 ____________________
10 ____________________
11 ____________________
12 ____________________
1 ____________________
2 ____________________
3 ____________________
4 ____________________
5 ____________________
6 ____________________
7 ____________________
8 ____________________
9 ____________________

daily checklist

- MORNING RITUAL
- DAILY DRESS-UP
- MINDFUL MOVEMENT
- EAT YOUR VEGGIES
- JOURNAL
- GOAL REVIEW
- GRATITUDE
- EVENING RITUAL
- ____________________

TUESDAY ____________________

7 ____________________
8 ____________________
9 ____________________
10 ____________________
11 ____________________
12 ____________________
1 ____________________
2 ____________________
3 ____________________
4 ____________________
5 ____________________
6 ____________________
7 ____________________
8 ____________________
9 ____________________

daily checklist

- MORNING RITUAL
- DAILY DRESS-UP
- MINDFUL MOVEMENT
- EAT YOUR VEGGIES
- JOURNAL
- GOAL REVIEW
- GRATITUDE
- EVENING RITUAL
- ____________________

WEDNESDAY ____________________

7 ____________________
8 ____________________
9 ____________________
10 ____________________
11 ____________________
12 ____________________
1 ____________________
2 ____________________
3 ____________________
4 ____________________
5 ____________________
6 ____________________
7 ____________________
8 ____________________
9 ____________________

daily checklist

- MORNING RITUAL
- DAILY DRESS-UP
- MINDFUL MOVEMENT
- EAT YOUR VEGGIES
- JOURNAL
- GOAL REVIEW
- GRATITUDE
- EVENING RITUAL
- ____________________

THURSDAY

7
8
9
10
11
12
1
2
3
4
5
6
7
8
9

daily checklist

- MORNING RITUAL
- DAILY DRESS-UP
- MINDFUL MOVEMENT
- EAT YOUR VEGGIES
- JOURNAL
- GOAL REVIEW
- GRATITUDE
- EVENING RITUAL

FRIDAY

7
8
9
10
11
12
1
2
3
4
5
6
7
8
9

daily checklist

- MORNING RITUAL
- DAILY DRESS-UP
- MINDFUL MOVEMENT
- EAT YOUR VEGGIES
- JOURNAL
- GOAL REVIEW
- GRATITUDE
- EVENING RITUAL

SATURDAY

7
8
9
10
11
12
1
2
3
4
5
6
7
8
9

daily checklist

- MORNING RITUAL
- DAILY DRESS-UP
- MINDFUL MOVEMENT
- EAT YOUR VEGGIES
- JOURNAL
- GOAL REVIEW
- GRATITUDE
- EVENING RITUAL

SUNDAY

7
8
9
10
11
12
1
2
3
4
5
6
7
8
9

daily checklist

- MORNING RITUAL
- DAILY DRESS-UP
- MINDFUL MOVEMENT
- EAT YOUR VEGGIES
- JOURNAL
- GOAL REVIEW
- GRATITUDE
- EVENING RITUAL

INTENTION:

weekly checklist

- ○ PLAN WEEK'S MITS
- ○ SOAK IN THE TUB
- ○ TAKE A DIGITAL DAY OFF
- ○ CLEAR CLUTTER
- ○ PEN A LOVE NOTE
- ○ BUY/PICK FRESH FLOWERS
- ○ TAKE AN ARTIST DATE
- ○ SAVOR A GREEN JUICE
- ○ ______

MITs

- ○ ______
- ○ ______
- ○ ______
- ○ ______
- ○ ______

wellness planning

M ______
T ______
W ______
TH ______
F ______
S ______
S ______

GRATITUDE:

MONDAY ______

7 ______
8 ______
9 ______
10 ______
11 ______
12 ______
1 ______
2 ______
3 ______
4 ______
5 ______
6 ______
7 ______
8 ______
9 ______

daily checklist

- ○ MORNING RITUAL
- ○ DAILY DRESS-UP
- ○ MINDFUL MOVEMENT
- ○ EAT YOUR VEGGIES
- ○ JOURNAL
- ○ GOAL REVIEW
- ○ GRATITUDE
- ○ EVENING RITUAL
- ○ ______

TUESDAY ______

7 ______
8 ______
9 ______
10 ______
11 ______
12 ______
1 ______
2 ______
3 ______
4 ______
5 ______
6 ______
7 ______
8 ______
9 ______

daily checklist

- ○ MORNING RITUAL
- ○ DAILY DRESS-UP
- ○ MINDFUL MOVEMENT
- ○ EAT YOUR VEGGIES
- ○ JOURNAL
- ○ GOAL REVIEW
- ○ GRATITUDE
- ○ EVENING RITUAL
- ○ ______

WEDNESDAY ______

7 ______
8 ______
9 ______
10 ______
11 ______
12 ______
1 ______
2 ______
3 ______
4 ______
5 ______
6 ______
7 ______
8 ______
9 ______

daily checklist

- ○ MORNING RITUAL
- ○ DAILY DRESS-UP
- ○ MINDFUL MOVEMENT
- ○ EAT YOUR VEGGIES
- ○ JOURNAL
- ○ GOAL REVIEW
- ○ GRATITUDE
- ○ EVENING RITUAL
- ○ ______

THURSDAY

7
8
9
10
11
12
1
2
3
4
5
6
7
8
9

daily checklist

- MORNING RITUAL
- DAILY DRESS-UP
- MINDFUL MOVEMENT
- EAT YOUR VEGGIES
- JOURNAL
- GOAL REVIEW
- GRATITUDE
- EVENING RITUAL

FRIDAY

7
8
9
10
11
12
1
2
3
4
5
6
7
8
9

daily checklist

- MORNING RITUAL
- DAILY DRESS-UP
- MINDFUL MOVEMENT
- EAT YOUR VEGGIES
- JOURNAL
- GOAL REVIEW
- GRATITUDE
- EVENING RITUAL

SATURDAY

7
8
9
10
11
12
1
2
3
4
5
6
7
8
9

daily checklist

- MORNING RITUAL
- DAILY DRESS-UP
- MINDFUL MOVEMENT
- EAT YOUR VEGGIES
- JOURNAL
- GOAL REVIEW
- GRATITUDE
- EVENING RITUAL

SUNDAY

7
8
9
10
11
12
1
2
3
4
5
6
7
8
9

daily checklist

- MORNING RITUAL
- DAILY DRESS-UP
- MINDFUL MOVEMENT
- EAT YOUR VEGGIES
- JOURNAL
- GOAL REVIEW
- GRATITUDE
- EVENING RITUAL

INTENTION:

weekly checklist

- PLAN WEEK'S MITS
- SOAK IN THE TUB
- TAKE A DIGITAL DAY OFF
- CLEAR CLUTTER
- PEN A LOVE NOTE
- BUY/PICK FRESH FLOWERS
- TAKE AN ARTIST DATE
- SAVOR A GREEN JUICE
- ____

MITs

- ____
- ____
- ____
- ____
- ____

wellness planning

M ____
T ____
W ____
TH ____
F ____
S ____
S ____

GRATITUDE:

MONDAY ____

7 ____
8 ____
9 ____
10 ____
11 ____
12 ____
1 ____
2 ____
3 ____
4 ____
5 ____
6 ____
7 ____
8 ____
9 ____

daily checklist

- MORNING RITUAL
- DAILY DRESS-UP
- MINDFUL MOVEMENT
- EAT YOUR VEGGIES
- JOURNAL
- GOAL REVIEW
- GRATITUDE
- EVENING RITUAL
- ____

TUESDAY ____

7 ____
8 ____
9 ____
10 ____
11 ____
12 ____
1 ____
2 ____
3 ____
4 ____
5 ____
6 ____
7 ____
8 ____
9 ____

daily checklist

- MORNING RITUAL
- DAILY DRESS-UP
- MINDFUL MOVEMENT
- EAT YOUR VEGGIES
- JOURNAL
- GOAL REVIEW
- GRATITUDE
- EVENING RITUAL
- ____

WEDNESDAY ____

7 ____
8 ____
9 ____
10 ____
11 ____
12 ____
1 ____
2 ____
3 ____
4 ____
5 ____
6 ____
7 ____
8 ____
9 ____

daily checklist

- MORNING RITUAL
- DAILY DRESS-UP
- MINDFUL MOVEMENT
- EAT YOUR VEGGIES
- JOURNAL
- GOAL REVIEW
- GRATITUDE
- EVENING RITUAL
- ____

THURSDAY

7
8
9
10
11
12
1
2
3
4
5
6
7
8
9

daily checklist

- MORNING RITUAL
- DAILY DRESS-UP
- MINDFUL MOVEMENT
- EAT YOUR VEGGIES
- JOURNAL
- GOAL REVIEW
- GRATITUDE
- EVENING RITUAL

FRIDAY

7
8
9
10
11
12
1
2
3
4
5
6
7
8
9

daily checklist

- MORNING RITUAL
- DAILY DRESS-UP
- MINDFUL MOVEMENT
- EAT YOUR VEGGIES
- JOURNAL
- GOAL REVIEW
- GRATITUDE
- EVENING RITUAL

SATURDAY

7
8
9
10
11
12
1
2
3
4
5
6
7
8
9

daily checklist

- MORNING RITUAL
- DAILY DRESS-UP
- MINDFUL MOVEMENT
- EAT YOUR VEGGIES
- JOURNAL
- GOAL REVIEW
- GRATITUDE
- EVENING RITUAL

SUNDAY

7
8
9
10
11
12
1
2
3
4
5
6
7
8
9

daily checklist

- MORNING RITUAL
- DAILY DRESS-UP
- MINDFUL MOVEMENT
- EAT YOUR VEGGIES
- JOURNAL
- GOAL REVIEW
- GRATITUDE
- EVENING RITUAL

INTENTION:

weekly checklist

- PLAN WEEK'S MITS
- SOAK IN THE TUB
- TAKE A DIGITAL DAY OFF
- CLEAR CLUTTER
- PEN A LOVE NOTE
- BUY/PICK FRESH FLOWERS
- TAKE AN ARTIST DATE
- SAVOR A GREEN JUICE
- ______

MITs

- ______
- ______
- ______
- ______
- ______

wellness planning

M ______
T ______
W ______
TH ______
F ______
S ______
S ______

GRATITUDE:

MONDAY ______

7 ______
8 ______
9 ______
10 ______
11 ______
12 ______
1 ______
2 ______
3 ______
4 ______
5 ______
6 ______
7 ______
8 ______
9 ______

daily checklist

- MORNING RITUAL
- DAILY DRESS-UP
- MINDFUL MOVEMENT
- EAT YOUR VEGGIES
- JOURNAL
- GOAL REVIEW
- GRATITUDE
- EVENING RITUAL
- ______

TUESDAY ______

7 ______
8 ______
9 ______
10 ______
11 ______
12 ______
1 ______
2 ______
3 ______
4 ______
5 ______
6 ______
7 ______
8 ______
9 ______

daily checklist

- MORNING RITUAL
- DAILY DRESS-UP
- MINDFUL MOVEMENT
- EAT YOUR VEGGIES
- JOURNAL
- GOAL REVIEW
- GRATITUDE
- EVENING RITUAL
- ______

WEDNESDAY ______

7 ______
8 ______
9 ______
10 ______
11 ______
12 ______
1 ______
2 ______
3 ______
4 ______
5 ______
6 ______
7 ______
8 ______
9 ______

daily checklist

- MORNING RITUAL
- DAILY DRESS-UP
- MINDFUL MOVEMENT
- EAT YOUR VEGGIES
- JOURNAL
- GOAL REVIEW
- GRATITUDE
- EVENING RITUAL
- ______

THURSDAY

7
8
9
10
11
12
1
2
3
4
5
6
7
8
9

daily checklist

- MORNING RITUAL
- DAILY DRESS-UP
- MINDFUL MOVEMENT
- EAT YOUR VEGGIES
- JOURNAL
- GOAL REVIEW
- GRATITUDE
- EVENING RITUAL

FRIDAY

7
8
9
10
11
12
1
2
3
4
5
6
7
8
9

daily checklist

- MORNING RITUAL
- DAILY DRESS-UP
- MINDFUL MOVEMENT
- EAT YOUR VEGGIES
- JOURNAL
- GOAL REVIEW
- GRATITUDE
- EVENING RITUAL

SATURDAY

7
8
9
10
11
12
1
2
3
4
5
6
7
8
9

daily checklist

- MORNING RITUAL
- DAILY DRESS-UP
- MINDFUL MOVEMENT
- EAT YOUR VEGGIES
- JOURNAL
- GOAL REVIEW
- GRATITUDE
- EVENING RITUAL

SUNDAY

7
8
9
10
11
12
1
2
3
4
5
6
7
8
9

daily checklist

- MORNING RITUAL
- DAILY DRESS-UP
- MINDFUL MOVEMENT
- EAT YOUR VEGGIES
- JOURNAL
- GOAL REVIEW
- GRATITUDE
- EVENING RITUAL

10 Roses
10€

month's dreams

DOODLE, LIST, COLLAGE, OR WRITE WHAT YOU'D LIKE TO MANIFEST THIS MONTH.

month's review

REVISIT YOUR MONTH'S DREAMS AND NOTE HOW THEY UNFOLDED FOR YOU.

30 days of tranquility

TRY THIS 30-DAY CHALLENGE TO INFUSE YOUR MONTH WITH SIMPLE PLEASURES.

1	2	3	4	5
SIT STILL FOR FIVE MINUTES	DO SIX SUN SALUTATIONS	WRITE A LOVE LETTER	APOLOGIZE	TELL THE TRUTH
6	**7**	**8**	**9**	**10**
CONSUME A GREEN DRINK	GO MEAT-FREE	WALK FOR 20 MINUTES	DO LEGS UP THE WALL	GIVE $10 TO CHARITY
11	**12**	**13**	**14**	**15**
PEN TWO JOURNAL PAGES	REVIEW YOUR YEAR'S DREAMS	CLEAR CLUTTER	GO ON AN ARTIST DATE	COLLAGE TWO PAGES
16	**17**	**18**	**19**	**20**
TREAT YOURSELF TO TEA	READ FOR 20 MINUTES	BUY YOURSELF FLOWERS	DANCE TO A FAVORITE TUNE	EXPRESS GRATITUDE
21	**22**	**23**	**24**	**25**
EAT ONLY UNPROCESSED FOODS	SOAK IN A BUBBLE BATH	MINDFULLY SIP A LIBATION	GET OUT IN NATURE	FORGO COMPLAINING
26	**27**	**28**	**29**	**30**
TAKE A DIGITAL DAY OFF	SNAP PHOTOS FROM YOUR DAY	MAKE A FAVORITE MEAL	HUG	BE FULLY PRESENT

habit tracking

NOTE HABITS YOU'RE TRYING TO ADD OR SUBTRACT AND TRACK THEM DAILY TO HELP WITH ACCOUNTABILITY. CELEBRATE YOUR SUCCESSES AND OBSERVE AREAS FOR GROWTH.

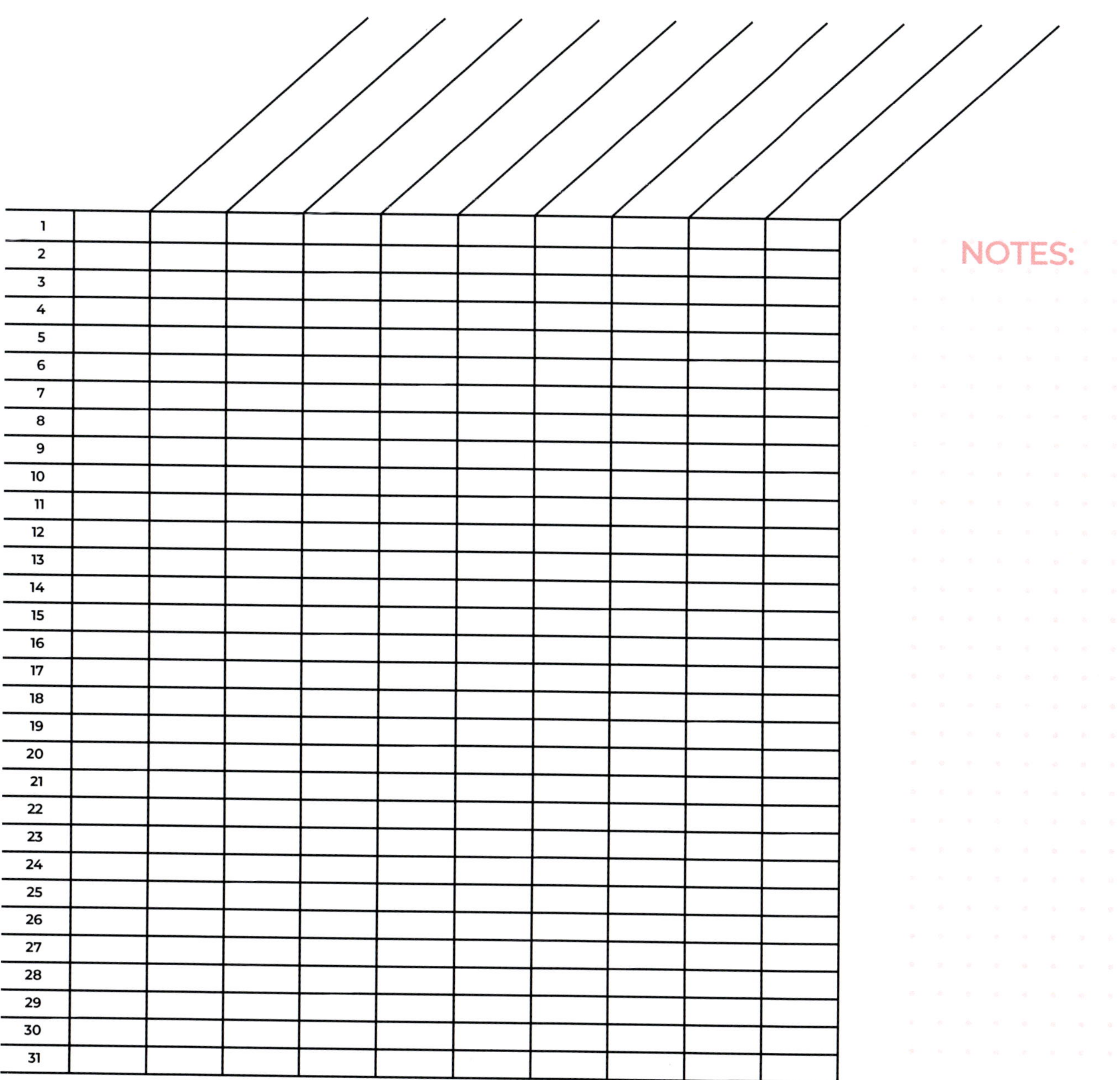

1										
2										
3										
4										
5										
6										
7										
8										
9										
10										
11										
12										
13										
14										
15										
16										
17										
18										
19										
20										
21										
22										
23										
24										
25										
26										
27										
28										
29										
30										
31										

NOTES:

moon phases

Notice your connection to the moon's cycles in these four phases: new, waxing, full, waning. Consider the prompts below as a way to tie into your Month's Dreams and provide space for monthly reflection.

new moon

A TIME FOR SETTING INTENTIONS.
I WANT . . .

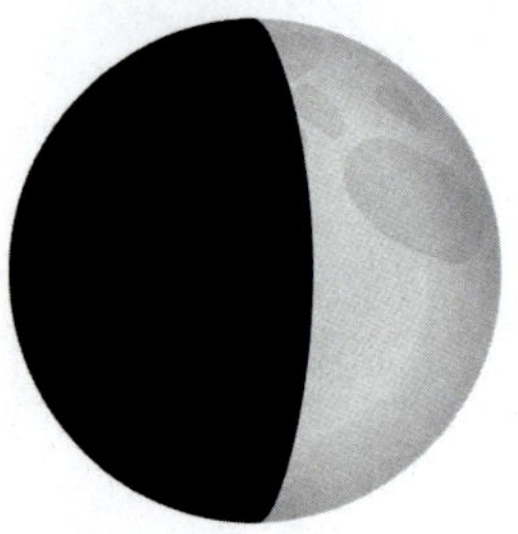

A TIME FOR ACTION. I WILL . . .

full moon

A TIME FOR HARVEST AND CLOSURE.
I RELEASE . . .

waning moon

A TIME FOR SOFTENING. I FEEL . . .

monthly planner

MONTH: ______________________ INTENTION: ______________________

SUNDAY	MONDAY	TUESDAY	WEDNESDAY	THURSDAY	FRIDAY	SATURDAY

MONTHLY TRANQUILITY TOOLS

- ❍ CRAFT MONTH'S DREAMS
- ❍ REVIEW BUDGET
- ❍ CREATE SOMETHING
- ❍ READ TWO BOOKS
- ❍ VOLUNTEER
- ❍ MANI/PEDI
- ❍ ENTERTAIN
- ❍ MASSAGE

INTENTION:

weekly checklist

- ❍ PLAN WEEK'S MITS
- ❍ SOAK IN THE TUB
- ❍ TAKE A DIGITAL DAY OFF
- ❍ CLEAR CLUTTER
- ❍ PEN A LOVE NOTE
- ❍ BUY/PICK FRESH FLOWERS
- ❍ TAKE AN ARTIST DATE
- ❍ SAVOR A GREEN JUICE
- ❍ ____

MITs

- ❍ ____
- ❍ ____
- ❍ ____
- ❍ ____
- ❍ ____

wellness planning

M ____
T ____
W ____
TH ____
F ____
S ____
S ____

GRATITUDE:

MONDAY ____

7 ____
8 ____
9 ____
10 ____
11 ____
12 ____
1 ____
2 ____
3 ____
4 ____
5 ____
6 ____
7 ____
8 ____
9 ____

daily checklist

- ❍ MORNING RITUAL
- ❍ DAILY DRESS-UP
- ❍ MINDFUL MOVEMENT
- ❍ EAT YOUR VEGGIES
- ❍ JOURNAL
- ❍ GOAL REVIEW
- ❍ GRATITUDE
- ❍ EVENING RITUAL
- ❍ ____

TUESDAY ____

7 ____
8 ____
9 ____
10 ____
11 ____
12 ____
1 ____
2 ____
3 ____
4 ____
5 ____
6 ____
7 ____
8 ____
9 ____

daily checklist

- ❍ MORNING RITUAL
- ❍ DAILY DRESS-UP
- ❍ MINDFUL MOVEMENT
- ❍ EAT YOUR VEGGIES
- ❍ JOURNAL
- ❍ GOAL REVIEW
- ❍ GRATITUDE
- ❍ EVENING RITUAL
- ❍ ____

WEDNESDAY ____

7 ____
8 ____
9 ____
10 ____
11 ____
12 ____
1 ____
2 ____
3 ____
4 ____
5 ____
6 ____
7 ____
8 ____
9 ____

daily checklist

- ❍ MORNING RITUAL
- ❍ DAILY DRESS-UP
- ❍ MINDFUL MOVEMENT
- ❍ EAT YOUR VEGGIES
- ❍ JOURNAL
- ❍ GOAL REVIEW
- ❍ GRATITUDE
- ❍ EVENING RITUAL
- ❍ ____

THURSDAY

7
8
9
10
11
12
1
2
3
4
5
6
7
8
9

daily checklist

- MORNING RITUAL
- DAILY DRESS-UP
- MINDFUL MOVEMENT
- EAT YOUR VEGGIES
- JOURNAL
- GOAL REVIEW
- GRATITUDE
- EVENING RITUAL

FRIDAY

7
8
9
10
11
12
1
2
3
4
5
6
7
8
9

daily checklist

- MORNING RITUAL
- DAILY DRESS-UP
- MINDFUL MOVEMENT
- EAT YOUR VEGGIES
- JOURNAL
- GOAL REVIEW
- GRATITUDE
- EVENING RITUAL

SATURDAY

7
8
9
10
11
12
1
2
3
4
5
6
7
8
9

daily checklist

- MORNING RITUAL
- DAILY DRESS-UP
- MINDFUL MOVEMENT
- EAT YOUR VEGGIES
- JOURNAL
- GOAL REVIEW
- GRATITUDE
- EVENING RITUAL

SUNDAY

7
8
9
10
11
12
1
2
3
4
5
6
7
8
9

daily checklist

- MORNING RITUAL
- DAILY DRESS-UP
- MINDFUL MOVEMENT
- EAT YOUR VEGGIES
- JOURNAL
- GOAL REVIEW
- GRATITUDE
- EVENING RITUAL

INTENTION:

weekly checklist

- PLAN WEEK'S MITS
- SOAK IN THE TUB
- TAKE A DIGITAL DAY OFF
- CLEAR CLUTTER
- PEN A LOVE NOTE
- BUY/PICK FRESH FLOWERS
- TAKE AN ARTIST DATE
- SAVOR A GREEN JUICE
- __________

MITs

wellness planning

M
T
W
TH
F
S
S

GRATITUDE:

MONDAY

7
8
9
10
11
12
1
2
3
4
5
6
7
8
9

daily checklist

- MORNING RITUAL
- DAILY DRESS-UP
- MINDFUL MOVEMENT
- EAT YOUR VEGGIES
- JOURNAL
- GOAL REVIEW
- GRATITUDE
- EVENING RITUAL

TUESDAY

7
8
9
10
11
12
1
2
3
4
5
6
7
8
9

daily checklist

- MORNING RITUAL
- DAILY DRESS-UP
- MINDFUL MOVEMENT
- EAT YOUR VEGGIES
- JOURNAL
- GOAL REVIEW
- GRATITUDE
- EVENING RITUAL

WEDNESDAY

7
8
9
10
11
12
1
2
3
4
5
6
7
8
9

daily checklist

- MORNING RITUAL
- DAILY DRESS-UP
- MINDFUL MOVEMENT
- EAT YOUR VEGGIES
- JOURNAL
- GOAL REVIEW
- GRATITUDE
- EVENING RITUAL

THURSDAY

7
8
9
10
11
12
1
2
3
4
5
6
7
8
9

daily checklist

- MORNING RITUAL
- DAILY DRESS-UP
- MINDFUL MOVEMENT
- EAT YOUR VEGGIES
- JOURNAL
- GOAL REVIEW
- GRATITUDE
- EVENING RITUAL

FRIDAY

7
8
9
10
11
12
1
2
3
4
5
6
7
8
9

daily checklist

- MORNING RITUAL
- DAILY DRESS-UP
- MINDFUL MOVEMENT
- EAT YOUR VEGGIES
- JOURNAL
- GOAL REVIEW
- GRATITUDE
- EVENING RITUAL

SATURDAY

7
8
9
10
11
12
1
2
3
4
5
6
7
8
9

daily checklist

- MORNING RITUAL
- DAILY DRESS-UP
- MINDFUL MOVEMENT
- EAT YOUR VEGGIES
- JOURNAL
- GOAL REVIEW
- GRATITUDE
- EVENING RITUAL

SUNDAY

7
8
9
10
11
12
1
2
3
4
5
6
7
8
9

daily checklist

- MORNING RITUAL
- DAILY DRESS-UP
- MINDFUL MOVEMENT
- EAT YOUR VEGGIES
- JOURNAL
- GOAL REVIEW
- GRATITUDE
- EVENING RITUAL

INTENTION:

weekly checklist

- PLAN WEEK'S MITS
- SOAK IN THE TUB
- TAKE A DIGITAL DAY OFF
- CLEAR CLUTTER
- PEN A LOVE NOTE
- BUY/PICK FRESH FLOWERS
- TAKE AN ARTIST DATE
- SAVOR A GREEN JUICE
- ____________

MITs

- ____________
- ____________
- ____________
- ____________
- ____________

wellness planning

M ____________
T ____________
W ____________
TH ____________
F ____________
S ____________
S ____________

GRATITUDE:

MONDAY ____________

7 ____________
8 ____________
9 ____________
10 ____________
11 ____________
12 ____________
1 ____________
2 ____________
3 ____________
4 ____________
5 ____________
6 ____________
7 ____________
8 ____________
9 ____________

daily checklist

- MORNING RITUAL
- DAILY DRESS-UP
- MINDFUL MOVEMENT
- EAT YOUR VEGGIES
- JOURNAL
- GOAL REVIEW
- GRATITUDE
- EVENING RITUAL
- ____________

TUESDAY ____________

7 ____________
8 ____________
9 ____________
10 ____________
11 ____________
12 ____________
1 ____________
2 ____________
3 ____________
4 ____________
5 ____________
6 ____________
7 ____________
8 ____________
9 ____________

daily checklist

- MORNING RITUAL
- DAILY DRESS-UP
- MINDFUL MOVEMENT
- EAT YOUR VEGGIES
- JOURNAL
- GOAL REVIEW
- GRATITUDE
- EVENING RITUAL
- ____________

WEDNESDAY ____________

7 ____________
8 ____________
9 ____________
10 ____________
11 ____________
12 ____________
1 ____________
2 ____________
3 ____________
4 ____________
5 ____________
6 ____________
7 ____________
8 ____________
9 ____________

daily checklist

- MORNING RITUAL
- DAILY DRESS-UP
- MINDFUL MOVEMENT
- EAT YOUR VEGGIES
- JOURNAL
- GOAL REVIEW
- GRATITUDE
- EVENING RITUAL
- ____________

THURSDAY ______

7 ______
8 ______
9 ______
10 ______
11 ______
12 ______
1 ______
2 ______
3 ______
4 ______
5 ______
6 ______
7 ______
8 ______
9 ______

daily checklist

- MORNING RITUAL
- DAILY DRESS-UP
- MINDFUL MOVEMENT
- EAT YOUR VEGGIES
- JOURNAL
- GOAL REVIEW
- GRATITUDE
- EVENING RITUAL

FRIDAY ______

7 ______
8 ______
9 ______
10 ______
11 ______
12 ______
1 ______
2 ______
3 ______
4 ______
5 ______
6 ______
7 ______
8 ______
9 ______

daily checklist

- MORNING RITUAL
- DAILY DRESS-UP
- MINDFUL MOVEMENT
- EAT YOUR VEGGIES
- JOURNAL
- GOAL REVIEW
- GRATITUDE
- EVENING RITUAL

SATURDAY ______

7 ______
8 ______
9 ______
10 ______
11 ______
12 ______
1 ______
2 ______
3 ______
4 ______
5 ______
6 ______
7 ______
8 ______
9 ______

daily checklist

- MORNING RITUAL
- DAILY DRESS-UP
- MINDFUL MOVEMENT
- EAT YOUR VEGGIES
- JOURNAL
- GOAL REVIEW
- GRATITUDE
- EVENING RITUAL

SUNDAY ______

7 ______
8 ______
9 ______
10 ______
11 ______
12 ______
1 ______
2 ______
3 ______
4 ______
5 ______
6 ______
7 ______
8 ______
9 ______

daily checklist

- MORNING RITUAL
- DAILY DRESS-UP
- MINDFUL MOVEMENT
- EAT YOUR VEGGIES
- JOURNAL
- GOAL REVIEW
- GRATITUDE
- EVENING RITUAL

INTENTION:

weekly checklist

- ❍ PLAN WEEK'S MITS
- ❍ SOAK IN THE TUB
- ❍ TAKE A DIGITAL DAY OFF
- ❍ CLEAR CLUTTER
- ❍ PEN A LOVE NOTE
- ❍ BUY/PICK FRESH FLOWERS
- ❍ TAKE AN ARTIST DATE
- ❍ SAVOR A GREEN JUICE
- ❍ ______

MITs

- ❍ ______
- ❍ ______
- ❍ ______
- ❍ ______
- ❍ ______

wellness planning

M ______
T ______
W ______
TH ______
F ______
S ______
S ______

GRATITUDE:

MONDAY ______

7 ______
8 ______
9 ______
10 ______
11 ______
12 ______
1 ______
2 ______
3 ______
4 ______
5 ______
6 ______
7 ______
8 ______
9 ______

daily checklist

- ❍ MORNING RITUAL
- ❍ DAILY DRESS-UP
- ❍ MINDFUL MOVEMENT
- ❍ EAT YOUR VEGGIES
- ❍ JOURNAL
- ❍ GOAL REVIEW
- ❍ GRATITUDE
- ❍ EVENING RITUAL
- ❍ ______

TUESDAY ______

7 ______
8 ______
9 ______
10 ______
11 ______
12 ______
1 ______
2 ______
3 ______
4 ______
5 ______
6 ______
7 ______
8 ______
9 ______

daily checklist

- ❍ MORNING RITUAL
- ❍ DAILY DRESS-UP
- ❍ MINDFUL MOVEMENT
- ❍ EAT YOUR VEGGIES
- ❍ JOURNAL
- ❍ GOAL REVIEW
- ❍ GRATITUDE
- ❍ EVENING RITUAL
- ❍ ______

WEDNESDAY ______

7 ______
8 ______
9 ______
10 ______
11 ______
12 ______
1 ______
2 ______
3 ______
4 ______
5 ______
6 ______
7 ______
8 ______
9 ______

daily checklist

- ❍ MORNING RITUAL
- ❍ DAILY DRESS-UP
- ❍ MINDFUL MOVEMENT
- ❍ EAT YOUR VEGGIES
- ❍ JOURNAL
- ❍ GOAL REVIEW
- ❍ GRATITUDE
- ❍ EVENING RITUAL
- ❍ ______

THURSDAY

7
8
9
10
11
12
1
2
3
4
5
6
7
8
9

daily checklist

- MORNING RITUAL
- DAILY DRESS-UP
- MINDFUL MOVEMENT
- EAT YOUR VEGGIES
- JOURNAL
- GOAL REVIEW
- GRATITUDE
- EVENING RITUAL

FRIDAY

7
8
9
10
11
12
1
2
3
4
5
6
7
8
9

daily checklist

- MORNING RITUAL
- DAILY DRESS-UP
- MINDFUL MOVEMENT
- EAT YOUR VEGGIES
- JOURNAL
- GOAL REVIEW
- GRATITUDE
- EVENING RITUAL

SATURDAY

7
8
9
10
11
12
1
2
3
4
5
6
7
8
9

daily checklist

- MORNING RITUAL
- DAILY DRESS-UP
- MINDFUL MOVEMENT
- EAT YOUR VEGGIES
- JOURNAL
- GOAL REVIEW
- GRATITUDE
- EVENING RITUAL

SUNDAY

7
8
9
10
11
12
1
2
3
4
5
6
7
8
9

daily checklist

- MORNING RITUAL
- DAILY DRESS-UP
- MINDFUL MOVEMENT
- EAT YOUR VEGGIES
- JOURNAL
- GOAL REVIEW
- GRATITUDE
- EVENING RITUAL

INTENTION:

weekly checklist

- PLAN WEEK'S MITS
- SOAK IN THE TUB
- TAKE A DIGITAL DAY OFF
- CLEAR CLUTTER
- PEN A LOVE NOTE
- BUY/PICK FRESH FLOWERS
- TAKE AN ARTIST DATE
- SAVOR A GREEN JUICE
- ______

MITs

- ______
- ______
- ______
- ______
- ______

wellness planning

M ______
T ______
W ______
TH ______
F ______
S ______
S ______

GRATITUDE:

MONDAY ______

7 ______
8 ______
9 ______
10 ______
11 ______
12 ______
1 ______
2 ______
3 ______
4 ______
5 ______
6 ______
7 ______
8 ______
9 ______

daily checklist

- MORNING RITUAL
- DAILY DRESS-UP
- MINDFUL MOVEMENT
- EAT YOUR VEGGIES
- JOURNAL
- GOAL REVIEW
- GRATITUDE
- EVENING RITUAL
- ______

TUESDAY ______

7 ______
8 ______
9 ______
10 ______
11 ______
12 ______
1 ______
2 ______
3 ______
4 ______
5 ______
6 ______
7 ______
8 ______
9 ______

daily checklist

- MORNING RITUAL
- DAILY DRESS-UP
- MINDFUL MOVEMENT
- EAT YOUR VEGGIES
- JOURNAL
- GOAL REVIEW
- GRATITUDE
- EVENING RITUAL
- ______

WEDNESDAY ______

7 ______
8 ______
9 ______
10 ______
11 ______
12 ______
1 ______
2 ______
3 ______
4 ______
5 ______
6 ______
7 ______
8 ______
9 ______

daily checklist

- MORNING RITUAL
- DAILY DRESS-UP
- MINDFUL MOVEMENT
- EAT YOUR VEGGIES
- JOURNAL
- GOAL REVIEW
- GRATITUDE
- EVENING RITUAL
- ______

THURSDAY

7
8
9
10
11
12
1
2
3
4
5
6
7
8
9

daily checklist

- MORNING RITUAL
- DAILY DRESS-UP
- MINDFUL MOVEMENT
- EAT YOUR VEGGIES
- JOURNAL
- GOAL REVIEW
- GRATITUDE
- EVENING RITUAL

FRIDAY

7
8
9
10
11
12
1
2
3
4
5
6
7
8
9

daily checklist

- MORNING RITUAL
- DAILY DRESS-UP
- MINDFUL MOVEMENT
- EAT YOUR VEGGIES
- JOURNAL
- GOAL REVIEW
- GRATITUDE
- EVENING RITUAL

SATURDAY

7
8
9
10
11
12
1
2
3
4
5
6
7
8
9

daily checklist

- MORNING RITUAL
- DAILY DRESS-UP
- MINDFUL MOVEMENT
- EAT YOUR VEGGIES
- JOURNAL
- GOAL REVIEW
- GRATITUDE
- EVENING RITUAL

SUNDAY

7
8
9
10
11
12
1
2
3
4
5
6
7
8
9

daily checklist

- MORNING RITUAL
- DAILY DRESS-UP
- MINDFUL MOVEMENT
- EAT YOUR VEGGIES
- JOURNAL
- GOAL REVIEW
- GRATITUDE
- EVENING RITUAL

WHEN IN
DOUBT,
TAKE A
BUBBLE
BATH.

seasonal life review

DATE: ____________

SEASONALLY REFLECT ON AREAS OF YOUR LIFE. RATE EACH ONE WITH YOUR LEVEL OF SATISFACTION 10 = BLISS, 5 = SO-SO, 0 = BOO.

Here are some additional areas to consider: social life, romance, family, education, health, fitness, meaning, activism. Next, take a moment to note the areas that ranked low and create three action steps to increase your tranquility in these areas. Be gentle. Plant seeds. Watch dreams take root.

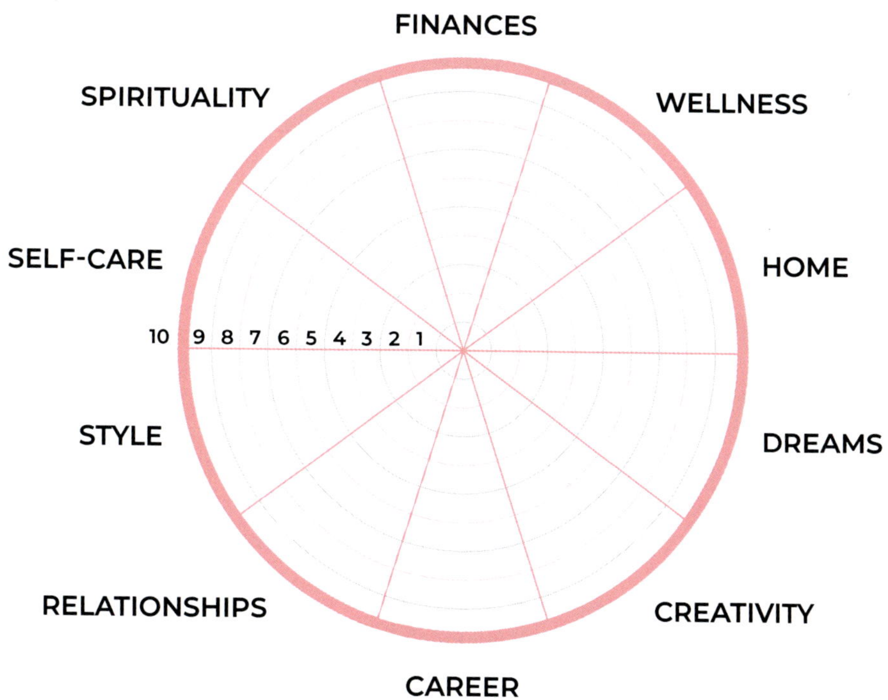

ACTION STEPS TO INCREASE AREAS THAT ARE LOWER THAN I'D LIKE:

L

month's dreams

DOODLE, LIST, COLLAGE, OR WRITE WHAT YOU'D LIKE TO MANIFEST THIS MONTH.

month's review

REVISIT YOUR MONTH'S DREAMS AND NOTE HOW THEY UNFOLDED FOR YOU.

30 days of tranquility

TRY THIS 30-DAY CHALLENGE TO INFUSE YOUR MONTH WITH SIMPLE PLEASURES.

1. SIT STILL FOR FIVE MINUTES
2. DO SIX SUN SALUTATIONS
3. WRITE A LOVE LETTER
4. APOLOGIZE
5. TELL THE TRUTH
6. CONSUME A GREEN DRINK
7. GO MEAT-FREE
8. WALK FOR 20 MINUTES
9. DO LEGS UP THE WALL
10. GIVE $10 TO CHARITY
11. PEN TWO JOURNAL PAGES
12. REVIEW YOUR YEAR'S DREAMS
13. CLEAR CLUTTER
14. GO ON AN ARTIST DATE
15. COLLAGE TWO PAGES
16. TREAT YOURSELF TO TEA
17. READ FOR 20 MINUTES
18. BUY YOURSELF FLOWERS
19. DANCE TO A FAVORITE TUNE
20. EXPRESS GRATITUDE
21. EAT ONLY UNPROCESSED FOODS
22. SOAK IN A BUBBLE BATH
23. MINDFULLY SIP A LIBATION
24. GET OUT IN NATURE
25. FORGO COMPLAINING
26. TAKE A DIGITAL DAY OFF
27. SNAP PHOTOS FROM YOUR DAY
28. MAKE A FAVORITE MEAL
29. HUG
30. BE FULLY PRESENT

habit tracking

NOTE HABITS YOU'RE TRYING TO ADD OR SUBTRACT AND TRACK THEM DAILY TO HELP WITH ACCOUNTABILITY. CELEBRATE YOUR SUCCESSES AND OBSERVE AREAS FOR GROWTH.

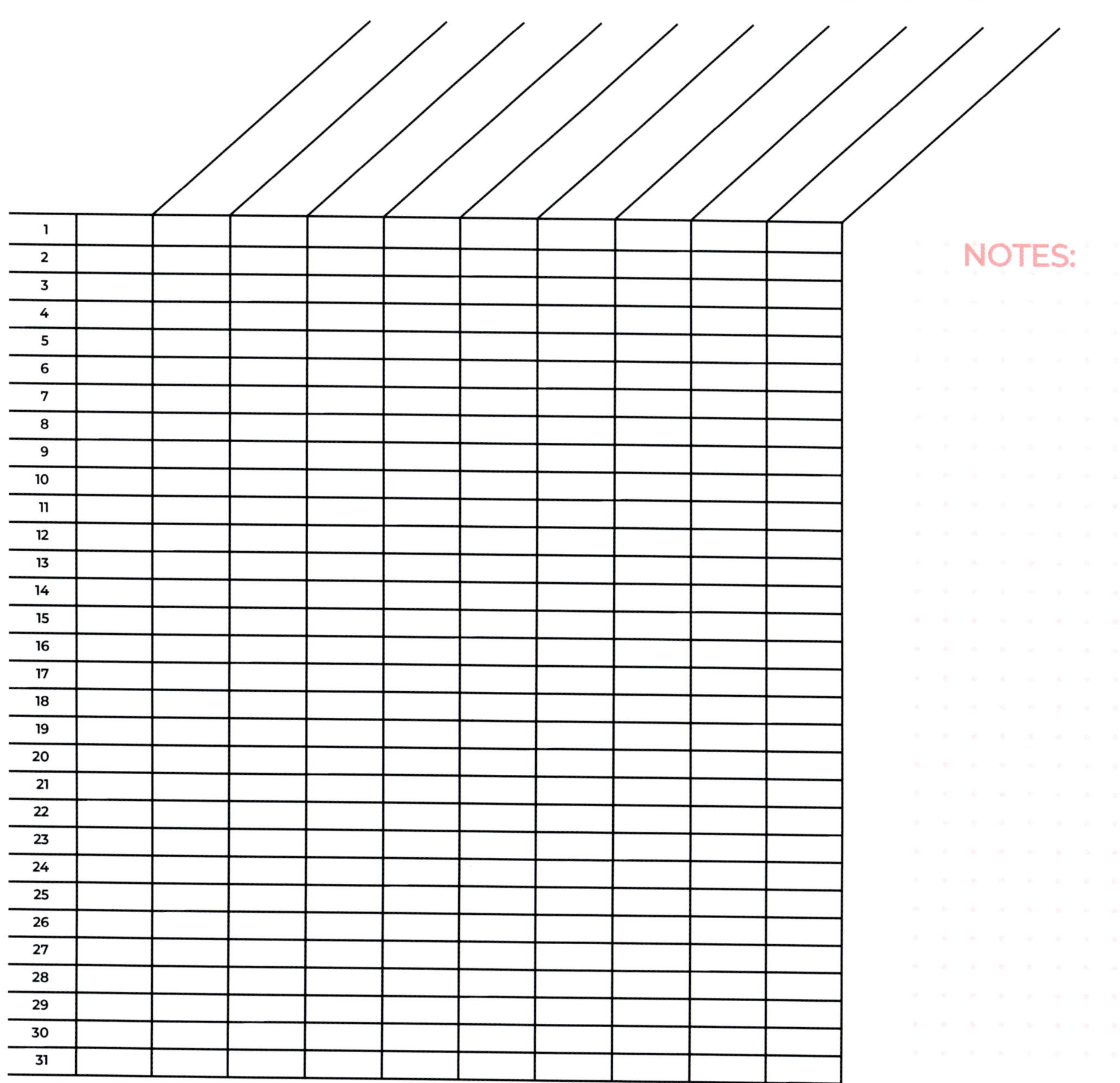

1										
2										
3										
4										
5										
6										
7										
8										
9										
10										
11										
12										
13										
14										
15										
16										
17										
18										
19										
20										
21										
22										
23										
24										
25										
26										
27										
28										
29										
30										
31										

NOTES:

moon phases

Notice your connection to the moon's cycles in these four phases: new, waxing, full, waning. Consider the prompts below as a way to tie into your Month's Dreams and provide space for monthly reflection.

new moon

A TIME FOR SETTING INTENTIONS.
I WANT . . .

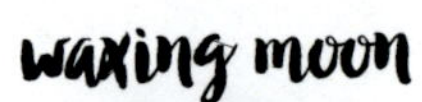

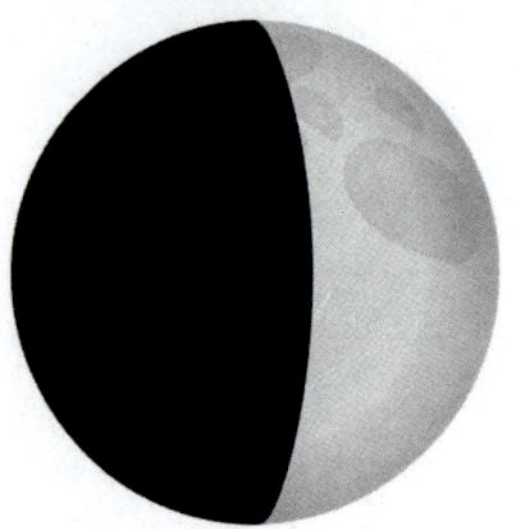

A TIME FOR ACTION. I WILL . . .

full moon

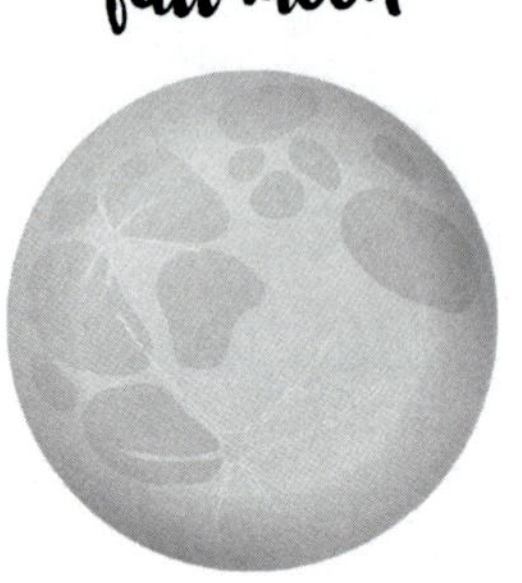

A TIME FOR HARVEST AND CLOSURE.
I RELEASE . . .

waning moon

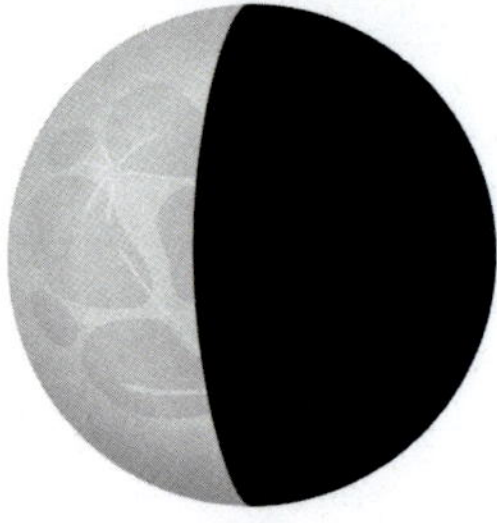

A TIME FOR SOFTENING. I FEEL . . .

monthly planner

MONTH: ______________________ INTENTION: ______________________

SUNDAY	MONDAY	TUESDAY	WEDNESDAY	THURSDAY	FRIDAY	SATURDAY

MONTHLY TRANQUILITY TOOLS

- ❍ CRAFT MONTH'S DREAMS
- ❍ REVIEW BUDGET
- ❍ CREATE SOMETHING
- ❍ READ TWO BOOKS
- ❍ VOLUNTEER
- ❍ MANI/PEDI
- ❍ ENTERTAIN
- ❍ MASSAGE

INTENTION:

weekly checklist

- PLAN WEEK'S MITS
- SOAK IN THE TUB
- TAKE A DIGITAL DAY OFF
- CLEAR CLUTTER
- PEN A LOVE NOTE
- BUY/PICK FRESH FLOWERS
- TAKE AN ARTIST DATE
- SAVOR A GREEN JUICE
- ____________

MITs

- ____________
- ____________
- ____________
- ____________
- ____________

wellness planning

M ____________
T ____________
W ____________
TH ____________
F ____________
S ____________
S ____________

GRATITUDE:

MONDAY ____________

7 ____________
8 ____________
9 ____________
10 ____________
11 ____________
12 ____________
1 ____________
2 ____________
3 ____________
4 ____________
5 ____________
6 ____________
7 ____________
8 ____________
9 ____________

daily checklist

- MORNING RITUAL
- DAILY DRESS-UP
- MINDFUL MOVEMENT
- EAT YOUR VEGGIES
- JOURNAL
- GOAL REVIEW
- GRATITUDE
- EVENING RITUAL
- ____________

TUESDAY ____________

7 ____________
8 ____________
9 ____________
10 ____________
11 ____________
12 ____________
1 ____________
2 ____________
3 ____________
4 ____________
5 ____________
6 ____________
7 ____________
8 ____________
9 ____________

daily checklist

- MORNING RITUAL
- DAILY DRESS-UP
- MINDFUL MOVEMENT
- EAT YOUR VEGGIES
- JOURNAL
- GOAL REVIEW
- GRATITUDE
- EVENING RITUAL
- ____________

WEDNESDAY ____________

7 ____________
8 ____________
9 ____________
10 ____________
11 ____________
12 ____________
1 ____________
2 ____________
3 ____________
4 ____________
5 ____________
6 ____________
7 ____________
8 ____________
9 ____________

daily checklist

- MORNING RITUAL
- DAILY DRESS-UP
- MINDFUL MOVEMENT
- EAT YOUR VEGGIES
- JOURNAL
- GOAL REVIEW
- GRATITUDE
- EVENING RITUAL
- ____________

THURSDAY

7
8
9
10
11
12
1
2
3
4
5
6
7
8
9

daily checklist

- MORNING RITUAL
- DAILY DRESS-UP
- MINDFUL MOVEMENT
- EAT YOUR VEGGIES
- JOURNAL
- GOAL REVIEW
- GRATITUDE
- EVENING RITUAL

FRIDAY

7
8
9
10
11
12
1
2
3
4
5
6
7
8
9

daily checklist

- MORNING RITUAL
- DAILY DRESS-UP
- MINDFUL MOVEMENT
- EAT YOUR VEGGIES
- JOURNAL
- GOAL REVIEW
- GRATITUDE
- EVENING RITUAL

SATURDAY

7
8
9
10
11
12
1
2
3
4
5
6
7
8
9

daily checklist

- MORNING RITUAL
- DAILY DRESS-UP
- MINDFUL MOVEMENT
- EAT YOUR VEGGIES
- JOURNAL
- GOAL REVIEW
- GRATITUDE
- EVENING RITUAL

SUNDAY

7
8
9
10
11
12
1
2
3
4
5
6
7
8
9

daily checklist

- MORNING RITUAL
- DAILY DRESS-UP
- MINDFUL MOVEMENT
- EAT YOUR VEGGIES
- JOURNAL
- GOAL REVIEW
- GRATITUDE
- EVENING RITUAL

INTENTION:

weekly checklist

- PLAN WEEK'S MITS
- SOAK IN THE TUB
- TAKE A DIGITAL DAY OFF
- CLEAR CLUTTER
- PEN A LOVE NOTE
- BUY/PICK FRESH FLOWERS
- TAKE AN ARTIST DATE
- SAVOR A GREEN JUICE
- ______

MITs

- ______
- ______
- ______
- ______
- ______

wellness planning

M ______
T ______
W ______
TH ______
F ______
S ______
S ______

GRATITUDE:

MONDAY ______

7 ______
8 ______
9 ______
10 ______
11 ______
12 ______
1 ______
2 ______
3 ______
4 ______
5 ______
6 ______
7 ______
8 ______
9 ______

daily checklist

- MORNING RITUAL
- DAILY DRESS-UP
- MINDFUL MOVEMENT
- EAT YOUR VEGGIES
- JOURNAL
- GOAL REVIEW
- GRATITUDE
- EVENING RITUAL
- ______

TUESDAY ______

7 ______
8 ______
9 ______
10 ______
11 ______
12 ______
1 ______
2 ______
3 ______
4 ______
5 ______
6 ______
7 ______
8 ______
9 ______

daily checklist

- MORNING RITUAL
- DAILY DRESS-UP
- MINDFUL MOVEMENT
- EAT YOUR VEGGIES
- JOURNAL
- GOAL REVIEW
- GRATITUDE
- EVENING RITUAL
- ______

WEDNESDAY ______

7 ______
8 ______
9 ______
10 ______
11 ______
12 ______
1 ______
2 ______
3 ______
4 ______
5 ______
6 ______
7 ______
8 ______
9 ______

daily checklist

- MORNING RITUAL
- DAILY DRESS-UP
- MINDFUL MOVEMENT
- EAT YOUR VEGGIES
- JOURNAL
- GOAL REVIEW
- GRATITUDE
- EVENING RITUAL
- ______

THURSDAY ____

7 ____
8 ____
9 ____
10 ____
11 ____
12 ____
1 ____
2 ____
3 ____
4 ____
5 ____
6 ____
7 ____
8 ____
9 ____

- ○ ____
- ○ ____
- ○ ____
- ○ ____
- ○ ____
- ○ ____
- ○ ____
- ○ ____
- ○ ____
- ○ ____

- ○ ____
- ○ ____
- ○ ____
- ○ ____
- ○ ____
- ○ ____

daily checklist

- ○ MORNING RITUAL
- ○ DAILY DRESS-UP
- ○ MINDFUL MOVEMENT
- ○ EAT YOUR VEGGIES
- ○ JOURNAL
- ○ GOAL REVIEW
- ○ GRATITUDE
- ○ EVENING RITUAL
- ○ ____

FRIDAY ____

7 ____
8 ____
9 ____
10 ____
11 ____
12 ____
1 ____
2 ____
3 ____
4 ____
5 ____
6 ____
7 ____
8 ____
9 ____

- ○ ____
- ○ ____
- ○ ____
- ○ ____
- ○ ____
- ○ ____
- ○ ____
- ○ ____
- ○ ____
- ○ ____

- ○ ____
- ○ ____
- ○ ____
- ○ ____
- ○ ____
- ○ ____

daily checklist

- ○ MORNING RITUAL
- ○ DAILY DRESS-UP
- ○ MINDFUL MOVEMENT
- ○ EAT YOUR VEGGIES
- ○ JOURNAL
- ○ GOAL REVIEW
- ○ GRATITUDE
- ○ EVENING RITUAL
- ○ ____

SATURDAY ____

7 ____
8 ____
9 ____
10 ____
11 ____
12 ____
1 ____
2 ____
3 ____
4 ____
5 ____
6 ____
7 ____
8 ____
9 ____

- ○ ____
- ○ ____
- ○ ____
- ○ ____
- ○ ____
- ○ ____
- ○ ____
- ○ ____
- ○ ____
- ○ ____

- ○ ____
- ○ ____
- ○ ____
- ○ ____
- ○ ____
- ○ ____

daily checklist

- ○ MORNING RITUAL
- ○ DAILY DRESS-UP
- ○ MINDFUL MOVEMENT
- ○ EAT YOUR VEGGIES
- ○ JOURNAL
- ○ GOAL REVIEW
- ○ GRATITUDE
- ○ EVENING RITUAL
- ○ ____

SUNDAY ____

7 ____
8 ____
9 ____
10 ____
11 ____
12 ____
1 ____
2 ____
3 ____
4 ____
5 ____
6 ____
7 ____
8 ____
9 ____

- ○ ____
- ○ ____
- ○ ____
- ○ ____
- ○ ____
- ○ ____
- ○ ____
- ○ ____
- ○ ____
- ○ ____

- ○ ____
- ○ ____
- ○ ____
- ○ ____
- ○ ____
- ○ ____

daily checklist

- ○ MORNING RITUAL
- ○ DAILY DRESS-UP
- ○ MINDFUL MOVEMENT
- ○ EAT YOUR VEGGIES
- ○ JOURNAL
- ○ GOAL REVIEW
- ○ GRATITUDE
- ○ EVENING RITUAL
- ○ ____

INTENTION:

weekly checklist

- PLAN WEEK'S MITS
- SOAK IN THE TUB
- TAKE A DIGITAL DAY OFF
- CLEAR CLUTTER
- PEN A LOVE NOTE
- BUY/PICK FRESH FLOWERS
- TAKE AN ARTIST DATE
- SAVOR A GREEN JUICE
- ______

MITs

- ______
- ______
- ______
- ______
- ______

wellness planning

M ______
T ______
W ______
TH ______
F ______
S ______
S ______

GRATITUDE:

MONDAY ______

7 ______
8 ______
9 ______
10 ______
11 ______
12 ______
1 ______
2 ______
3 ______
4 ______
5 ______
6 ______
7 ______
8 ______
9 ______

daily checklist

- MORNING RITUAL
- DAILY DRESS-UP
- MINDFUL MOVEMENT
- EAT YOUR VEGGIES
- JOURNAL
- GOAL REVIEW
- GRATITUDE
- EVENING RITUAL
- ______

TUESDAY ______

7 ______
8 ______
9 ______
10 ______
11 ______
12 ______
1 ______
2 ______
3 ______
4 ______
5 ______
6 ______
7 ______
8 ______
9 ______

daily checklist

- MORNING RITUAL
- DAILY DRESS-UP
- MINDFUL MOVEMENT
- EAT YOUR VEGGIES
- JOURNAL
- GOAL REVIEW
- GRATITUDE
- EVENING RITUAL
- ______

WEDNESDAY ______

7 ______
8 ______
9 ______
10 ______
11 ______
12 ______
1 ______
2 ______
3 ______
4 ______
5 ______
6 ______
7 ______
8 ______
9 ______

daily checklist

- MORNING RITUAL
- DAILY DRESS-UP
- MINDFUL MOVEMENT
- EAT YOUR VEGGIES
- JOURNAL
- GOAL REVIEW
- GRATITUDE
- EVENING RITUAL
- ______

THURSDAY

7
8
9
10
11
12
1
2
3
4
5
6
7
8
9

daily checklist

- MORNING RITUAL
- DAILY DRESS-UP
- MINDFUL MOVEMENT
- EAT YOUR VEGGIES
- JOURNAL
- GOAL REVIEW
- GRATITUDE
- EVENING RITUAL

FRIDAY

7
8
9
10
11
12
1
2
3
4
5
6
7
8
9

daily checklist

- MORNING RITUAL
- DAILY DRESS-UP
- MINDFUL MOVEMENT
- EAT YOUR VEGGIES
- JOURNAL
- GOAL REVIEW
- GRATITUDE
- EVENING RITUAL

SATURDAY

7
8
9
10
11
12
1
2
3
4
5
6
7
8
9

daily checklist

- MORNING RITUAL
- DAILY DRESS-UP
- MINDFUL MOVEMENT
- EAT YOUR VEGGIES
- JOURNAL
- GOAL REVIEW
- GRATITUDE
- EVENING RITUAL

SUNDAY

7
8
9
10
11
12
1
2
3
4
5
6
7
8
9

daily checklist

- MORNING RITUAL
- DAILY DRESS-UP
- MINDFUL MOVEMENT
- EAT YOUR VEGGIES
- JOURNAL
- GOAL REVIEW
- GRATITUDE
- EVENING RITUAL

INTENTION:

weekly checklist

- ❍ PLAN WEEK'S MITS
- ❍ SOAK IN THE TUB
- ❍ TAKE A DIGITAL DAY OFF
- ❍ CLEAR CLUTTER
- ❍ PEN A LOVE NOTE
- ❍ BUY/PICK FRESH FLOWERS
- ❍ TAKE AN ARTIST DATE
- ❍ SAVOR A GREEN JUICE
- ❍ ____________

MITs

- ❍ ____________
- ❍ ____________
- ❍ ____________
- ❍ ____________
- ❍ ____________

wellness planning

M ____________
T ____________
W ____________
TH ____________
F ____________
S ____________
S ____________

GRATITUDE:

MONDAY ____________

7 ____________
8 ____________
9 ____________
10 ____________
11 ____________
12 ____________
1 ____________
2 ____________
3 ____________
4 ____________
5 ____________
6 ____________
7 ____________
8 ____________
9 ____________

- ❍ ____________
- ❍ ____________
- ❍ ____________
- ❍ ____________
- ❍ ____________
- ❍ ____________
- ❍ ____________
- ❍ ____________
- ❍ ____________
- ❍ ____________

- ❍ ____________
- ❍ ____________
- ❍ ____________
- ❍ ____________
- ❍ ____________
- ❍ ____________

daily checklist

- ❍ MORNING RITUAL
- ❍ DAILY DRESS-UP
- ❍ MINDFUL MOVEMENT
- ❍ EAT YOUR VEGGIES
- ❍ JOURNAL
- ❍ GOAL REVIEW
- ❍ GRATITUDE
- ❍ EVENING RITUAL
- ❍ ____________

TUESDAY ____________

7 ____________
8 ____________
9 ____________
10 ____________
11 ____________
12 ____________
1 ____________
2 ____________
3 ____________
4 ____________
5 ____________
6 ____________
7 ____________
8 ____________
9 ____________

- ❍ ____________
- ❍ ____________
- ❍ ____________
- ❍ ____________
- ❍ ____________
- ❍ ____________
- ❍ ____________
- ❍ ____________
- ❍ ____________
- ❍ ____________

- ❍ ____________
- ❍ ____________
- ❍ ____________
- ❍ ____________
- ❍ ____________
- ❍ ____________

daily checklist

- ❍ MORNING RITUAL
- ❍ DAILY DRESS-UP
- ❍ MINDFUL MOVEMENT
- ❍ EAT YOUR VEGGIES
- ❍ JOURNAL
- ❍ GOAL REVIEW
- ❍ GRATITUDE
- ❍ EVENING RITUAL
- ❍ ____________

WEDNESDAY ____________

7 ____________
8 ____________
9 ____________
10 ____________
11 ____________
12 ____________
1 ____________
2 ____________
3 ____________
4 ____________
5 ____________
6 ____________
7 ____________
8 ____________
9 ____________

- ❍ ____________
- ❍ ____________
- ❍ ____________
- ❍ ____________
- ❍ ____________
- ❍ ____________
- ❍ ____________
- ❍ ____________
- ❍ ____________
- ❍ ____________

- ❍ ____________
- ❍ ____________
- ❍ ____________
- ❍ ____________
- ❍ ____________
- ❍ ____________

daily checklist

- ❍ MORNING RITUAL
- ❍ DAILY DRESS-UP
- ❍ MINDFUL MOVEMENT
- ❍ EAT YOUR VEGGIES
- ❍ JOURNAL
- ❍ GOAL REVIEW
- ❍ GRATITUDE
- ❍ EVENING RITUAL
- ❍ ____________

THURSDAY

7
8
9
10
11
12
1
2
3
4
5
6
7
8
9

daily checklist

- MORNING RITUAL
- DAILY DRESS-UP
- MINDFUL MOVEMENT
- EAT YOUR VEGGIES
- JOURNAL
- GOAL REVIEW
- GRATITUDE
- EVENING RITUAL

FRIDAY

7
8
9
10
11
12
1
2
3
4
5
6
7
8
9

daily checklist

- MORNING RITUAL
- DAILY DRESS-UP
- MINDFUL MOVEMENT
- EAT YOUR VEGGIES
- JOURNAL
- GOAL REVIEW
- GRATITUDE
- EVENING RITUAL

SATURDAY

7
8
9
10
11
12
1
2
3
4
5
6
7
8
9

daily checklist

- MORNING RITUAL
- DAILY DRESS-UP
- MINDFUL MOVEMENT
- EAT YOUR VEGGIES
- JOURNAL
- GOAL REVIEW
- GRATITUDE
- EVENING RITUAL

SUNDAY

7
8
9
10
11
12
1
2
3
4
5
6
7
8
9

daily checklist

- MORNING RITUAL
- DAILY DRESS-UP
- MINDFUL MOVEMENT
- EAT YOUR VEGGIES
- JOURNAL
- GOAL REVIEW
- GRATITUDE
- EVENING RITUAL

INTENTION:

weekly checklist

- ❍ PLAN WEEK'S MITS
- ❍ SOAK IN THE TUB
- ❍ TAKE A DIGITAL DAY OFF
- ❍ CLEAR CLUTTER
- ❍ PEN A LOVE NOTE
- ❍ BUY/PICK FRESH FLOWERS
- ❍ TAKE AN ARTIST DATE
- ❍ SAVOR A GREEN JUICE
- ❍ ____

MITs

- ❍ ____
- ❍ ____
- ❍ ____
- ❍ ____
- ❍ ____

wellness planning

M ____
T ____
W ____
TH ____
F ____
S ____
S ____

GRATITUDE:

MONDAY ____

7 ____
8 ____
9 ____
10 ____
11 ____
12 ____
1 ____
2 ____
3 ____
4 ____
5 ____
6 ____
7 ____
8 ____
9 ____

daily checklist

- ❍ MORNING RITUAL
- ❍ DAILY DRESS-UP
- ❍ MINDFUL MOVEMENT
- ❍ EAT YOUR VEGGIES
- ❍ JOURNAL
- ❍ GOAL REVIEW
- ❍ GRATITUDE
- ❍ EVENING RITUAL
- ❍ ____

TUESDAY ____

7 ____
8 ____
9 ____
10 ____
11 ____
12 ____
1 ____
2 ____
3 ____
4 ____
5 ____
6 ____
7 ____
8 ____
9 ____

daily checklist

- ❍ MORNING RITUAL
- ❍ DAILY DRESS-UP
- ❍ MINDFUL MOVEMENT
- ❍ EAT YOUR VEGGIES
- ❍ JOURNAL
- ❍ GOAL REVIEW
- ❍ GRATITUDE
- ❍ EVENING RITUAL
- ❍ ____

WEDNESDAY ____

7 ____
8 ____
9 ____
10 ____
11 ____
12 ____
1 ____
2 ____
3 ____
4 ____
5 ____
6 ____
7 ____
8 ____
9 ____

daily checklist

- ❍ MORNING RITUAL
- ❍ DAILY DRESS-UP
- ❍ MINDFUL MOVEMENT
- ❍ EAT YOUR VEGGIES
- ❍ JOURNAL
- ❍ GOAL REVIEW
- ❍ GRATITUDE
- ❍ EVENING RITUAL
- ❍ ____

THURSDAY ______
7
8
9
10
11
12
1
2
3
4
5
6
7
8
9

daily checklist
- MORNING RITUAL
- DAILY DRESS-UP
- MINDFUL MOVEMENT
- EAT YOUR VEGGIES
- JOURNAL
- GOAL REVIEW
- GRATITUDE
- EVENING RITUAL

FRIDAY ______
7
8
9
10
11
12
1
2
3
4
5
6
7
8
9

daily checklist
- MORNING RITUAL
- DAILY DRESS-UP
- MINDFUL MOVEMENT
- EAT YOUR VEGGIES
- JOURNAL
- GOAL REVIEW
- GRATITUDE
- EVENING RITUAL

SATURDAY ______
7
8
9
10
11
12
1
2
3
4
5
6
7
8
9

daily checklist
- MORNING RITUAL
- DAILY DRESS-UP
- MINDFUL MOVEMENT
- EAT YOUR VEGGIES
- JOURNAL
- GOAL REVIEW
- GRATITUDE
- EVENING RITUAL

SUNDAY ______
7
8
9
10
11
12
1
2
3
4
5
6
7
8
9

daily checklist
- MORNING RITUAL
- DAILY DRESS-UP
- MINDFUL MOVEMENT
- EAT YOUR VEGGIES
- JOURNAL
- GOAL REVIEW
- GRATITUDE
- EVENING RITUAL

month's dreams

DOODLE, LIST, COLLAGE, OR WRITE WHAT YOU'D LIKE TO MANIFEST THIS MONTH.

month's review

REVISIT YOUR MONTH'S DREAMS AND NOTE HOW THEY UNFOLDED FOR YOU.

30 days of tranquility

TRY THIS 30-DAY CHALLENGE TO INFUSE YOUR MONTH WITH SIMPLE PLEASURES.

1
SIT STILL FOR FIVE MINUTES

2
DO SIX SUN SALUTATIONS

3
WRITE A LOVE LETTER

4
APOLOGIZE

5
TELL THE TRUTH

6
CONSUME A GREEN DRINK

7
GO MEAT-FREE

8
WALK FOR 20 MINUTES

9
DO LEGS UP THE WALL

10
GIVE $10 TO CHARITY

11
PEN TWO JOURNAL PAGES

12
REVIEW YOUR YEAR'S DREAMS

13
CLEAR CLUTTER

14
GO ON AN ARTIST DATE

15
COLLAGE TWO PAGES

16
TREAT YOURSELF TO TEA

17
READ FOR 20 MINUTES

18
BUY YOURSELF FLOWERS

19
DANCE TO A FAVORITE TUNE

20
EXPRESS GRATITUDE

21
EAT ONLY UNPROCESSED FOODS

22
SOAK IN A BUBBLE BATH

23
MINDFULLY SIP A LIBATION

24
GET OUT IN NATURE

25
FORGO COMPLAINING

26
TAKE A DIGITAL DAY OFF

27
SNAP PHOTOS FROM YOUR DAY

28
MAKE A FAVORITE MEAL

29
HUG

30
BE FULLY PRESENT

habit tracking

NOTE HABITS YOU'RE TRYING TO ADD OR SUBTRACT AND TRACK THEM DAILY TO HELP WITH ACCOUNTABILITY. CELEBRATE YOUR SUCCESSES AND OBSERVE AREAS FOR GROWTH.

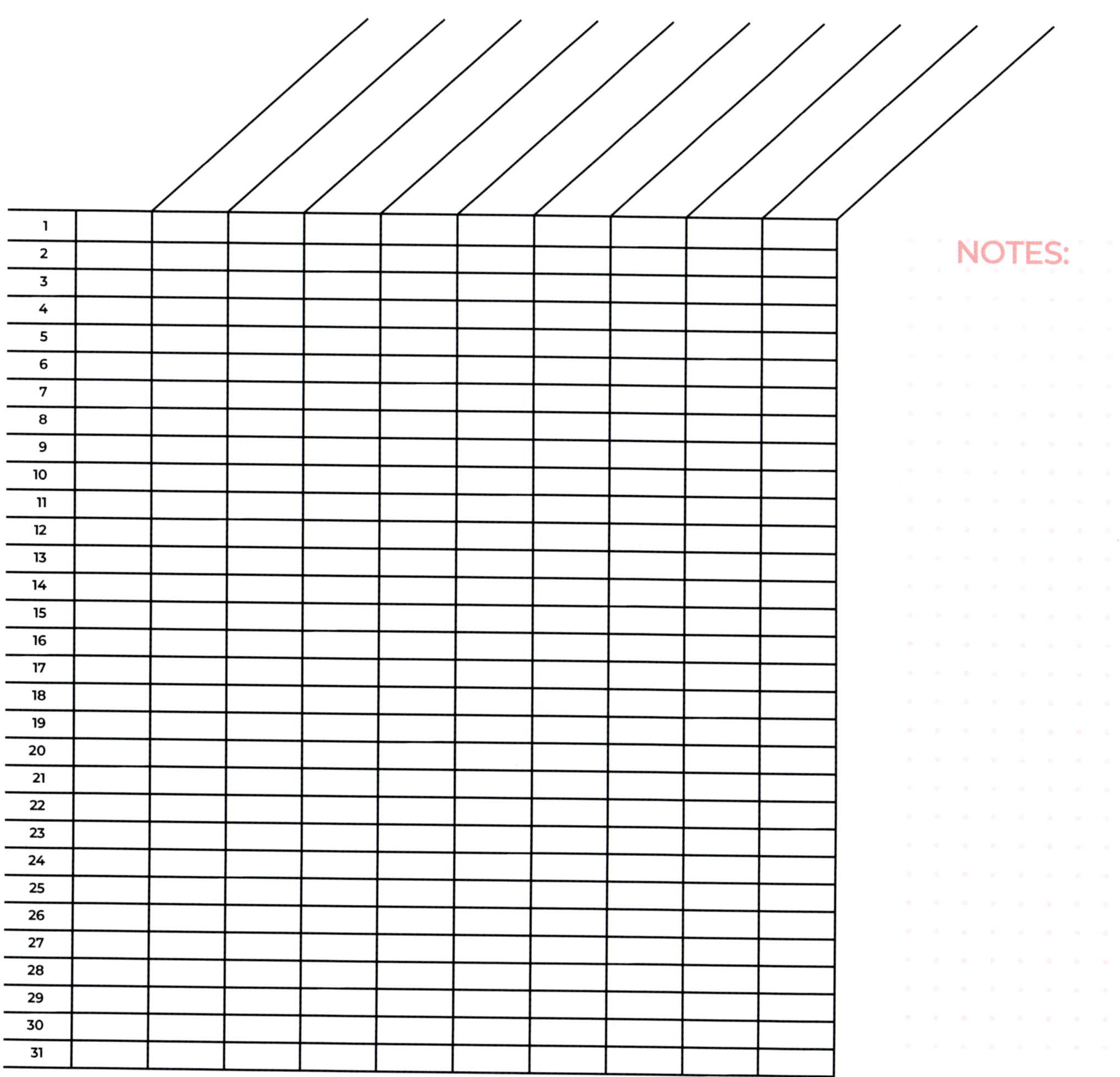

1									
2									
3									
4									
5									
6									
7									
8									
9									
10									
11									
12									
13									
14									
15									
16									
17									
18									
19									
20									
21									
22									
23									
24									
25									
26									
27									
28									
29									
30									
31									

NOTES:

moon phases

N*otice your connection to the moon's cycles in these four phases: new, waxing, full, waning. Consider the prompts below as a way to tie into your Month's Dreams and provide space for monthly reflection.*

new moon

A TIME FOR SETTING INTENTIONS.
I WANT . . .

waxing moon

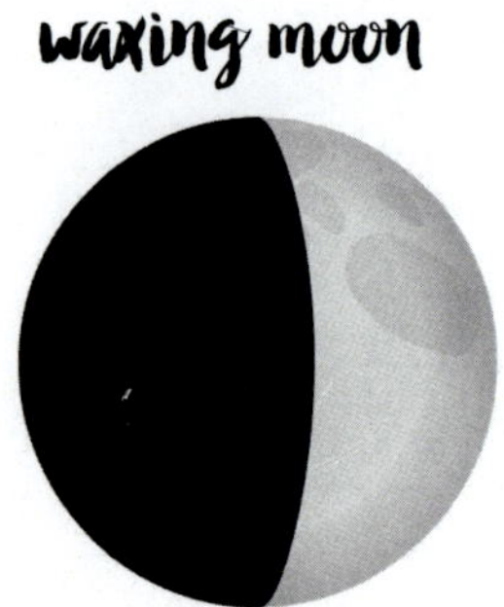

A TIME FOR ACTION. I WILL . . .

full moon

A TIME FOR HARVEST AND CLOSURE.
I RELEASE . . .

waning moon

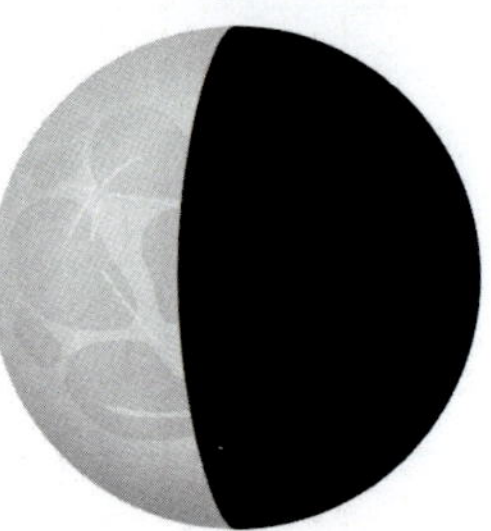

A TIME FOR SOFTENING. I FEEL . . .

monthly planner

MONTH: ______________________ INTENTION: ______________________

SUNDAY	MONDAY	TUESDAY	WEDNESDAY	THURSDAY	FRIDAY	SATURDAY

MONTHLY TRANQUILITY TOOLS

- ❍ CRAFT MONTH'S DREAMS
- ❍ REVIEW BUDGET
- ❍ CREATE SOMETHING
- ❍ READ TWO BOOKS
- ❍ VOLUNTEER
- ❍ MANI/PEDI
- ❍ ENTERTAIN
- ❍ MASSAGE

INTENTION:

weekly checklist

- PLAN WEEK'S MITS
- SOAK IN THE TUB
- TAKE A DIGITAL DAY OFF
- CLEAR CLUTTER
- PEN A LOVE NOTE
- BUY/PICK FRESH FLOWERS
- TAKE AN ARTIST DATE
- SAVOR A GREEN JUICE
- ______

MITS

- ______
- ______
- ______
- ______
- ______

wellness planning

M ______
T ______
W ______
TH ______
F ______
S ______
S ______

GRATITUDE:

MONDAY ______

7 ______
8 ______
9 ______
10 ______
11 ______
12 ______
1 ______
2 ______
3 ______
4 ______
5 ______
6 ______
7 ______
8 ______
9 ______

daily checklist

- MORNING RITUAL
- DAILY DRESS-UP
- MINDFUL MOVEMENT
- EAT YOUR VEGGIES
- JOURNAL
- GOAL REVIEW
- GRATITUDE
- EVENING RITUAL
- ______

TUESDAY ______

7 ______
8 ______
9 ______
10 ______
11 ______
12 ______
1 ______
2 ______
3 ______
4 ______
5 ______
6 ______
7 ______
8 ______
9 ______

daily checklist

- MORNING RITUAL
- DAILY DRESS-UP
- MINDFUL MOVEMENT
- EAT YOUR VEGGIES
- JOURNAL
- GOAL REVIEW
- GRATITUDE
- EVENING RITUAL
- ______

WEDNESDAY ______

7 ______
8 ______
9 ______
10 ______
11 ______
12 ______
1 ______
2 ______
3 ______
4 ______
5 ______
6 ______
7 ______
8 ______
9 ______

daily checklist

- MORNING RITUAL
- DAILY DRESS-UP
- MINDFUL MOVEMENT
- EAT YOUR VEGGIES
- JOURNAL
- GOAL REVIEW
- GRATITUDE
- EVENING RITUAL
- ______

THURSDAY

7
8
9
10
11
12
1
2
3
4
5
6
7
8
9

daily checklist

- MORNING RITUAL
- DAILY DRESS-UP
- MINDFUL MOVEMENT
- EAT YOUR VEGGIES
- JOURNAL
- GOAL REVIEW
- GRATITUDE
- EVENING RITUAL

FRIDAY

7
8
9
10
11
12
1
2
3
4
5
6
7
8
9

daily checklist

- MORNING RITUAL
- DAILY DRESS-UP
- MINDFUL MOVEMENT
- EAT YOUR VEGGIES
- JOURNAL
- GOAL REVIEW
- GRATITUDE
- EVENING RITUAL

SATURDAY

7
8
9
10
11
12
1
2
3
4
5
6
7
8
9

daily checklist

- MORNING RITUAL
- DAILY DRESS-UP
- MINDFUL MOVEMENT
- EAT YOUR VEGGIES
- JOURNAL
- GOAL REVIEW
- GRATITUDE
- EVENING RITUAL

SUNDAY

7
8
9
10
11
12
1
2
3
4
5
6
7
8
9

daily checklist

- MORNING RITUAL
- DAILY DRESS-UP
- MINDFUL MOVEMENT
- EAT YOUR VEGGIES
- JOURNAL
- GOAL REVIEW
- GRATITUDE
- EVENING RITUAL

INTENTION:

weekly checklist

- PLAN WEEK'S MITS
- SOAK IN THE TUB
- TAKE A DIGITAL DAY OFF
- CLEAR CLUTTER
- PEN A LOVE NOTE
- BUY/PICK FRESH FLOWERS
- TAKE AN ARTIST DATE
- SAVOR A GREEN JUICE
- ____________

MITs

- ____________
- ____________
- ____________
- ____________
- ____________

wellness planning

M ____________
T ____________
W ____________
TH ____________
F ____________
S ____________
S ____________

GRATITUDE:

MONDAY ____________

7 ____________
8 ____________
9 ____________
10 ____________
11 ____________
12 ____________
1 ____________
2 ____________
3 ____________
4 ____________
5 ____________
6 ____________
7 ____________
8 ____________
9 ____________

daily checklist

- MORNING RITUAL
- DAILY DRESS-UP
- MINDFUL MOVEMENT
- EAT YOUR VEGGIES
- JOURNAL
- GOAL REVIEW
- GRATITUDE
- EVENING RITUAL
- ____________

TUESDAY ____________

7 ____________
8 ____________
9 ____________
10 ____________
11 ____________
12 ____________
1 ____________
2 ____________
3 ____________
4 ____________
5 ____________
6 ____________
7 ____________
8 ____________
9 ____________

daily checklist

- MORNING RITUAL
- DAILY DRESS-UP
- MINDFUL MOVEMENT
- EAT YOUR VEGGIES
- JOURNAL
- GOAL REVIEW
- GRATITUDE
- EVENING RITUAL
- ____________

WEDNESDAY ____________

7 ____________
8 ____________
9 ____________
10 ____________
11 ____________
12 ____________
1 ____________
2 ____________
3 ____________
4 ____________
5 ____________
6 ____________
7 ____________
8 ____________
9 ____________

daily checklist

- MORNING RITUAL
- DAILY DRESS-UP
- MINDFUL MOVEMENT
- EAT YOUR VEGGIES
- JOURNAL
- GOAL REVIEW
- GRATITUDE
- EVENING RITUAL
- ____________

THURSDAY

7
8
9
10
11
12
1
2
3
4
5
6
7
8
9

daily checklist

- MORNING RITUAL
- DAILY DRESS-UP
- MINDFUL MOVEMENT
- EAT YOUR VEGGIES
- JOURNAL
- GOAL REVIEW
- GRATITUDE
- EVENING RITUAL

FRIDAY

7
8
9
10
11
12
1
2
3
4
5
6
7
8
9

daily checklist

- MORNING RITUAL
- DAILY DRESS-UP
- MINDFUL MOVEMENT
- EAT YOUR VEGGIES
- JOURNAL
- GOAL REVIEW
- GRATITUDE
- EVENING RITUAL

SATURDAY

7
8
9
10
11
12
1
2
3
4
5
6
7
8
9

daily checklist

- MORNING RITUAL
- DAILY DRESS-UP
- MINDFUL MOVEMENT
- EAT YOUR VEGGIES
- JOURNAL
- GOAL REVIEW
- GRATITUDE
- EVENING RITUAL

SUNDAY

7
8
9
10
11
12
1
2
3
4
5
6
7
8
9

daily checklist

- MORNING RITUAL
- DAILY DRESS-UP
- MINDFUL MOVEMENT
- EAT YOUR VEGGIES
- JOURNAL
- GOAL REVIEW
- GRATITUDE
- EVENING RITUAL

INTENTION:

weekly checklist

- ❍ PLAN WEEK'S MITS
- ❍ SOAK IN THE TUB
- ❍ TAKE A DIGITAL DAY OFF
- ❍ CLEAR CLUTTER
- ❍ PEN A LOVE NOTE
- ❍ BUY/PICK FRESH FLOWERS
- ❍ TAKE AN ARTIST DATE
- ❍ SAVOR A GREEN JUICE
- ❍ ____________

MITs

- ❍ ____________
- ❍ ____________
- ❍ ____________
- ❍ ____________
- ❍ ____________

wellness planning

M ____________
T ____________
W ____________
TH ____________
F ____________
S ____________
S ____________

GRATITUDE:

MONDAY ____________

7 ____________
8 ____________
9 ____________
10 ____________
11 ____________
12 ____________
1 ____________
2 ____________
3 ____________
4 ____________
5 ____________
6 ____________
7 ____________
8 ____________
9 ____________

daily checklist

- ❍ MORNING RITUAL
- ❍ DAILY DRESS-UP
- ❍ MINDFUL MOVEMENT
- ❍ EAT YOUR VEGGIES
- ❍ JOURNAL
- ❍ GOAL REVIEW
- ❍ GRATITUDE
- ❍ EVENING RITUAL
- ❍ ____________

TUESDAY ____________

7 ____________
8 ____________
9 ____________
10 ____________
11 ____________
12 ____________
1 ____________
2 ____________
3 ____________
4 ____________
5 ____________
6 ____________
7 ____________
8 ____________
9 ____________

daily checklist

- ❍ MORNING RITUAL
- ❍ DAILY DRESS-UP
- ❍ MINDFUL MOVEMENT
- ❍ EAT YOUR VEGGIES
- ❍ JOURNAL
- ❍ GOAL REVIEW
- ❍ GRATITUDE
- ❍ EVENING RITUAL
- ❍ ____________

WEDNESDAY ____________

7 ____________
8 ____________
9 ____________
10 ____________
11 ____________
12 ____________
1 ____________
2 ____________
3 ____________
4 ____________
5 ____________
6 ____________
7 ____________
8 ____________
9 ____________

daily checklist

- ❍ MORNING RITUAL
- ❍ DAILY DRESS-UP
- ❍ MINDFUL MOVEMENT
- ❍ EAT YOUR VEGGIES
- ❍ JOURNAL
- ❍ GOAL REVIEW
- ❍ GRATITUDE
- ❍ EVENING RITUAL
- ❍ ____________

THURSDAY ______

7 ______
8 ______
9 ______
10 ______
11 ______
12 ______
1 ______
2 ______
3 ______
4 ______
5 ______
6 ______
7 ______
8 ______
9 ______

daily checklist

- MORNING RITUAL
- DAILY DRESS-UP
- MINDFUL MOVEMENT
- EAT YOUR VEGGIES
- JOURNAL
- GOAL REVIEW
- GRATITUDE
- EVENING RITUAL

FRIDAY ______

7 ______
8 ______
9 ______
10 ______
11 ______
12 ______
1 ______
2 ______
3 ______
4 ______
5 ______
6 ______
7 ______
8 ______
9 ______

daily checklist

- MORNING RITUAL
- DAILY DRESS-UP
- MINDFUL MOVEMENT
- EAT YOUR VEGGIES
- JOURNAL
- GOAL REVIEW
- GRATITUDE
- EVENING RITUAL

SATURDAY ______

7 ______
8 ______
9 ______
10 ______
11 ______
12 ______
1 ______
2 ______
3 ______
4 ______
5 ______
6 ______
7 ______
8 ______
9 ______

daily checklist

- MORNING RITUAL
- DAILY DRESS-UP
- MINDFUL MOVEMENT
- EAT YOUR VEGGIES
- JOURNAL
- GOAL REVIEW
- GRATITUDE
- EVENING RITUAL

SUNDAY ______

7 ______
8 ______
9 ______
10 ______
11 ______
12 ______
1 ______
2 ______
3 ______
4 ______
5 ______
6 ______
7 ______
8 ______
9 ______

daily checklist

- MORNING RITUAL
- DAILY DRESS-UP
- MINDFUL MOVEMENT
- EAT YOUR VEGGIES
- JOURNAL
- GOAL REVIEW
- GRATITUDE
- EVENING RITUAL

INTENTION:

weekly checklist

- PLAN WEEK'S MITS
- SOAK IN THE TUB
- TAKE A DIGITAL DAY OFF
- CLEAR CLUTTER
- PEN A LOVE NOTE
- BUY/PICK FRESH FLOWERS
- TAKE AN ARTIST DATE
- SAVOR A GREEN JUICE
- ______

MITs

- ______
- ______
- ______
- ______
- ______

wellness planning

M ______
T ______
W ______
TH ______
F ______
S ______
S ______

GRATITUDE:

MONDAY ______

7 ______
8 ______
9 ______
10 ______
11 ______
12 ______
1 ______
2 ______
3 ______
4 ______
5 ______
6 ______
7 ______
8 ______
9 ______

daily checklist

- MORNING RITUAL
- DAILY DRESS-UP
- MINDFUL MOVEMENT
- EAT YOUR VEGGIES
- JOURNAL
- GOAL REVIEW
- GRATITUDE
- EVENING RITUAL
- ______

TUESDAY ______

7 ______
8 ______
9 ______
10 ______
11 ______
12 ______
1 ______
2 ______
3 ______
4 ______
5 ______
6 ______
7 ______
8 ______
9 ______

daily checklist

- MORNING RITUAL
- DAILY DRESS-UP
- MINDFUL MOVEMENT
- EAT YOUR VEGGIES
- JOURNAL
- GOAL REVIEW
- GRATITUDE
- EVENING RITUAL
- ______

WEDNESDAY ______

7 ______
8 ______
9 ______
10 ______
11 ______
12 ______
1 ______
2 ______
3 ______
4 ______
5 ______
6 ______
7 ______
8 ______
9 ______

daily checklist

- MORNING RITUAL
- DAILY DRESS-UP
- MINDFUL MOVEMENT
- EAT YOUR VEGGIES
- JOURNAL
- GOAL REVIEW
- GRATITUDE
- EVENING RITUAL
- ______

THURSDAY ______

7 ______
8 ______
9 ______
10 ______
11 ______
12 ______
1 ______
2 ______
3 ______
4 ______
5 ______
6 ______
7 ______
8 ______
9 ______

daily checklist

- MORNING RITUAL
- DAILY DRESS-UP
- MINDFUL MOVEMENT
- EAT YOUR VEGGIES
- JOURNAL
- GOAL REVIEW
- GRATITUDE
- EVENING RITUAL

FRIDAY ______

7 ______
8 ______
9 ______
10 ______
11 ______
12 ______
1 ______
2 ______
3 ______
4 ______
5 ______
6 ______
7 ______
8 ______
9 ______

daily checklist

- MORNING RITUAL
- DAILY DRESS-UP
- MINDFUL MOVEMENT
- EAT YOUR VEGGIES
- JOURNAL
- GOAL REVIEW
- GRATITUDE
- EVENING RITUAL

SATURDAY ______

7 ______
8 ______
9 ______
10 ______
11 ______
12 ______
1 ______
2 ______
3 ______
4 ______
5 ______
6 ______
7 ______
8 ______
9 ______

daily checklist

- MORNING RITUAL
- DAILY DRESS-UP
- MINDFUL MOVEMENT
- EAT YOUR VEGGIES
- JOURNAL
- GOAL REVIEW
- GRATITUDE
- EVENING RITUAL

SUNDAY ______

7 ______
8 ______
9 ______
10 ______
11 ______
12 ______
1 ______
2 ______
3 ______
4 ______
5 ______
6 ______
7 ______
8 ______
9 ______

daily checklist

- MORNING RITUAL
- DAILY DRESS-UP
- MINDFUL MOVEMENT
- EAT YOUR VEGGIES
- JOURNAL
- GOAL REVIEW
- GRATITUDE
- EVENING RITUAL

INTENTION:

weekly checklist

- ❍ PLAN WEEK'S MITS
- ❍ SOAK IN THE TUB
- ❍ TAKE A DIGITAL DAY OFF
- ❍ CLEAR CLUTTER
- ❍ PEN A LOVE NOTE
- ❍ BUY/PICK FRESH FLOWERS
- ❍ TAKE AN ARTIST DATE
- ❍ SAVOR A GREEN JUICE
- ❍ ____________________

MITs

- ❍ ____________________
- ❍ ____________________
- ❍ ____________________
- ❍ ____________________
- ❍ ____________________

wellness planning

M ____________________

T ____________________

W ____________________

TH ____________________

F ____________________

S ____________________

S ____________________

GRATITUDE:

MONDAY ____________________

7 ____________________

8 ____________________

9 ____________________

10 ____________________

11 ____________________

12 ____________________

1 ____________________

2 ____________________

3 ____________________

4 ____________________

5 ____________________

6 ____________________

7 ____________________

8 ____________________

9 ____________________

- ❍ ____________________
- ❍ ____________________
- ❍ ____________________
- ❍ ____________________
- ❍ ____________________
- ❍ ____________________
- ❍ ____________________
- ❍ ____________________
- ❍ ____________________
- ❍ ____________________

- ❍ ____________________
- ❍ ____________________
- ❍ ____________________
- ❍ ____________________
- ❍ ____________________
- ❍ ____________________

daily checklist

- ❍ MORNING RITUAL
- ❍ DAILY DRESS-UP
- ❍ MINDFUL MOVEMENT
- ❍ EAT YOUR VEGGIES
- ❍ JOURNAL
- ❍ GOAL REVIEW
- ❍ GRATITUDE
- ❍ EVENING RITUAL
- ❍ ____________________

TUESDAY ____________________

7 ____________________

8 ____________________

9 ____________________

10 ____________________

11 ____________________

12 ____________________

1 ____________________

2 ____________________

3 ____________________

4 ____________________

5 ____________________

6 ____________________

7 ____________________

8 ____________________

9 ____________________

- ❍ ____________________
- ❍ ____________________
- ❍ ____________________
- ❍ ____________________
- ❍ ____________________
- ❍ ____________________
- ❍ ____________________
- ❍ ____________________
- ❍ ____________________
- ❍ ____________________

- ❍ ____________________
- ❍ ____________________
- ❍ ____________________
- ❍ ____________________
- ❍ ____________________
- ❍ ____________________

daily checklist

- ❍ MORNING RITUAL
- ❍ DAILY DRESS-UP
- ❍ MINDFUL MOVEMENT
- ❍ EAT YOUR VEGGIES
- ❍ JOURNAL
- ❍ GOAL REVIEW
- ❍ GRATITUDE
- ❍ EVENING RITUAL
- ❍ ____________________

WEDNESDAY ____________________

7 ____________________

8 ____________________

9 ____________________

10 ____________________

11 ____________________

12 ____________________

1 ____________________

2 ____________________

3 ____________________

4 ____________________

5 ____________________

6 ____________________

7 ____________________

8 ____________________

9 ____________________

- ❍ ____________________
- ❍ ____________________
- ❍ ____________________
- ❍ ____________________
- ❍ ____________________
- ❍ ____________________
- ❍ ____________________
- ❍ ____________________
- ❍ ____________________
- ❍ ____________________

- ❍ ____________________
- ❍ ____________________
- ❍ ____________________
- ❍ ____________________
- ❍ ____________________
- ❍ ____________________

daily checklist

- ❍ MORNING RITUAL
- ❍ DAILY DRESS-UP
- ❍ MINDFUL MOVEMENT
- ❍ EAT YOUR VEGGIES
- ❍ JOURNAL
- ❍ GOAL REVIEW
- ❍ GRATITUDE
- ❍ EVENING RITUAL
- ❍ ____________________

THURSDAY

7
8
9
10
11
12
1
2
3
4
5
6
7
8
9

daily checklist

- MORNING RITUAL
- DAILY DRESS-UP
- MINDFUL MOVEMENT
- EAT YOUR VEGGIES
- JOURNAL
- GOAL REVIEW
- GRATITUDE
- EVENING RITUAL

FRIDAY

7
8
9
10
11
12
1
2
3
4
5
6
7
8
9

daily checklist

- MORNING RITUAL
- DAILY DRESS-UP
- MINDFUL MOVEMENT
- EAT YOUR VEGGIES
- JOURNAL
- GOAL REVIEW
- GRATITUDE
- EVENING RITUAL

SATURDAY

7
8
9
10
11
12
1
2
3
4
5
6
7
8
9

daily checklist

- MORNING RITUAL
- DAILY DRESS-UP
- MINDFUL MOVEMENT
- EAT YOUR VEGGIES
- JOURNAL
- GOAL REVIEW
- GRATITUDE
- EVENING RITUAL

SUNDAY

7
8
9
10
11
12
1
2
3
4
5
6
7
8
9

daily checklist

- MORNING RITUAL
- DAILY DRESS-UP
- MINDFUL MOVEMENT
- EAT YOUR VEGGIES
- JOURNAL
- GOAL REVIEW
- GRATITUDE
- EVENING RITUAL

What I Need
to Succeed!

month's dreams

DOODLE, LIST, COLLAGE, OR WRITE WHAT YOU'D LIKE TO MANIFEST THIS MONTH.

month's review

REVISIT YOUR MONTH'S DREAMS AND NOTE HOW THEY UNFOLDED FOR YOU.

30 days of tranquility

TRY THIS 30-DAY CHALLENGE TO INFUSE YOUR MONTH WITH SIMPLE PLEASURES.

1. SIT STILL FOR FIVE MINUTES
2. DO SIX SUN SALUTATIONS
3. WRITE A LOVE LETTER
4. APOLOGIZE
5. TELL THE TRUTH
6. CONSUME A GREEN DRINK
7. GO MEAT-FREE
8. WALK FOR 20 MINUTES
9. DO LEGS UP THE WALL
10. GIVE $10 TO CHARITY
11. PEN TWO JOURNAL PAGES
12. REVIEW YOUR YEAR'S DREAMS
13. CLEAR CLUTTER
14. GO ON AN ARTIST DATE
15. COLLAGE TWO PAGES
16. TREAT YOURSELF TO TEA
17. READ FOR 20 MINUTES
18. BUY YOURSELF FLOWERS
19. DANCE TO A FAVORITE TUNE
20. EXPRESS GRATITUDE
21. EAT ONLY UNPROCESSED FOODS
22. SOAK IN A BUBBLE BATH
23. MINDFULLY SIP A LIBATION
24. GET OUT IN NATURE
25. FORGO COMPLAINING
26. TAKE A DIGITAL DAY OFF
27. SNAP PHOTOS FROM YOUR DAY
28. MAKE A FAVORITE MEAL
29. HUG
30. BE FULLY PRESENT

habit tracking

NOTE HABITS YOU'RE TRYING TO ADD OR SUBTRACT AND TRACK THEM DAILY TO HELP WITH ACCOUNTABILITY. CELEBRATE YOUR SUCCESSES AND OBSERVE AREAS FOR GROWTH.

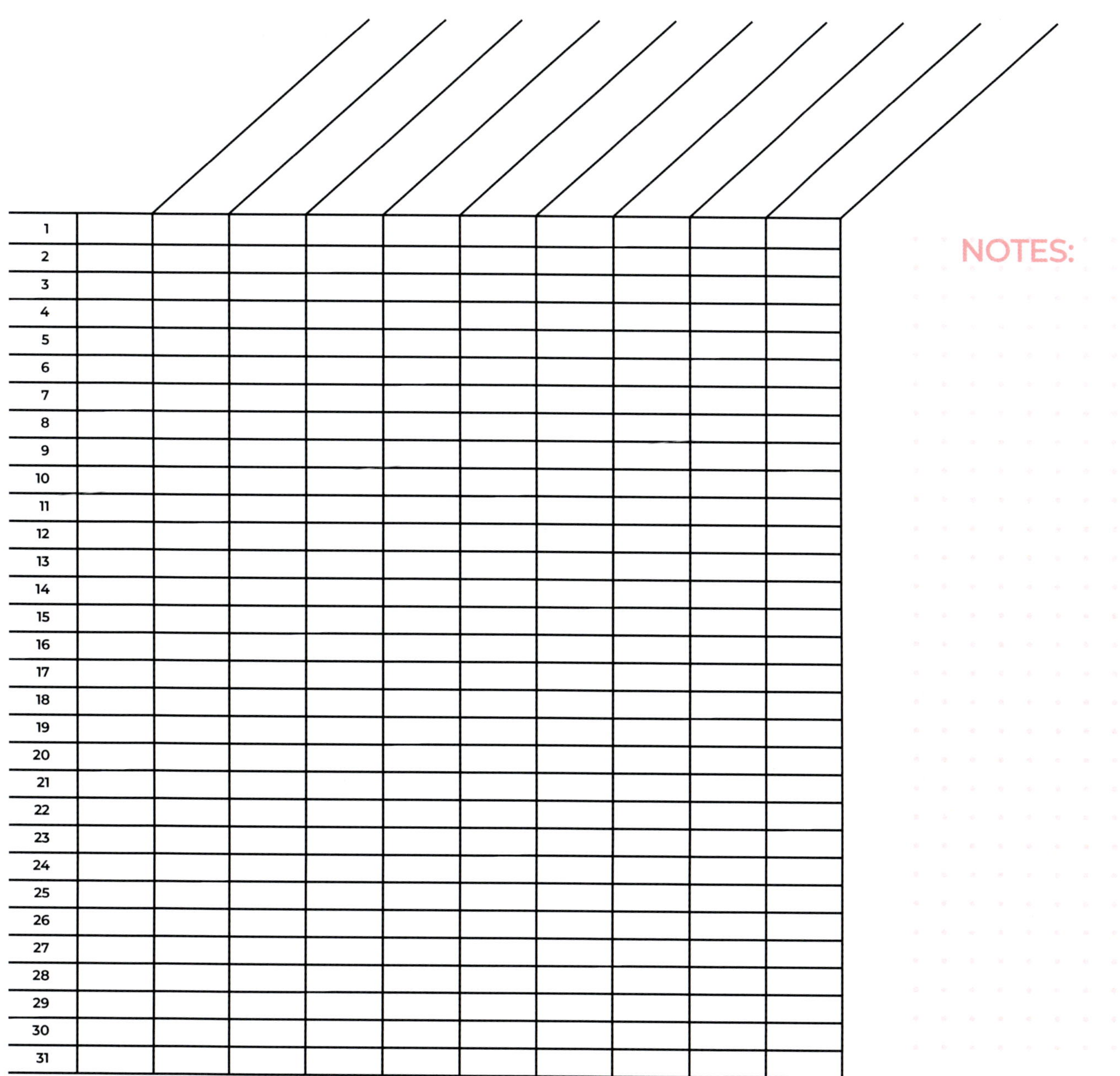

1										
2										
3										
4										
5										
6										
7										
8										
9										
10										
11										
12										
13										
14										
15										
16										
17										
18										
19										
20										
21										
22										
23										
24										
25										
26										
27										
28										
29										
30										
31										

NOTES:

moon phases

Notice your connection to the moon's cycles in these four phases: new, waxing, full, waning. Consider the prompts below as a way to tie into your Month's Dreams and provide space for monthly reflection.

new moon

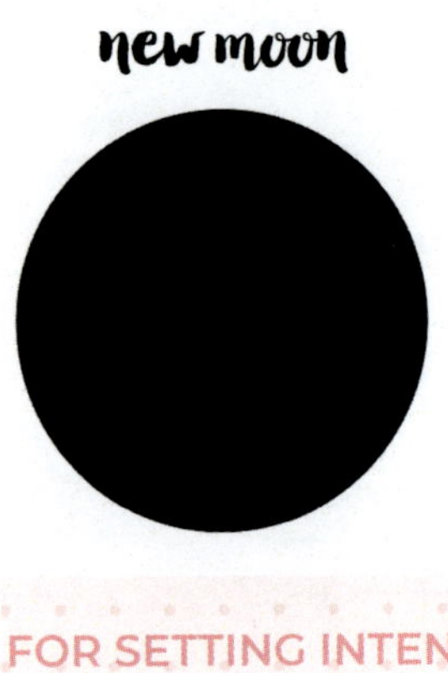

A TIME FOR SETTING INTENTIONS. I WANT . . .

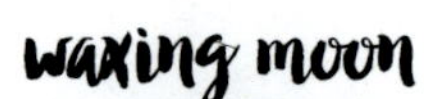

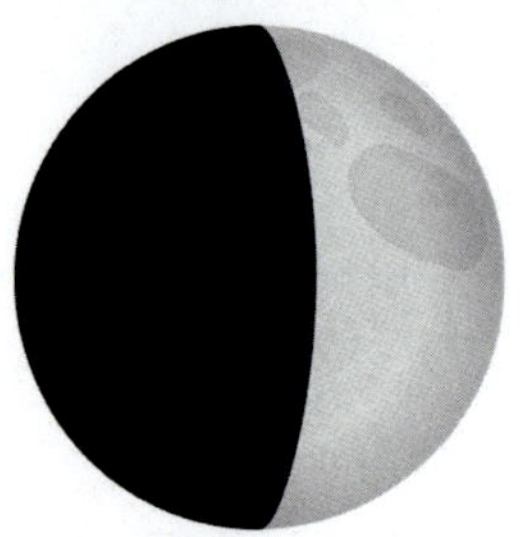

A TIME FOR ACTION. I WILL . . .

full moon

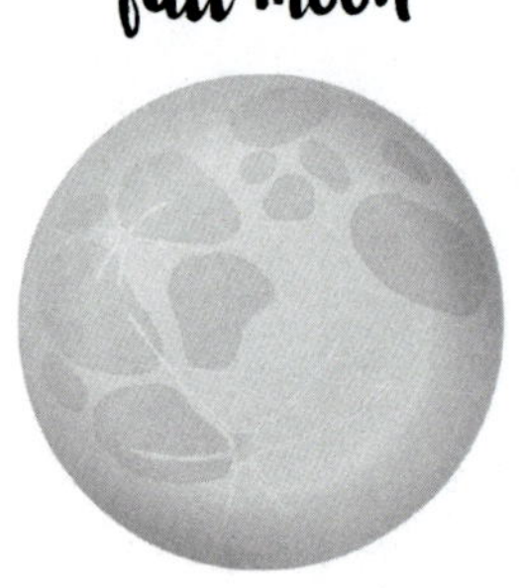

A TIME FOR HARVEST AND CLOSURE. I RELEASE . . .

waning moon

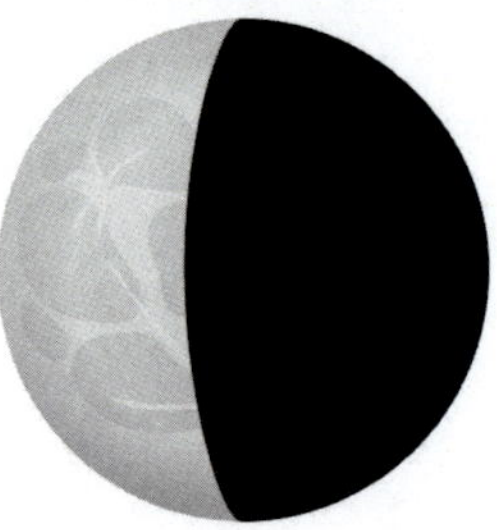

A TIME FOR SOFTENING. I FEEL . . .

monthly planner

MONTH: ______________________ INTENTION: ______________________

SUNDAY	MONDAY	TUESDAY	WEDNESDAY	THURSDAY	FRIDAY	SATURDAY

MONTHLY TRANQUILITY TOOLS

- ❍ CRAFT MONTH'S DREAMS
- ❍ REVIEW BUDGET
- ❍ CREATE SOMETHING
- ❍ READ TWO BOOKS
- ❍ VOLUNTEER
- ❍ MANI/PEDI
- ❍ ENTERTAIN
- ❍ MASSAGE

INTENTION:

weekly checklist

- ❍ PLAN WEEK'S MITS
- ❍ SOAK IN THE TUB
- ❍ TAKE A DIGITAL DAY OFF
- ❍ CLEAR CLUTTER
- ❍ PEN A LOVE NOTE
- ❍ BUY/PICK FRESH FLOWERS
- ❍ TAKE AN ARTIST DATE
- ❍ SAVOR A GREEN JUICE
- ❍ ____

MITs

- ❍ ____
- ❍ ____
- ❍ ____
- ❍ ____
- ❍ ____

wellness planning

M ____
T ____
W ____
TH ____
F ____
S ____
S ____

GRATITUDE:

MONDAY ____

7 ____
8 ____
9 ____
10 ____
11 ____
12 ____
1 ____
2 ____
3 ____
4 ____
5 ____
6 ____
7 ____
8 ____
9 ____

daily checklist

- ❍ MORNING RITUAL
- ❍ DAILY DRESS-UP
- ❍ MINDFUL MOVEMENT
- ❍ EAT YOUR VEGGIES
- ❍ JOURNAL
- ❍ GOAL REVIEW
- ❍ GRATITUDE
- ❍ EVENING RITUAL
- ❍ ____

TUESDAY ____

7 ____
8 ____
9 ____
10 ____
11 ____
12 ____
1 ____
2 ____
3 ____
4 ____
5 ____
6 ____
7 ____
8 ____
9 ____

daily checklist

- ❍ MORNING RITUAL
- ❍ DAILY DRESS-UP
- ❍ MINDFUL MOVEMENT
- ❍ EAT YOUR VEGGIES
- ❍ JOURNAL
- ❍ GOAL REVIEW
- ❍ GRATITUDE
- ❍ EVENING RITUAL
- ❍ ____

WEDNESDAY ____

7 ____
8 ____
9 ____
10 ____
11 ____
12 ____
1 ____
2 ____
3 ____
4 ____
5 ____
6 ____
7 ____
8 ____
9 ____

daily checklist

- ❍ MORNING RITUAL
- ❍ DAILY DRESS-UP
- ❍ MINDFUL MOVEMENT
- ❍ EAT YOUR VEGGIES
- ❍ JOURNAL
- ❍ GOAL REVIEW
- ❍ GRATITUDE
- ❍ EVENING RITUAL
- ❍ ____

THURSDAY

7
8
9
10
11
12
1
2
3
4
5
6
7
8
9

daily checklist

- MORNING RITUAL
- DAILY DRESS-UP
- MINDFUL MOVEMENT
- EAT YOUR VEGGIES
- JOURNAL
- GOAL REVIEW
- GRATITUDE
- EVENING RITUAL

FRIDAY

7
8
9
10
11
12
1
2
3
4
5
6
7
8
9

daily checklist

- MORNING RITUAL
- DAILY DRESS-UP
- MINDFUL MOVEMENT
- EAT YOUR VEGGIES
- JOURNAL
- GOAL REVIEW
- GRATITUDE
- EVENING RITUAL

SATURDAY

7
8
9
10
11
12
1
2
3
4
5
6
7
8
9

daily checklist

- MORNING RITUAL
- DAILY DRESS-UP
- MINDFUL MOVEMENT
- EAT YOUR VEGGIES
- JOURNAL
- GOAL REVIEW
- GRATITUDE
- EVENING RITUAL

SUNDAY

7
8
9
10
11
12
1
2
3
4
5
6
7
8
9

daily checklist

- MORNING RITUAL
- DAILY DRESS-UP
- MINDFUL MOVEMENT
- EAT YOUR VEGGIES
- JOURNAL
- GOAL REVIEW
- GRATITUDE
- EVENING RITUAL

INTENTION:

weekly checklist

- PLAN WEEK'S MITS
- SOAK IN THE TUB
- TAKE A DIGITAL DAY OFF
- CLEAR CLUTTER
- PEN A LOVE NOTE
- BUY/PICK FRESH FLOWERS
- TAKE AN ARTIST DATE
- SAVOR A GREEN JUICE
- ________

MITs

- ________
- ________
- ________
- ________
- ________

wellness planning

M ________
T ________
W ________
TH ________
F ________
S ________
S ________

GRATITUDE:

MONDAY ________

7 ________
8 ________
9 ________
10 ________
11 ________
12 ________
1 ________
2 ________
3 ________
4 ________
5 ________
6 ________
7 ________
8 ________
9 ________

daily checklist

- MORNING RITUAL
- DAILY DRESS-UP
- MINDFUL MOVEMENT
- EAT YOUR VEGGIES
- JOURNAL
- GOAL REVIEW
- GRATITUDE
- EVENING RITUAL
- ________

TUESDAY ________

7 ________
8 ________
9 ________
10 ________
11 ________
12 ________
1 ________
2 ________
3 ________
4 ________
5 ________
6 ________
7 ________
8 ________
9 ________

daily checklist

- MORNING RITUAL
- DAILY DRESS-UP
- MINDFUL MOVEMENT
- EAT YOUR VEGGIES
- JOURNAL
- GOAL REVIEW
- GRATITUDE
- EVENING RITUAL
- ________

WEDNESDAY ________

7 ________
8 ________
9 ________
10 ________
11 ________
12 ________
1 ________
2 ________
3 ________
4 ________
5 ________
6 ________
7 ________
8 ________
9 ________

daily checklist

- MORNING RITUAL
- DAILY DRESS-UP
- MINDFUL MOVEMENT
- EAT YOUR VEGGIES
- JOURNAL
- GOAL REVIEW
- GRATITUDE
- EVENING RITUAL
- ________

THURSDAY

7
8
9
10
11
12
1
2
3
4
5
6
7
8
9

daily checklist

- MORNING RITUAL
- DAILY DRESS-UP
- MINDFUL MOVEMENT
- EAT YOUR VEGGIES
- JOURNAL
- GOAL REVIEW
- GRATITUDE
- EVENING RITUAL

FRIDAY

7
8
9
10
11
12
1
2
3
4
5
6
7
8
9

daily checklist

- MORNING RITUAL
- DAILY DRESS-UP
- MINDFUL MOVEMENT
- EAT YOUR VEGGIES
- JOURNAL
- GOAL REVIEW
- GRATITUDE
- EVENING RITUAL

SATURDAY

7
8
9
10
11
12
1
2
3
4
5
6
7
8
9

daily checklist

- MORNING RITUAL
- DAILY DRESS-UP
- MINDFUL MOVEMENT
- EAT YOUR VEGGIES
- JOURNAL
- GOAL REVIEW
- GRATITUDE
- EVENING RITUAL

SUNDAY

7
8
9
10
11
12
1
2
3
4
5
6
7
8
9

daily checklist

- MORNING RITUAL
- DAILY DRESS-UP
- MINDFUL MOVEMENT
- EAT YOUR VEGGIES
- JOURNAL
- GOAL REVIEW
- GRATITUDE
- EVENING RITUAL

INTENTION:

weekly checklist

- PLAN WEEK'S MITS
- SOAK IN THE TUB
- TAKE A DIGITAL DAY OFF
- CLEAR CLUTTER
- PEN A LOVE NOTE
- BUY/PICK FRESH FLOWERS
- TAKE AN ARTIST DATE
- SAVOR A GREEN JUICE
- ____

MITS

- ____
- ____
- ____
- ____
- ____

wellness planning

M ____
T ____
W ____
TH ____
F ____
S ____
S ____

GRATITUDE:

MONDAY ____

7 ____
8 ____
9 ____
10 ____
11 ____
12 ____
1 ____
2 ____
3 ____
4 ____
5 ____
6 ____
7 ____
8 ____
9 ____

daily checklist

- MORNING RITUAL
- DAILY DRESS-UP
- MINDFUL MOVEMENT
- EAT YOUR VEGGIES
- JOURNAL
- GOAL REVIEW
- GRATITUDE
- EVENING RITUAL
- ____

TUESDAY ____

7 ____
8 ____
9 ____
10 ____
11 ____
12 ____
1 ____
2 ____
3 ____
4 ____
5 ____
6 ____
7 ____
8 ____
9 ____

daily checklist

- MORNING RITUAL
- DAILY DRESS-UP
- MINDFUL MOVEMENT
- EAT YOUR VEGGIES
- JOURNAL
- GOAL REVIEW
- GRATITUDE
- EVENING RITUAL
- ____

WEDNESDAY ____

7 ____
8 ____
9 ____
10 ____
11 ____
12 ____
1 ____
2 ____
3 ____
4 ____
5 ____
6 ____
7 ____
8 ____
9 ____

daily checklist

- MORNING RITUAL
- DAILY DRESS-UP
- MINDFUL MOVEMENT
- EAT YOUR VEGGIES
- JOURNAL
- GOAL REVIEW
- GRATITUDE
- EVENING RITUAL
- ____

THURSDAY

7
8
9
10
11
12
1
2
3
4
5
6
7
8
9

daily checklist

- MORNING RITUAL
- DAILY DRESS-UP
- MINDFUL MOVEMENT
- EAT YOUR VEGGIES
- JOURNAL
- GOAL REVIEW
- GRATITUDE
- EVENING RITUAL

FRIDAY

7
8
9
10
11
12
1
2
3
4
5
6
7
8
9

daily checklist

- MORNING RITUAL
- DAILY DRESS-UP
- MINDFUL MOVEMENT
- EAT YOUR VEGGIES
- JOURNAL
- GOAL REVIEW
- GRATITUDE
- EVENING RITUAL

SATURDAY

7
8
9
10
11
12
1
2
3
4
5
6
7
8
9

daily checklist

- MORNING RITUAL
- DAILY DRESS-UP
- MINDFUL MOVEMENT
- EAT YOUR VEGGIES
- JOURNAL
- GOAL REVIEW
- GRATITUDE
- EVENING RITUAL

SUNDAY

7
8
9
10
11
12
1
2
3
4
5
6
7
8
9

daily checklist

- MORNING RITUAL
- DAILY DRESS-UP
- MINDFUL MOVEMENT
- EAT YOUR VEGGIES
- JOURNAL
- GOAL REVIEW
- GRATITUDE
- EVENING RITUAL

INTENTION:

weekly checklist

- PLAN WEEK'S MITS
- SOAK IN THE TUB
- TAKE A DIGITAL DAY OFF
- CLEAR CLUTTER
- PEN A LOVE NOTE
- BUY/PICK FRESH FLOWERS
- TAKE AN ARTIST DATE
- SAVOR A GREEN JUICE
- ______

MITS

wellness planning

M
T
W
TH
F
S
S

GRATITUDE:

MONDAY

7
8
9
10
11
12
1
2
3
4
5
6
7
8
9

daily checklist

- MORNING RITUAL
- DAILY DRESS-UP
- MINDFUL MOVEMENT
- EAT YOUR VEGGIES
- JOURNAL
- GOAL REVIEW
- GRATITUDE
- EVENING RITUAL
- ______

TUESDAY

7
8
9
10
11
12
1
2
3
4
5
6
7
8
9

daily checklist

- MORNING RITUAL
- DAILY DRESS-UP
- MINDFUL MOVEMENT
- EAT YOUR VEGGIES
- JOURNAL
- GOAL REVIEW
- GRATITUDE
- EVENING RITUAL
- ______

WEDNESDAY

7
8
9
10
11
12
1
2
3
4
5
6
7
8
9

daily checklist

- MORNING RITUAL
- DAILY DRESS-UP
- MINDFUL MOVEMENT
- EAT YOUR VEGGIES
- JOURNAL
- GOAL REVIEW
- GRATITUDE
- EVENING RITUAL
- ______

THURSDAY ______

7 ______
8 ______
9 ______
10 ______
11 ______
12 ______
1 ______
2 ______
3 ______
4 ______
5 ______
6 ______
7 ______
8 ______
9 ______

daily checklist

- MORNING RITUAL
- DAILY DRESS-UP
- MINDFUL MOVEMENT
- EAT YOUR VEGGIES
- JOURNAL
- GOAL REVIEW
- GRATITUDE
- EVENING RITUAL

FRIDAY ______

7 ______
8 ______
9 ______
10 ______
11 ______
12 ______
1 ______
2 ______
3 ______
4 ______
5 ______
6 ______
7 ______
8 ______
9 ______

daily checklist

- MORNING RITUAL
- DAILY DRESS-UP
- MINDFUL MOVEMENT
- EAT YOUR VEGGIES
- JOURNAL
- GOAL REVIEW
- GRATITUDE
- EVENING RITUAL

SATURDAY ______

7 ______
8 ______
9 ______
10 ______
11 ______
12 ______
1 ______
2 ______
3 ______
4 ______
5 ______
6 ______
7 ______
8 ______
9 ______

daily checklist

- MORNING RITUAL
- DAILY DRESS-UP
- MINDFUL MOVEMENT
- EAT YOUR VEGGIES
- JOURNAL
- GOAL REVIEW
- GRATITUDE
- EVENING RITUAL

SUNDAY ______

7 ______
8 ______
9 ______
10 ______
11 ______
12 ______
1 ______
2 ______
3 ______
4 ______
5 ______
6 ______
7 ______
8 ______
9 ______

daily checklist

- MORNING RITUAL
- DAILY DRESS-UP
- MINDFUL MOVEMENT
- EAT YOUR VEGGIES
- JOURNAL
- GOAL REVIEW
- GRATITUDE
- EVENING RITUAL

INTENTION:

weekly checklist

- PLAN WEEK'S MITS
- SOAK IN THE TUB
- TAKE A DIGITAL DAY OFF
- CLEAR CLUTTER
- PEN A LOVE NOTE
- BUY/PICK FRESH FLOWERS
- TAKE AN ARTIST DATE
- SAVOR A GREEN JUICE
- ______

MITs

wellness planning

M
T
W
TH
F
S
S

GRATITUDE:

MONDAY

7 8 9 10 11 12 1 2 3 4 5 6 7 8 9

daily checklist

- MORNING RITUAL
- DAILY DRESS-UP
- MINDFUL MOVEMENT
- EAT YOUR VEGGIES
- JOURNAL
- GOAL REVIEW
- GRATITUDE
- EVENING RITUAL

TUESDAY

7 8 9 10 11 12 1 2 3 4 5 6 7 8 9

daily checklist

- MORNING RITUAL
- DAILY DRESS-UP
- MINDFUL MOVEMENT
- EAT YOUR VEGGIES
- JOURNAL
- GOAL REVIEW
- GRATITUDE
- EVENING RITUAL

WEDNESDAY

7 8 9 10 11 12 1 2 3 4 5 6 7 8 9

daily checklist

- MORNING RITUAL
- DAILY DRESS-UP
- MINDFUL MOVEMENT
- EAT YOUR VEGGIES
- JOURNAL
- GOAL REVIEW
- GRATITUDE
- EVENING RITUAL

THURSDAY

7
8
9
10
11
12
1
2
3
4
5
6
7
8
9

daily checklist

- MORNING RITUAL
- DAILY DRESS-UP
- MINDFUL MOVEMENT
- EAT YOUR VEGGIES
- JOURNAL
- GOAL REVIEW
- GRATITUDE
- EVENING RITUAL

FRIDAY

7
8
9
10
11
12
1
2
3
4
5
6
7
8
9

daily checklist

- MORNING RITUAL
- DAILY DRESS-UP
- MINDFUL MOVEMENT
- EAT YOUR VEGGIES
- JOURNAL
- GOAL REVIEW
- GRATITUDE
- EVENING RITUAL

SATURDAY

7
8
9
10
11
12
1
2
3
4
5
6
7
8
9

daily checklist

- MORNING RITUAL
- DAILY DRESS-UP
- MINDFUL MOVEMENT
- EAT YOUR VEGGIES
- JOURNAL
- GOAL REVIEW
- GRATITUDE
- EVENING RITUAL

SUNDAY

7
8
9
10
11
12
1
2
3
4
5
6
7
8
9

daily checklist

- MORNING RITUAL
- DAILY DRESS-UP
- MINDFUL MOVEMENT
- EAT YOUR VEGGIES
- JOURNAL
- GOAL REVIEW
- GRATITUDE
- EVENING RITUAL

LOVE

IS

THE

ANSWER.

seasonal life review

DATE: ____________

SEASONALLY REFLECT ON AREAS OF YOUR LIFE. RATE EACH ONE WITH YOUR LEVEL OF SATISFACTION 10 = BLISS, 5 = SO-SO, 0 = BOO.

Here are some additional areas to consider: social life, romance, family, education, health, fitness, meaning, activism. Next, take a moment to note the areas that ranked low and create three action steps to increase your tranquility in these areas. Be gentle. Plant seeds. Watch dreams take root.

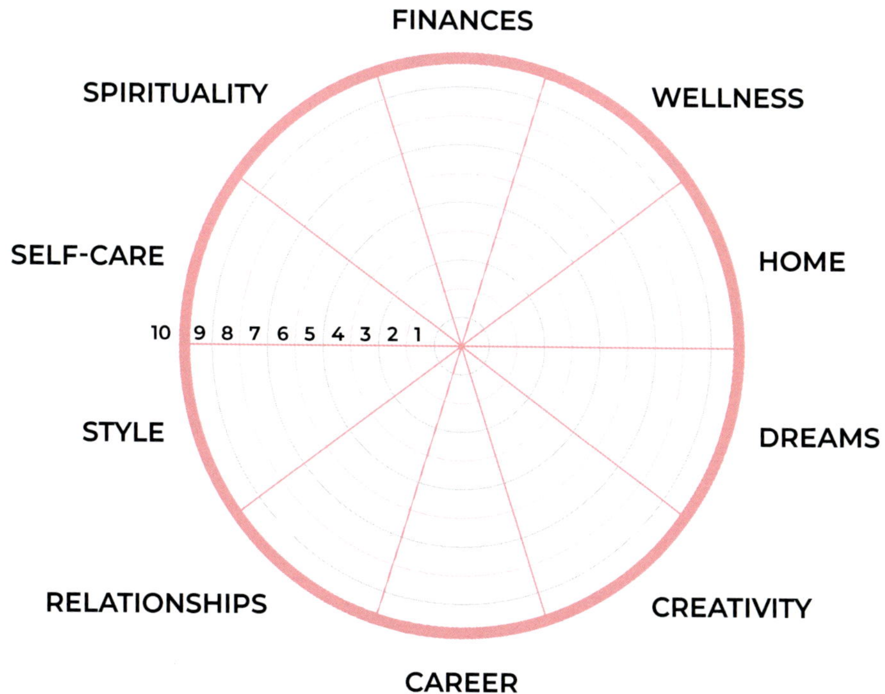

ACTION STEPS TO INCREASE AREAS THAT ARE LOWER THAN I'D LIKE:

month's dreams

DOODLE, LIST, COLLAGE, OR WRITE WHAT YOU'D LIKE TO MANIFEST THIS MONTH.

month's review

REVISIT YOUR MONTH'S DREAMS AND NOTE HOW THEY UNFOLDED FOR YOU.

30 days of tranquility

TRY THIS 30-DAY CHALLENGE TO INFUSE YOUR MONTH WITH SIMPLE PLEASURES.

1 SIT STILL FOR FIVE MINUTES	2 DO SIX SUN SALUTATIONS	3 WRITE A LOVE LETTER	4 APOLOGIZE	5 TELL THE TRUTH
6 CONSUME A GREEN DRINK	7 GO MEAT-FREE	8 WALK FOR 20 MINUTES	9 DO LEGS UP THE WALL	10 GIVE $10 TO CHARITY
11 PEN TWO JOURNAL PAGES	12 REVIEW YOUR YEAR'S DREAMS	13 CLEAR CLUTTER	14 GO ON AN ARTIST DATE	15 COLLAGE TWO PAGES
16 TREAT YOURSELF TO TEA	17 READ FOR 20 MINUTES	18 BUY YOURSELF FLOWERS	19 DANCE TO A FAVORITE TUNE	20 EXPRESS GRATITUDE
21 EAT ONLY UNPROCESSED FOODS	22 SOAK IN A BUBBLE BATH	23 MINDFULLY SIP A LIBATION	24 GET OUT IN NATURE	25 FORGO COMPLAINING
26 TAKE A DIGITAL DAY OFF	27 SNAP PHOTOS FROM YOUR DAY	28 MAKE A FAVORITE MEAL	29 HUG	30 BE FULLY PRESENT

habit tracking

NOTE HABITS YOU'RE TRYING TO ADD OR SUBTRACT AND TRACK THEM DAILY TO HELP WITH ACCOUNTABILITY. CELEBRATE YOUR SUCCESSES AND OBSERVE AREAS FOR GROWTH.

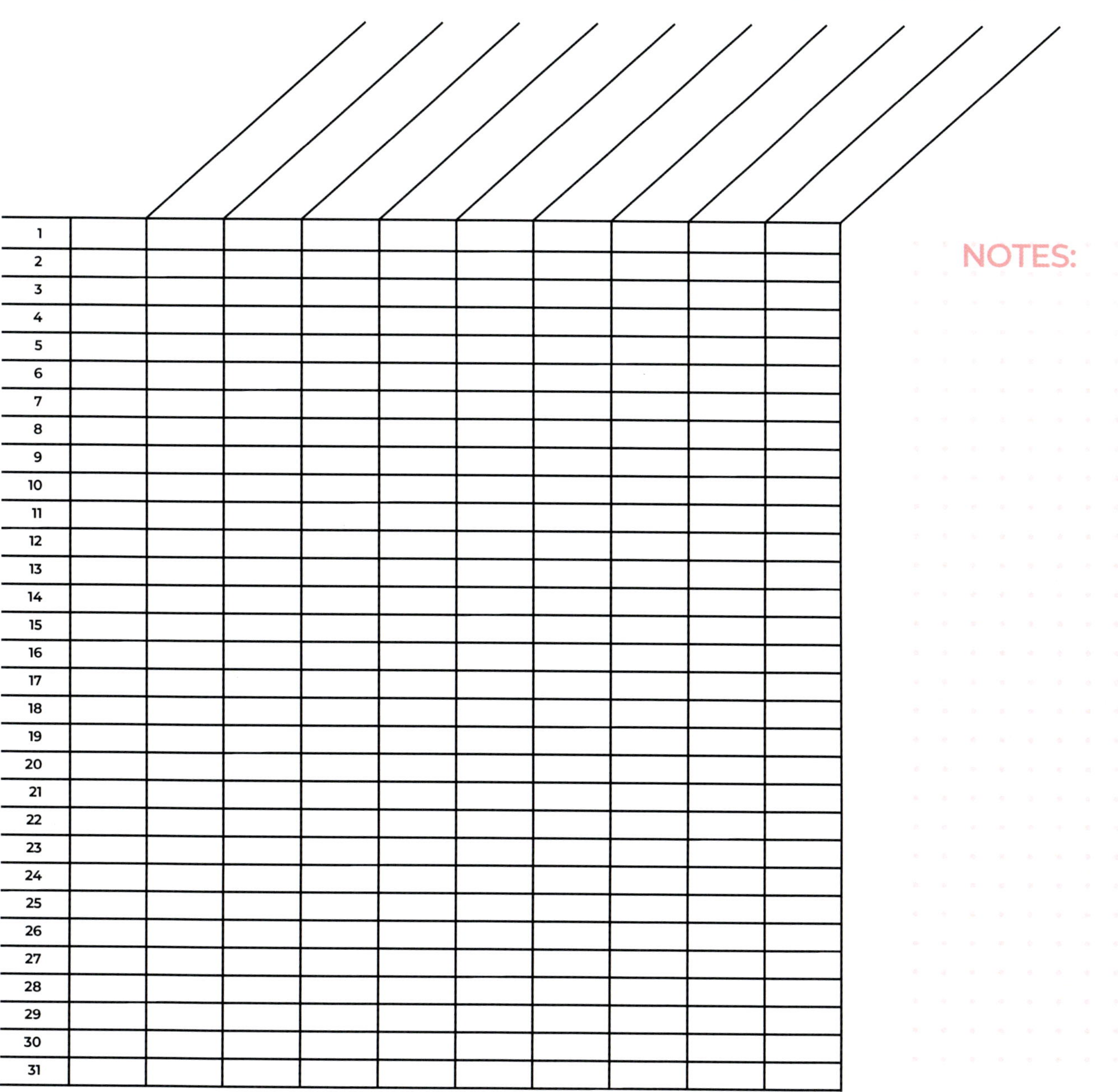

moon phases

N*otice your connection to the moon's cycles in these four phases: new, waxing, full, waning. Consider the prompts below as a way to tie into your Month's Dreams and provide space for monthly reflection.*

new moon

A TIME FOR SETTING INTENTIONS.
I WANT . . .

waxing moon

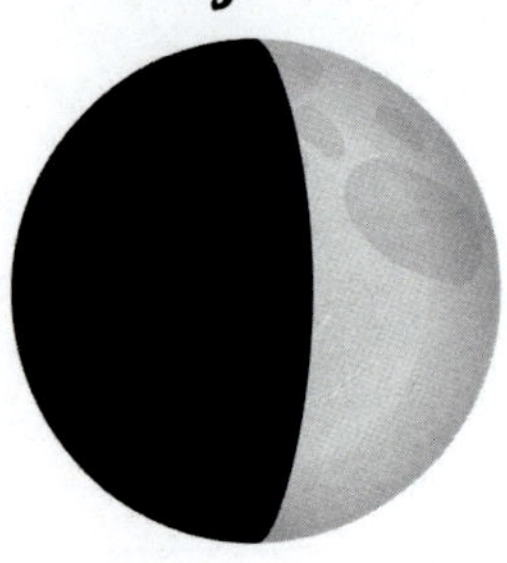

A TIME FOR ACTION. I WILL . . .

A TIME FOR HARVEST AND CLOSURE.
I RELEASE . . .

waning moon

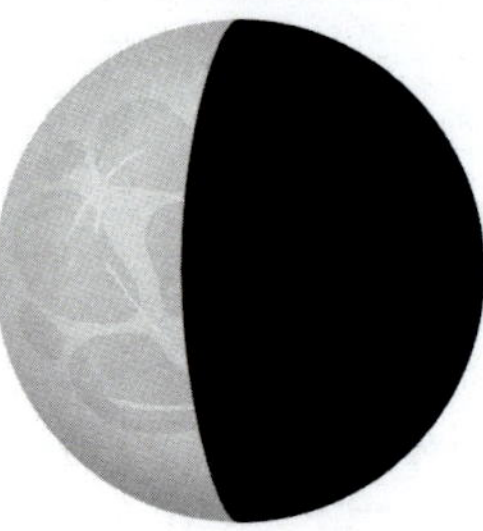

A TIME FOR SOFTENING. I FEEL . . .

monthly planner

MONTH: ______________________ INTENTION: ______________________

SUNDAY	MONDAY	TUESDAY	WEDNESDAY	THURSDAY	FRIDAY	SATURDAY

MONTHLY TRANQUILITY TOOLS

- ❍ CRAFT MONTH'S DREAMS
- ❍ REVIEW BUDGET
- ❍ CREATE SOMETHING
- ❍ READ TWO BOOKS
- ❍ VOLUNTEER
- ❍ MANI/PEDI
- ❍ ENTERTAIN
- ❍ MASSAGE

INTENTION:

weekly checklist

- PLAN WEEK'S MITS
- SOAK IN THE TUB
- TAKE A DIGITAL DAY OFF
- CLEAR CLUTTER
- PEN A LOVE NOTE
- BUY/PICK FRESH FLOWERS
- TAKE AN ARTIST DATE
- SAVOR A GREEN JUICE
- ______

MITs

- ______
- ______
- ______
- ______
- ______

wellness planning

M ______
T ______
W ______
TH ______
F ______
S ______
S ______

GRATITUDE:

MONDAY ______

7 ______
8 ______
9 ______
10 ______
11 ______
12 ______
1 ______
2 ______
3 ______
4 ______
5 ______
6 ______
7 ______
8 ______
9 ______

daily checklist

- MORNING RITUAL
- DAILY DRESS-UP
- MINDFUL MOVEMENT
- EAT YOUR VEGGIES
- JOURNAL
- GOAL REVIEW
- GRATITUDE
- EVENING RITUAL
- ______

TUESDAY ______

7 ______
8 ______
9 ______
10 ______
11 ______
12 ______
1 ______
2 ______
3 ______
4 ______
5 ______
6 ______
7 ______
8 ______
9 ______

daily checklist

- MORNING RITUAL
- DAILY DRESS-UP
- MINDFUL MOVEMENT
- EAT YOUR VEGGIES
- JOURNAL
- GOAL REVIEW
- GRATITUDE
- EVENING RITUAL
- ______

WEDNESDAY ______

7 ______
8 ______
9 ______
10 ______
11 ______
12 ______
1 ______
2 ______
3 ______
4 ______
5 ______
6 ______
7 ______
8 ______
9 ______

daily checklist

- MORNING RITUAL
- DAILY DRESS-UP
- MINDFUL MOVEMENT
- EAT YOUR VEGGIES
- JOURNAL
- GOAL REVIEW
- GRATITUDE
- EVENING RITUAL
- ______

THURSDAY ______

7
8
9
10
11
12
1
2
3
4
5
6
7
8
9

daily checklist

- MORNING RITUAL
- DAILY DRESS-UP
- MINDFUL MOVEMENT
- EAT YOUR VEGGIES
- JOURNAL
- GOAL REVIEW
- GRATITUDE
- EVENING RITUAL

FRIDAY ______

7
8
9
10
11
12
1
2
3
4
5
6
7
8
9

daily checklist

- MORNING RITUAL
- DAILY DRESS-UP
- MINDFUL MOVEMENT
- EAT YOUR VEGGIES
- JOURNAL
- GOAL REVIEW
- GRATITUDE
- EVENING RITUAL

SATURDAY ______

7
8
9
10
11
12
1
2
3
4
5
6
7
8
9

daily checklist

- MORNING RITUAL
- DAILY DRESS-UP
- MINDFUL MOVEMENT
- EAT YOUR VEGGIES
- JOURNAL
- GOAL REVIEW
- GRATITUDE
- EVENING RITUAL

SUNDAY ______

7
8
9
10
11
12
1
2
3
4
5
6
7
8
9

daily checklist

- MORNING RITUAL
- DAILY DRESS-UP
- MINDFUL MOVEMENT
- EAT YOUR VEGGIES
- JOURNAL
- GOAL REVIEW
- GRATITUDE
- EVENING RITUAL

INTENTION:

weekly checklist

- PLAN WEEK'S MITS
- SOAK IN THE TUB
- TAKE A DIGITAL DAY OFF
- CLEAR CLUTTER
- PEN A LOVE NOTE
- BUY/PICK FRESH FLOWERS
- TAKE AN ARTIST DATE
- SAVOR A GREEN JUICE
- ___

MITs

- ___
- ___
- ___
- ___
- ___

wellness planning

M ___
T ___
W ___
TH ___
F ___
S ___
S ___

GRATITUDE:

MONDAY ___

7 ___
8 ___
9 ___
10 ___
11 ___
12 ___
1 ___
2 ___
3 ___
4 ___
5 ___
6 ___
7 ___
8 ___
9 ___

daily checklist

- MORNING RITUAL
- DAILY DRESS-UP
- MINDFUL MOVEMENT
- EAT YOUR VEGGIES
- JOURNAL
- GOAL REVIEW
- GRATITUDE
- EVENING RITUAL
- ___

TUESDAY ___

7 ___
8 ___
9 ___
10 ___
11 ___
12 ___
1 ___
2 ___
3 ___
4 ___
5 ___
6 ___
7 ___
8 ___
9 ___

daily checklist

- MORNING RITUAL
- DAILY DRESS-UP
- MINDFUL MOVEMENT
- EAT YOUR VEGGIES
- JOURNAL
- GOAL REVIEW
- GRATITUDE
- EVENING RITUAL
- ___

WEDNESDAY ___

7 ___
8 ___
9 ___
10 ___
11 ___
12 ___
1 ___
2 ___
3 ___
4 ___
5 ___
6 ___
7 ___
8 ___
9 ___

daily checklist

- MORNING RITUAL
- DAILY DRESS-UP
- MINDFUL MOVEMENT
- EAT YOUR VEGGIES
- JOURNAL
- GOAL REVIEW
- GRATITUDE
- EVENING RITUAL
- ___

THURSDAY ________

7 ________
8 ________
9 ________
10 ________
11 ________
12 ________
1 ________
2 ________
3 ________
4 ________
5 ________
6 ________
7 ________
8 ________
9 ________

- ❍ ________
- ❍ ________
- ❍ ________
- ❍ ________
- ❍ ________
- ❍ ________
- ❍ ________
- ❍ ________
- ❍ ________
- ❍ ________

- ❍ ________
- ❍ ________
- ❍ ________
- ❍ ________
- ❍ ________
- ❍ ________

daily checklist

- ❍ MORNING RITUAL
- ❍ DAILY DRESS-UP
- ❍ MINDFUL MOVEMENT
- ❍ EAT YOUR VEGGIES
- ❍ JOURNAL
- ❍ GOAL REVIEW
- ❍ GRATITUDE
- ❍ EVENING RITUAL
- ❍ ________

FRIDAY ________

7 ________
8 ________
9 ________
10 ________
11 ________
12 ________
1 ________
2 ________
3 ________
4 ________
5 ________
6 ________
7 ________
8 ________
9 ________

- ❍ ________
- ❍ ________
- ❍ ________
- ❍ ________
- ❍ ________
- ❍ ________
- ❍ ________
- ❍ ________
- ❍ ________
- ❍ ________

- ❍ ________
- ❍ ________
- ❍ ________
- ❍ ________
- ❍ ________
- ❍ ________

daily checklist

- ❍ MORNING RITUAL
- ❍ DAILY DRESS-UP
- ❍ MINDFUL MOVEMENT
- ❍ EAT YOUR VEGGIES
- ❍ JOURNAL
- ❍ GOAL REVIEW
- ❍ GRATITUDE
- ❍ EVENING RITUAL
- ❍ ________

SATURDAY ________

7 ________
8 ________
9 ________
10 ________
11 ________
12 ________
1 ________
2 ________
3 ________
4 ________
5 ________
6 ________
7 ________
8 ________
9 ________

- ❍ ________
- ❍ ________
- ❍ ________
- ❍ ________
- ❍ ________
- ❍ ________
- ❍ ________
- ❍ ________
- ❍ ________
- ❍ ________

- ❍ ________
- ❍ ________
- ❍ ________
- ❍ ________
- ❍ ________
- ❍ ________

daily checklist

- ❍ MORNING RITUAL
- ❍ DAILY DRESS-UP
- ❍ MINDFUL MOVEMENT
- ❍ EAT YOUR VEGGIES
- ❍ JOURNAL
- ❍ GOAL REVIEW
- ❍ GRATITUDE
- ❍ EVENING RITUAL
- ❍ ________

SUNDAY ________

7 ________
8 ________
9 ________
10 ________
11 ________
12 ________
1 ________
2 ________
3 ________
4 ________
5 ________
6 ________
7 ________
8 ________
9 ________

- ❍ ________
- ❍ ________
- ❍ ________
- ❍ ________
- ❍ ________
- ❍ ________
- ❍ ________
- ❍ ________
- ❍ ________
- ❍ ________

- ❍ ________
- ❍ ________
- ❍ ________
- ❍ ________
- ❍ ________
- ❍ ________

daily checklist

- ❍ MORNING RITUAL
- ❍ DAILY DRESS-UP
- ❍ MINDFUL MOVEMENT
- ❍ EAT YOUR VEGGIES
- ❍ JOURNAL
- ❍ GOAL REVIEW
- ❍ GRATITUDE
- ❍ EVENING RITUAL
- ❍ ________

INTENTION:

weekly checklist

- PLAN WEEK'S MITS
- SOAK IN THE TUB
- TAKE A DIGITAL DAY OFF
- CLEAR CLUTTER
- PEN A LOVE NOTE
- BUY/PICK FRESH FLOWERS
- TAKE AN ARTIST DATE
- SAVOR A GREEN JUICE
- ____________

MITs

- ____________
- ____________
- ____________
- ____________
- ____________

wellness planning

M ____________
T ____________
W ____________
TH ____________
F ____________
S ____________
S ____________

GRATITUDE:

MONDAY ____________

7 ____________
8 ____________
9 ____________
10 ____________
11 ____________
12 ____________
1 ____________
2 ____________
3 ____________
4 ____________
5 ____________
6 ____________
7 ____________
8 ____________
9 ____________

daily checklist

- MORNING RITUAL
- DAILY DRESS-UP
- MINDFUL MOVEMENT
- EAT YOUR VEGGIES
- JOURNAL
- GOAL REVIEW
- GRATITUDE
- EVENING RITUAL
- ____________

TUESDAY ____________

7 ____________
8 ____________
9 ____________
10 ____________
11 ____________
12 ____________
1 ____________
2 ____________
3 ____________
4 ____________
5 ____________
6 ____________
7 ____________
8 ____________
9 ____________

daily checklist

- MORNING RITUAL
- DAILY DRESS-UP
- MINDFUL MOVEMENT
- EAT YOUR VEGGIES
- JOURNAL
- GOAL REVIEW
- GRATITUDE
- EVENING RITUAL
- ____________

WEDNESDAY ____________

7 ____________
8 ____________
9 ____________
10 ____________
11 ____________
12 ____________
1 ____________
2 ____________
3 ____________
4 ____________
5 ____________
6 ____________
7 ____________
8 ____________
9 ____________

daily checklist

- MORNING RITUAL
- DAILY DRESS-UP
- MINDFUL MOVEMENT
- EAT YOUR VEGGIES
- JOURNAL
- GOAL REVIEW
- GRATITUDE
- EVENING RITUAL
- ____________

THURSDAY

7
8
9
10
11
12
1
2
3
4
5
6
7
8
9

daily checklist

- MORNING RITUAL
- DAILY DRESS-UP
- MINDFUL MOVEMENT
- EAT YOUR VEGGIES
- JOURNAL
- GOAL REVIEW
- GRATITUDE
- EVENING RITUAL

FRIDAY

7
8
9
10
11
12
1
2
3
4
5
6
7
8
9

daily checklist

- MORNING RITUAL
- DAILY DRESS-UP
- MINDFUL MOVEMENT
- EAT YOUR VEGGIES
- JOURNAL
- GOAL REVIEW
- GRATITUDE
- EVENING RITUAL

SATURDAY

7
8
9
10
11
12
1
2
3
4
5
6
7
8
9

daily checklist

- MORNING RITUAL
- DAILY DRESS-UP
- MINDFUL MOVEMENT
- EAT YOUR VEGGIES
- JOURNAL
- GOAL REVIEW
- GRATITUDE
- EVENING RITUAL

SUNDAY

7
8
9
10
11
12
1
2
3
4
5
6
7
8
9

daily checklist

- MORNING RITUAL
- DAILY DRESS-UP
- MINDFUL MOVEMENT
- EAT YOUR VEGGIES
- JOURNAL
- GOAL REVIEW
- GRATITUDE
- EVENING RITUAL

INTENTION:

weekly checklist

- PLAN WEEK'S MITS
- SOAK IN THE TUB
- TAKE A DIGITAL DAY OFF
- CLEAR CLUTTER
- PEN A LOVE NOTE
- BUY/PICK FRESH FLOWERS
- TAKE AN ARTIST DATE
- SAVOR A GREEN JUICE
- ________

MITS

- ________
- ________
- ________
- ________
- ________

wellness planning

M ________
T ________
W ________
TH ________
F ________
S ________
S ________

GRATITUDE:

MONDAY ________

7 ________
8 ________
9 ________
10 ________
11 ________
12 ________
1 ________
2 ________
3 ________
4 ________
5 ________
6 ________
7 ________
8 ________
9 ________

daily checklist

- MORNING RITUAL
- DAILY DRESS-UP
- MINDFUL MOVEMENT
- EAT YOUR VEGGIES
- JOURNAL
- GOAL REVIEW
- GRATITUDE
- EVENING RITUAL
- ________

TUESDAY ________

7 ________
8 ________
9 ________
10 ________
11 ________
12 ________
1 ________
2 ________
3 ________
4 ________
5 ________
6 ________
7 ________
8 ________
9 ________

daily checklist

- MORNING RITUAL
- DAILY DRESS-UP
- MINDFUL MOVEMENT
- EAT YOUR VEGGIES
- JOURNAL
- GOAL REVIEW
- GRATITUDE
- EVENING RITUAL
- ________

WEDNESDAY ________

7 ________
8 ________
9 ________
10 ________
11 ________
12 ________
1 ________
2 ________
3 ________
4 ________
5 ________
6 ________
7 ________
8 ________
9 ________

daily checklist

- MORNING RITUAL
- DAILY DRESS-UP
- MINDFUL MOVEMENT
- EAT YOUR VEGGIES
- JOURNAL
- GOAL REVIEW
- GRATITUDE
- EVENING RITUAL
- ________

THURSDAY

7
8
9
10
11
12
1
2
3
4
5
6
7
8
9

daily checklist

- MORNING RITUAL
- DAILY DRESS-UP
- MINDFUL MOVEMENT
- EAT YOUR VEGGIES
- JOURNAL
- GOAL REVIEW
- GRATITUDE
- EVENING RITUAL

FRIDAY

7
8
9
10
11
12
1
2
3
4
5
6
7
8
9

daily checklist

- MORNING RITUAL
- DAILY DRESS-UP
- MINDFUL MOVEMENT
- EAT YOUR VEGGIES
- JOURNAL
- GOAL REVIEW
- GRATITUDE
- EVENING RITUAL

SATURDAY

7
8
9
10
11
12
1
2
3
4
5
6
7
8
9

daily checklist

- MORNING RITUAL
- DAILY DRESS-UP
- MINDFUL MOVEMENT
- EAT YOUR VEGGIES
- JOURNAL
- GOAL REVIEW
- GRATITUDE
- EVENING RITUAL

SUNDAY

7
8
9
10
11
12
1
2
3
4
5
6
7
8
9

daily checklist

- MORNING RITUAL
- DAILY DRESS-UP
- MINDFUL MOVEMENT
- EAT YOUR VEGGIES
- JOURNAL
- GOAL REVIEW
- GRATITUDE
- EVENING RITUAL

INTENTION:

weekly checklist

- PLAN WEEK'S MITS
- SOAK IN THE TUB
- TAKE A DIGITAL DAY OFF
- CLEAR CLUTTER
- PEN A LOVE NOTE
- BUY/PICK FRESH FLOWERS
- TAKE AN ARTIST DATE
- SAVOR A GREEN JUICE
- __________

MITs

- __________
- __________
- __________
- __________
- __________

wellness planning

M __________
T __________
W __________
TH __________
F __________
S __________
S __________

GRATITUDE:

MONDAY ______	TUESDAY ______	WEDNESDAY ______
7	7	7
8	8	8
9	9	9
10	10	10
11	11	11
12	12	12
1	1	1
2	2	2
3	3	3
4	4	4
5	5	5
6	6	6
7	7	7
8	8	8
9	9	9

daily checklist

- MORNING RITUAL
- DAILY DRESS-UP
- MINDFUL MOVEMENT
- EAT YOUR VEGGIES
- JOURNAL
- GOAL REVIEW
- GRATITUDE
- EVENING RITUAL
- __________

daily checklist

- MORNING RITUAL
- DAILY DRESS-UP
- MINDFUL MOVEMENT
- EAT YOUR VEGGIES
- JOURNAL
- GOAL REVIEW
- GRATITUDE
- EVENING RITUAL
- __________

daily checklist

- MORNING RITUAL
- DAILY DRESS-UP
- MINDFUL MOVEMENT
- EAT YOUR VEGGIES
- JOURNAL
- GOAL REVIEW
- GRATITUDE
- EVENING RITUAL
- __________

THURSDAY

7
8
9
10
11
12
1
2
3
4
5
6
7
8
9

daily checklist

- MORNING RITUAL
- DAILY DRESS-UP
- MINDFUL MOVEMENT
- EAT YOUR VEGGIES
- JOURNAL
- GOAL REVIEW
- GRATITUDE
- EVENING RITUAL

FRIDAY

7
8
9
10
11
12
1
2
3
4
5
6
7
8
9

daily checklist

- MORNING RITUAL
- DAILY DRESS-UP
- MINDFUL MOVEMENT
- EAT YOUR VEGGIES
- JOURNAL
- GOAL REVIEW
- GRATITUDE
- EVENING RITUAL

SATURDAY

7
8
9
10
11
12
1
2
3
4
5
6
7
8
9

daily checklist

- MORNING RITUAL
- DAILY DRESS-UP
- MINDFUL MOVEMENT
- EAT YOUR VEGGIES
- JOURNAL
- GOAL REVIEW
- GRATITUDE
- EVENING RITUAL

SUNDAY

7
8
9
10
11
12
1
2
3
4
5
6
7
8
9

daily checklist

- MORNING RITUAL
- DAILY DRESS-UP
- MINDFUL MOVEMENT
- EAT YOUR VEGGIES
- JOURNAL
- GOAL REVIEW
- GRATITUDE
- EVENING RITUAL

month's dreams

DOODLE, LIST, COLLAGE, OR WRITE WHAT YOU'D LIKE TO MANIFEST THIS MONTH.

month's review

REVISIT YOUR MONTH'S DREAMS AND NOTE HOW THEY UNFOLDED FOR YOU.

30 days of tranquility

TRY THIS 30-DAY CHALLENGE TO INFUSE YOUR MONTH WITH SIMPLE PLEASURES.

1 SIT STILL FOR FIVE MINUTES

2 DO SIX SUN SALUTATIONS

3 WRITE A LOVE LETTER

4 APOLOGIZE

5 TELL THE TRUTH

6 CONSUME A GREEN DRINK

7 GO MEAT-FREE

8 WALK FOR 20 MINUTES

9 DO LEGS UP THE WALL

10 GIVE $10 TO CHARITY

11 PEN TWO JOURNAL PAGES

12 REVIEW YOUR YEAR'S DREAMS

13 CLEAR CLUTTER

14 GO ON AN ARTIST DATE

15 COLLAGE TWO PAGES

16 TREAT YOURSELF TO TEA

17 READ FOR 20 MINUTES

18 BUY YOURSELF FLOWERS

19 DANCE TO A FAVORITE TUNE

20 EXPRESS GRATITUDE

21 EAT ONLY UNPROCESSED FOODS

22 SOAK IN A BUBBLE BATH

23 MINDFULLY SIP A LIBATION

24 GET OUT IN NATURE

25 FORGO COMPLAINING

26 TAKE A DIGITAL DAY OFF

27 SNAP PHOTOS FROM YOUR DAY

28 MAKE A FAVORITE MEAL

29 HUG

30 BE FULLY PRESENT

habit tracking

NOTE HABITS YOU'RE TRYING TO ADD OR SUBTRACT AND TRACK THEM DAILY TO HELP WITH ACCOUNTABILITY. CELEBRATE YOUR SUCCESSES AND OBSERVE AREAS FOR GROWTH.

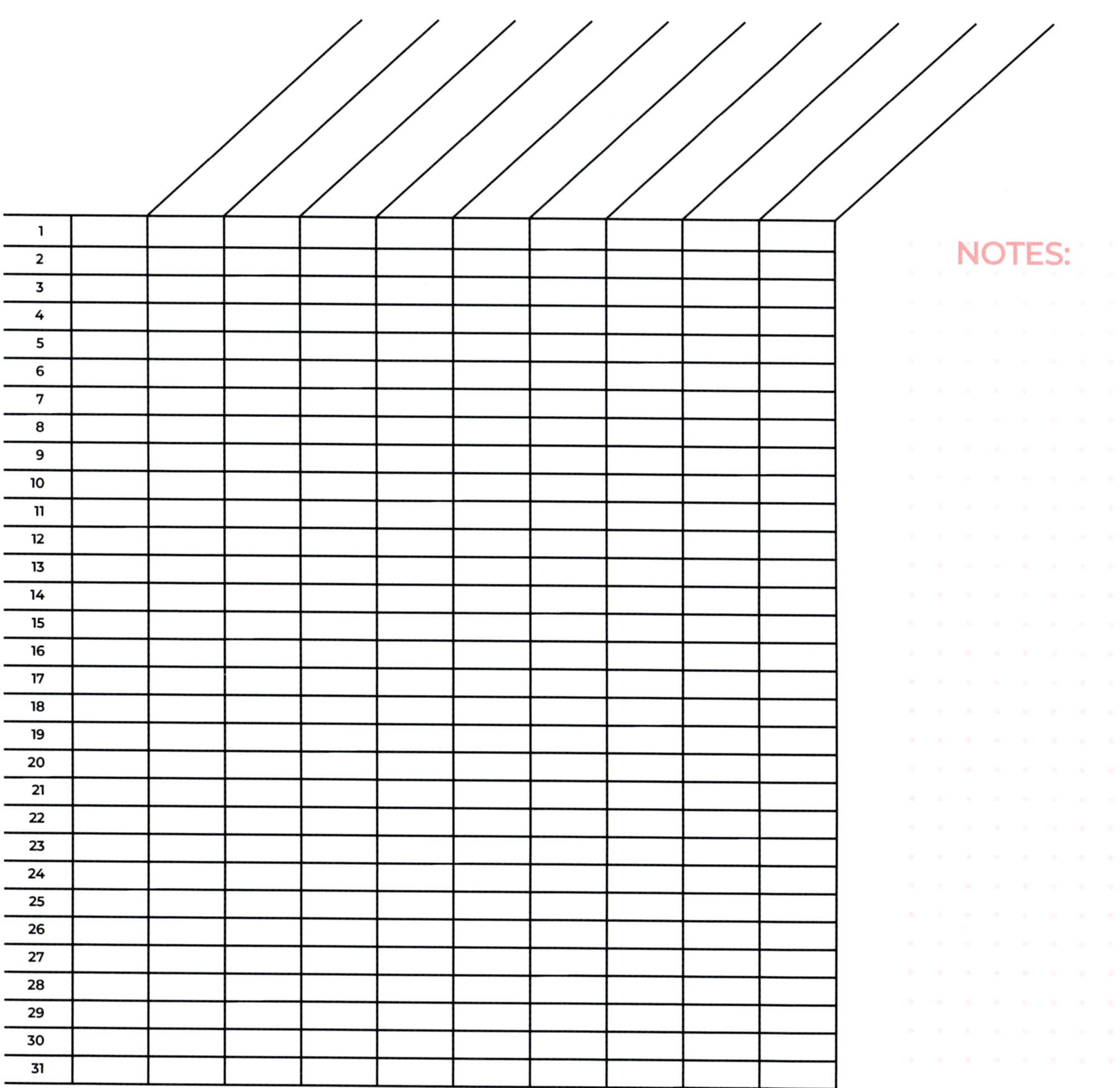

1										
2										
3										
4										
5										
6										
7										
8										
9										
10										
11										
12										
13										
14										
15										
16										
17										
18										
19										
20										
21										
22										
23										
24										
25										
26										
27										
28										
29										
30										
31										

NOTES:

moon phases

Notice your connection to the moon's cycles in these four phases: new, waxing, full, waning. Consider the prompts below as a way to tie into your Month's Dreams and provide space for monthly reflection.

new moon

A TIME FOR SETTING INTENTIONS. I WANT . . .

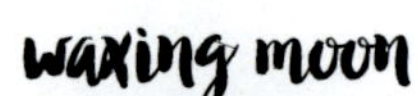

A TIME FOR ACTION. I WILL . . .

full moon

A TIME FOR HARVEST AND CLOSURE. I RELEASE . . .

waning moon

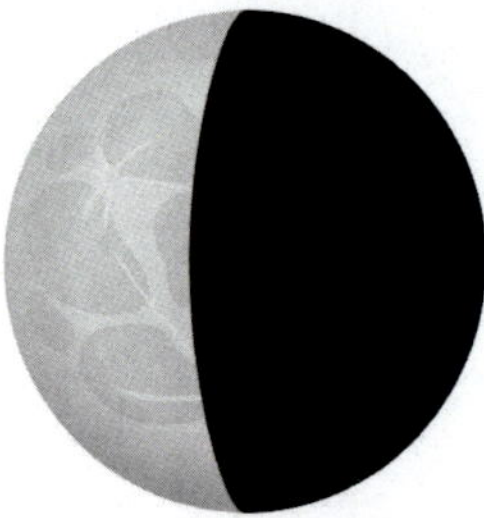

A TIME FOR SOFTENING. I FEEL . . .

monthly planner

MONTH: ____________________ INTENTION: ____________________

SUNDAY	MONDAY	TUESDAY	WEDNESDAY	THURSDAY	FRIDAY	SATURDAY

MONTHLY TRANQUILITY TOOLS

- ❍ CRAFT MONTH'S DREAMS
- ❍ REVIEW BUDGET
- ❍ CREATE SOMETHING
- ❍ READ TWO BOOKS
- ❍ VOLUNTEER
- ❍ MANI/PEDI
- ❍ ENTERTAIN
- ❍ MASSAGE

INTENTION:

weekly checklist

- PLAN WEEK'S MITS
- SOAK IN THE TUB
- TAKE A DIGITAL DAY OFF
- CLEAR CLUTTER
- PEN A LOVE NOTE
- BUY/PICK FRESH FLOWERS
- TAKE AN ARTIST DATE
- SAVOR A GREEN JUICE
- ______

MITs

- ______
- ______
- ______
- ______
- ______

wellness planning

M ______
T ______
W ______
TH ______
F ______
S ______
S ______

GRATITUDE:

MONDAY ______

7 ______
8 ______
9 ______
10 ______
11 ______
12 ______
1 ______
2 ______
3 ______
4 ______
5 ______
6 ______
7 ______
8 ______
9 ______

daily checklist

- MORNING RITUAL
- DAILY DRESS-UP
- MINDFUL MOVEMENT
- EAT YOUR VEGGIES
- JOURNAL
- GOAL REVIEW
- GRATITUDE
- EVENING RITUAL
- ______

TUESDAY ______

7 ______
8 ______
9 ______
10 ______
11 ______
12 ______
1 ______
2 ______
3 ______
4 ______
5 ______
6 ______
7 ______
8 ______
9 ______

daily checklist

- MORNING RITUAL
- DAILY DRESS-UP
- MINDFUL MOVEMENT
- EAT YOUR VEGGIES
- JOURNAL
- GOAL REVIEW
- GRATITUDE
- EVENING RITUAL
- ______

WEDNESDAY ______

7 ______
8 ______
9 ______
10 ______
11 ______
12 ______
1 ______
2 ______
3 ______
4 ______
5 ______
6 ______
7 ______
8 ______
9 ______

daily checklist

- MORNING RITUAL
- DAILY DRESS-UP
- MINDFUL MOVEMENT
- EAT YOUR VEGGIES
- JOURNAL
- GOAL REVIEW
- GRATITUDE
- EVENING RITUAL
- ______

THURSDAY	FRIDAY	SATURDAY	SUNDAY
7	7	7	7
8	8	8	8
9	9	9	9
10	10	10	10
11	11	11	11
12	12	12	12
1	1	1	1
2	2	2	2
3	3	3	3
4	4	4	4
5	5	5	5
6	6	6	6
7	7	7	7
8	8	8	8
9	9	9	9

daily checklist

- MORNING RITUAL
- DAILY DRESS-UP
- MINDFUL MOVEMENT
- EAT YOUR VEGGIES
- JOURNAL
- GOAL REVIEW
- GRATITUDE
- EVENING RITUAL

daily checklist

- MORNING RITUAL
- DAILY DRESS-UP
- MINDFUL MOVEMENT
- EAT YOUR VEGGIES
- JOURNAL
- GOAL REVIEW
- GRATITUDE
- EVENING RITUAL

daily checklist

- MORNING RITUAL
- DAILY DRESS-UP
- MINDFUL MOVEMENT
- EAT YOUR VEGGIES
- JOURNAL
- GOAL REVIEW
- GRATITUDE
- EVENING RITUAL

daily checklist

- MORNING RITUAL
- DAILY DRESS-UP
- MINDFUL MOVEMENT
- EAT YOUR VEGGIES
- JOURNAL
- GOAL REVIEW
- GRATITUDE
- EVENING RITUAL

INTENTION:

weekly checklist

- PLAN WEEK'S MITS
- SOAK IN THE TUB
- TAKE A DIGITAL DAY OFF
- CLEAR CLUTTER
- PEN A LOVE NOTE
- BUY/PICK FRESH FLOWERS
- TAKE AN ARTIST DATE
- SAVOR A GREEN JUICE
- __________

MITs

wellness planning

M
T
W
TH
F
S
S

GRATITUDE:

MONDAY __________

7
8
9
10
11
12
1
2
3
4
5
6
7
8
9

daily checklist

- MORNING RITUAL
- DAILY DRESS-UP
- MINDFUL MOVEMENT
- EAT YOUR VEGGIES
- JOURNAL
- GOAL REVIEW
- GRATITUDE
- EVENING RITUAL
- __________

TUESDAY __________

7
8
9
10
11
12
1
2
3
4
5
6
7
8
9

daily checklist

- MORNING RITUAL
- DAILY DRESS-UP
- MINDFUL MOVEMENT
- EAT YOUR VEGGIES
- JOURNAL
- GOAL REVIEW
- GRATITUDE
- EVENING RITUAL
- __________

WEDNESDAY __________

7
8
9
10
11
12
1
2
3
4
5
6
7
8
9

daily checklist

- MORNING RITUAL
- DAILY DRESS-UP
- MINDFUL MOVEMENT
- EAT YOUR VEGGIES
- JOURNAL
- GOAL REVIEW
- GRATITUDE
- EVENING RITUAL
- __________

THURSDAY

7
8
9
10
11
12
1
2
3
4
5
6
7
8
9

daily checklist

- MORNING RITUAL
- DAILY DRESS-UP
- MINDFUL MOVEMENT
- EAT YOUR VEGGIES
- JOURNAL
- GOAL REVIEW
- GRATITUDE
- EVENING RITUAL

FRIDAY

7
8
9
10
11
12
1
2
3
4
5
6
7
8
9

daily checklist

- MORNING RITUAL
- DAILY DRESS-UP
- MINDFUL MOVEMENT
- EAT YOUR VEGGIES
- JOURNAL
- GOAL REVIEW
- GRATITUDE
- EVENING RITUAL

SATURDAY

7
8
9
10
11
12
1
2
3
4
5
6
7
8
9

daily checklist

- MORNING RITUAL
- DAILY DRESS-UP
- MINDFUL MOVEMENT
- EAT YOUR VEGGIES
- JOURNAL
- GOAL REVIEW
- GRATITUDE
- EVENING RITUAL

SUNDAY

7
8
9
10
11
12
1
2
3
4
5
6
7
8
9

daily checklist

- MORNING RITUAL
- DAILY DRESS-UP
- MINDFUL MOVEMENT
- EAT YOUR VEGGIES
- JOURNAL
- GOAL REVIEW
- GRATITUDE
- EVENING RITUAL

INTENTION:

weekly checklist

- PLAN WEEK'S MITS
- SOAK IN THE TUB
- TAKE A DIGITAL DAY OFF
- CLEAR CLUTTER
- PEN A LOVE NOTE
- BUY/PICK FRESH FLOWERS
- TAKE AN ARTIST DATE
- SAVOR A GREEN JUICE

MITS

wellness planning

M

T

W

TH

F

S

S

GRATITUDE:

MONDAY

7 8 9 10 11 12 1 2 3 4 5 6 7 8 9

daily checklist

- MORNING RITUAL
- DAILY DRESS-UP
- MINDFUL MOVEMENT
- EAT YOUR VEGGIES
- JOURNAL
- GOAL REVIEW
- GRATITUDE
- EVENING RITUAL

TUESDAY

7 8 9 10 11 12 1 2 3 4 5 6 7 8 9

daily checklist

- MORNING RITUAL
- DAILY DRESS-UP
- MINDFUL MOVEMENT
- EAT YOUR VEGGIES
- JOURNAL
- GOAL REVIEW
- GRATITUDE
- EVENING RITUAL

WEDNESDAY

7 8 9 10 11 12 1 2 3 4 5 6 7 8 9

daily checklist

- MORNING RITUAL
- DAILY DRESS-UP
- MINDFUL MOVEMENT
- EAT YOUR VEGGIES
- JOURNAL
- GOAL REVIEW
- GRATITUDE
- EVENING RITUAL

THURSDAY

7
8
9
10
11
12
1
2
3
4
5
6
7
8
9

daily checklist

- MORNING RITUAL
- DAILY DRESS-UP
- MINDFUL MOVEMENT
- EAT YOUR VEGGIES
- JOURNAL
- GOAL REVIEW
- GRATITUDE
- EVENING RITUAL

FRIDAY

7
8
9
10
11
12
1
2
3
4
5
6
7
8
9

daily checklist

- MORNING RITUAL
- DAILY DRESS-UP
- MINDFUL MOVEMENT
- EAT YOUR VEGGIES
- JOURNAL
- GOAL REVIEW
- GRATITUDE
- EVENING RITUAL

SATURDAY

7
8
9
10
11
12
1
2
3
4
5
6
7
8
9

daily checklist

- MORNING RITUAL
- DAILY DRESS-UP
- MINDFUL MOVEMENT
- EAT YOUR VEGGIES
- JOURNAL
- GOAL REVIEW
- GRATITUDE
- EVENING RITUAL

SUNDAY

7
8
9
10
11
12
1
2
3
4
5
6
7
8
9

daily checklist

- MORNING RITUAL
- DAILY DRESS-UP
- MINDFUL MOVEMENT
- EAT YOUR VEGGIES
- JOURNAL
- GOAL REVIEW
- GRATITUDE
- EVENING RITUAL

INTENTION:

weekly checklist

- PLAN WEEK'S MITS
- SOAK IN THE TUB
- TAKE A DIGITAL DAY OFF
- CLEAR CLUTTER
- PEN A LOVE NOTE
- BUY/PICK FRESH FLOWERS
- TAKE AN ARTIST DATE
- SAVOR A GREEN JUICE
- __________

MITs

wellness planning

M

T

W

TH

F

S

S

GRATITUDE:

MONDAY

7
8
9
10
11
12
1
2
3
4
5
6
7
8
9

daily checklist

- MORNING RITUAL
- DAILY DRESS-UP
- MINDFUL MOVEMENT
- EAT YOUR VEGGIES
- JOURNAL
- GOAL REVIEW
- GRATITUDE
- EVENING RITUAL

TUESDAY

7
8
9
10
11
12
1
2
3
4
5
6
7
8
9

daily checklist

- MORNING RITUAL
- DAILY DRESS-UP
- MINDFUL MOVEMENT
- EAT YOUR VEGGIES
- JOURNAL
- GOAL REVIEW
- GRATITUDE
- EVENING RITUAL

WEDNESDAY

7
8
9
10
11
12
1
2
3
4
5
6
7
8
9

daily checklist

- MORNING RITUAL
- DAILY DRESS-UP
- MINDFUL MOVEMENT
- EAT YOUR VEGGIES
- JOURNAL
- GOAL REVIEW
- GRATITUDE
- EVENING RITUAL

THURSDAY

7
8
9
10
11
12
1
2
3
4
5
6
7
8
9

daily checklist

- MORNING RITUAL
- DAILY DRESS-UP
- MINDFUL MOVEMENT
- EAT YOUR VEGGIES
- JOURNAL
- GOAL REVIEW
- GRATITUDE
- EVENING RITUAL

FRIDAY

7
8
9
10
11
12
1
2
3
4
5
6
7
8
9

daily checklist

- MORNING RITUAL
- DAILY DRESS-UP
- MINDFUL MOVEMENT
- EAT YOUR VEGGIES
- JOURNAL
- GOAL REVIEW
- GRATITUDE
- EVENING RITUAL

SATURDAY

7
8
9
10
11
12
1
2
3
4
5
6
7
8
9

daily checklist

- MORNING RITUAL
- DAILY DRESS-UP
- MINDFUL MOVEMENT
- EAT YOUR VEGGIES
- JOURNAL
- GOAL REVIEW
- GRATITUDE
- EVENING RITUAL

SUNDAY

7
8
9
10
11
12
1
2
3
4
5
6
7
8
9

daily checklist

- MORNING RITUAL
- DAILY DRESS-UP
- MINDFUL MOVEMENT
- EAT YOUR VEGGIES
- JOURNAL
- GOAL REVIEW
- GRATITUDE
- EVENING RITUAL

INTENTION:

MONDAY

7
8
9
10
11
12
1
2
3
4
5
6
7
8
9

TUESDAY

7
8
9
10
11
12
1
2
3
4
5
6
7
8
9

WEDNESDAY

7
8
9
10
11
12
1
2
3
4
5
6
7
8
9

weekly checklist

- PLAN WEEK'S MITS
- SOAK IN THE TUB
- TAKE A DIGITAL DAY OFF
- CLEAR CLUTTER
- PEN A LOVE NOTE
- BUY/PICK FRESH FLOWERS
- TAKE AN ARTIST DATE
- SAVOR A GREEN JUICE

MITs

wellness planning

M
T
W
TH
F
S
S

GRATITUDE:

daily checklist

- MORNING RITUAL
- DAILY DRESS-UP
- MINDFUL MOVEMENT
- EAT YOUR VEGGIES
- JOURNAL
- GOAL REVIEW
- GRATITUDE
- EVENING RITUAL

daily checklist

- MORNING RITUAL
- DAILY DRESS-UP
- MINDFUL MOVEMENT
- EAT YOUR VEGGIES
- JOURNAL
- GOAL REVIEW
- GRATITUDE
- EVENING RITUAL

daily checklist

- MORNING RITUAL
- DAILY DRESS-UP
- MINDFUL MOVEMENT
- EAT YOUR VEGGIES
- JOURNAL
- GOAL REVIEW
- GRATITUDE
- EVENING RITUAL

THURSDAY

7
8
9
10
11
12
1
2
3
4
5
6
7
8
9

daily checklist

- MORNING RITUAL
- DAILY DRESS-UP
- MINDFUL MOVEMENT
- EAT YOUR VEGGIES
- JOURNAL
- GOAL REVIEW
- GRATITUDE
- EVENING RITUAL

FRIDAY

7
8
9
10
11
12
1
2
3
4
5
6
7
8
9

daily checklist

- MORNING RITUAL
- DAILY DRESS-UP
- MINDFUL MOVEMENT
- EAT YOUR VEGGIES
- JOURNAL
- GOAL REVIEW
- GRATITUDE
- EVENING RITUAL

SATURDAY

7
8
9
10
11
12
1
2
3
4
5
6
7
8
9

daily checklist

- MORNING RITUAL
- DAILY DRESS-UP
- MINDFUL MOVEMENT
- EAT YOUR VEGGIES
- JOURNAL
- GOAL REVIEW
- GRATITUDE
- EVENING RITUAL

SUNDAY

7
8
9
10
11
12
1
2
3
4
5
6
7
8
9

daily checklist

- MORNING RITUAL
- DAILY DRESS-UP
- MINDFUL MOVEMENT
- EAT YOUR VEGGIES
- JOURNAL
- GOAL REVIEW
- GRATITUDE
- EVENING RITUAL

month's dreams

DOODLE, LIST, COLLAGE, OR WRITE WHAT YOU'D LIKE TO MANIFEST THIS MONTH.

month's review

REVISIT YOUR MONTH'S DREAMS AND NOTE HOW THEY UNFOLDED FOR YOU.

30 days of tranquility

TRY THIS 30-DAY CHALLENGE TO INFUSE YOUR MONTH WITH SIMPLE PLEASURES.

1. SIT STILL FOR FIVE MINUTES
2. DO SIX SUN SALUTATIONS
3. WRITE A LOVE LETTER
4. APOLOGIZE
5. TELL THE TRUTH
6. CONSUME A GREEN DRINK
7. GO MEAT-FREE
8. WALK FOR 20 MINUTES
9. DO LEGS UP THE WALL
10. GIVE $10 TO CHARITY
11. PEN TWO JOURNAL PAGES
12. REVIEW YOUR YEAR'S DREAMS
13. CLEAR CLUTTER
14. GO ON AN ARTIST DATE
15. COLLAGE TWO PAGES
16. TREAT YOURSELF TO TEA
17. READ FOR 20 MINUTES
18. BUY YOURSELF FLOWERS
19. DANCE TO A FAVORITE TUNE
20. EXPRESS GRATITUDE
21. EAT ONLY UNPROCESSED FOODS
22. SOAK IN A BUBBLE BATH
23. MINDFULLY SIP A LIBATION
24. GET OUT IN NATURE
25. FORGO COMPLAINING
26. TAKE A DIGITAL DAY OFF
27. SNAP PHOTOS FROM YOUR DAY
28. MAKE A FAVORITE MEAL
29. HUG
30. BE FULLY PRESENT

habit tracking

NOTE HABITS YOU'RE TRYING TO ADD OR SUBTRACT AND TRACK THEM DAILY TO HELP WITH ACCOUNTABILITY. CELEBRATE YOUR SUCCESSES AND OBSERVE AREAS FOR GROWTH.

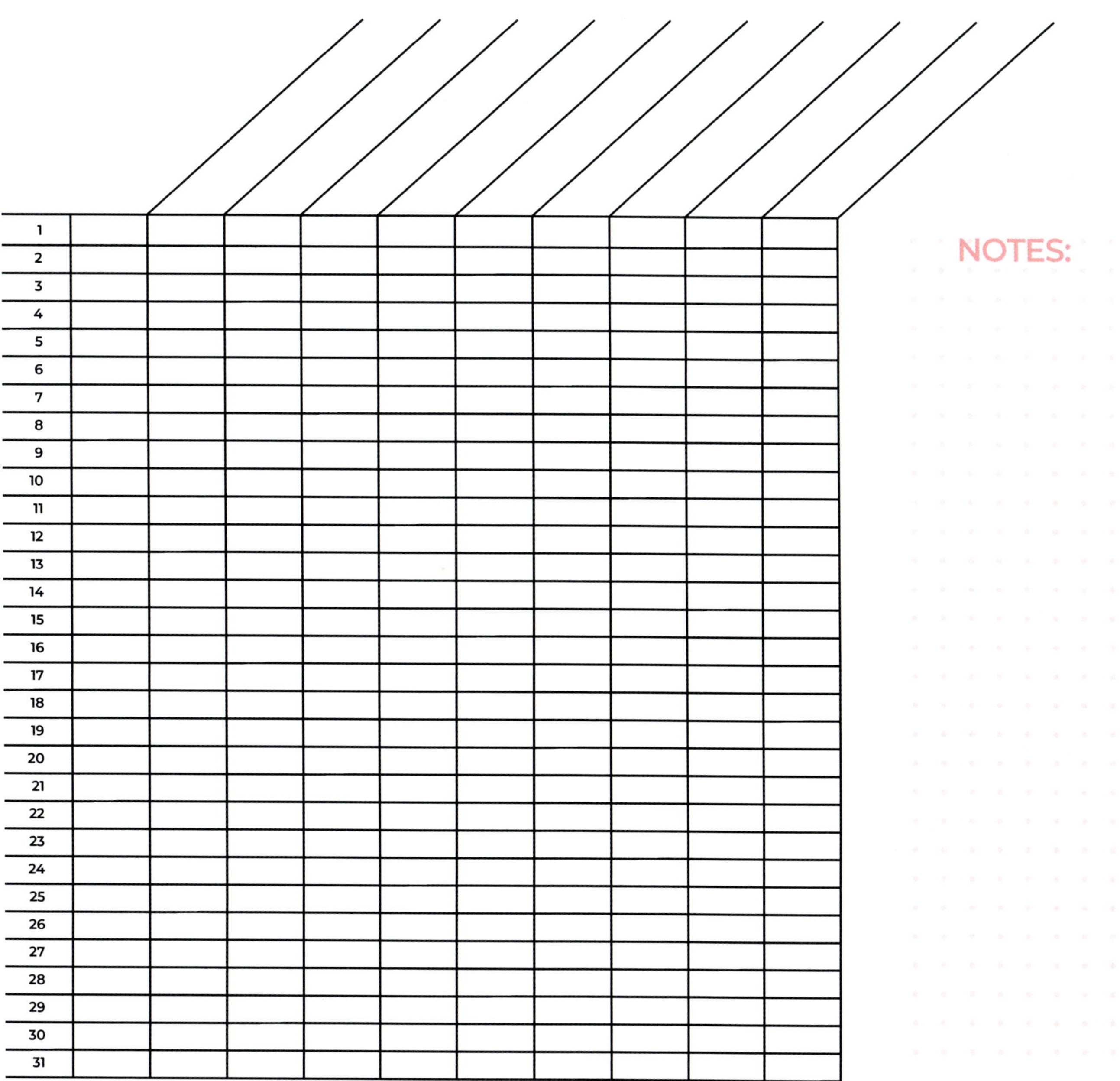

1										
2										
3										
4										
5										
6										
7										
8										
9										
10										
11										
12										
13										
14										
15										
16										
17										
18										
19										
20										
21										
22										
23										
24										
25										
26										
27										
28										
29										
30										
31										

NOTES:

moon phases

Notice your connection to the moon's cycles in these four phases: new, waxing, full, waning. Consider the prompts below as a way to tie into your Month's Dreams and provide space for monthly reflection.

new moon

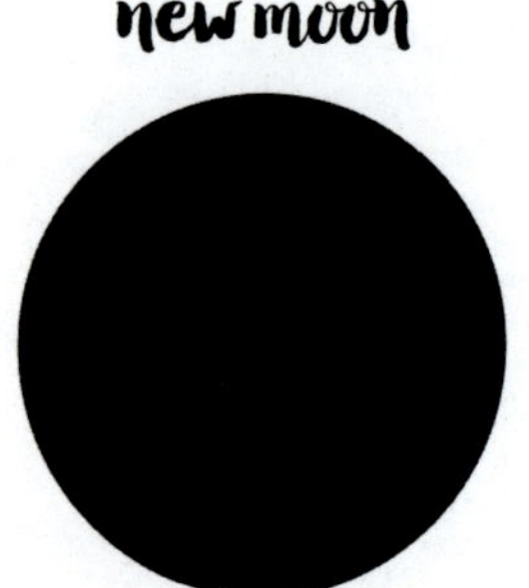

A TIME FOR SETTING INTENTIONS.
I WANT . . .

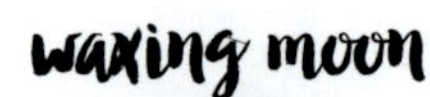

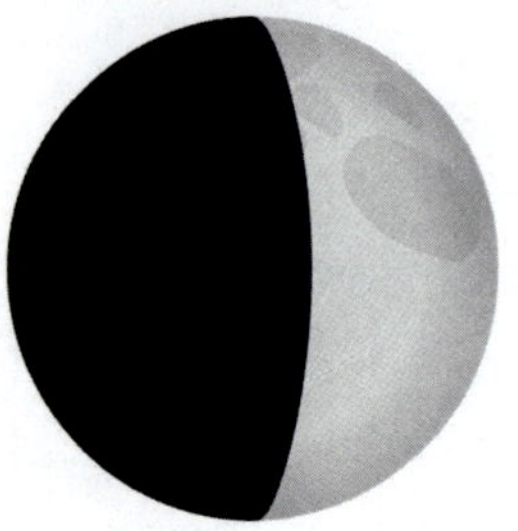

A TIME FOR ACTION. I WILL . . .

full moon

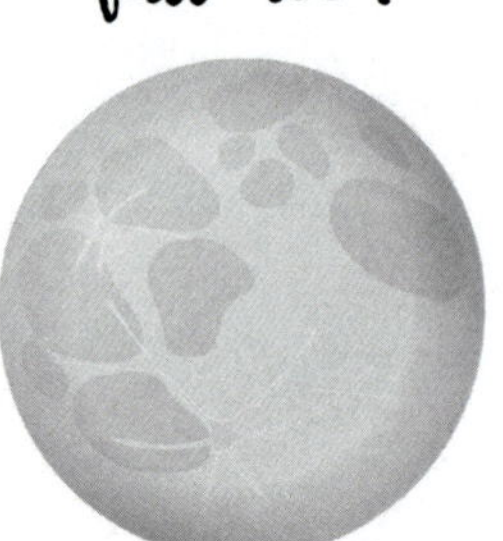

A TIME FOR HARVEST AND CLOSURE.
I RELEASE . . .

waning moon

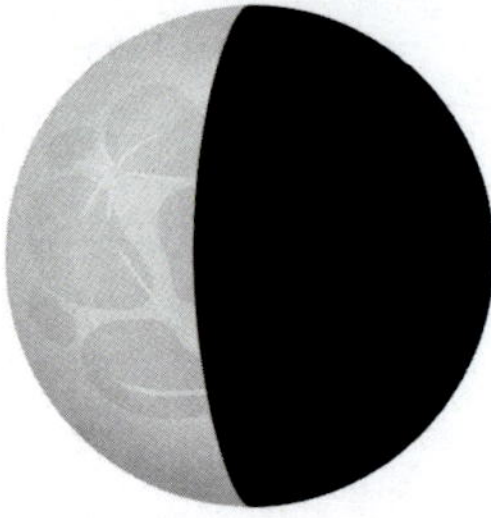

A TIME FOR SOFTENING. I FEEL . . .

monthly planner

MONTH: ____________________ INTENTION: ____________________

SUNDAY	MONDAY	TUESDAY	WEDNESDAY	THURSDAY	FRIDAY	SATURDAY

MONTHLY TRANQUILITY TOOLS

- ❍ CRAFT MONTH'S DREAMS
- ❍ REVIEW BUDGET
- ❍ CREATE SOMETHING
- ❍ READ TWO BOOKS
- ❍ VOLUNTEER
- ❍ MANI/PEDI
- ❍ ENTERTAIN
- ❍ MASSAGE

INTENTION:

weekly checklist

- PLAN WEEK'S MITS
- SOAK IN THE TUB
- TAKE A DIGITAL DAY OFF
- CLEAR CLUTTER
- PEN A LOVE NOTE
- BUY/PICK FRESH FLOWERS
- TAKE AN ARTIST DATE
- SAVOR A GREEN JUICE
- ______

MITS

- ______
- ______
- ______
- ______
- ______

wellness planning

M ______
T ______
W ______
TH ______
F ______
S ______
S ______

GRATITUDE:

MONDAY ______

7 ______
8 ______
9 ______
10 ______
11 ______
12 ______
1 ______
2 ______
3 ______
4 ______
5 ______
6 ______
7 ______
8 ______
9 ______

daily checklist

- MORNING RITUAL
- DAILY DRESS-UP
- MINDFUL MOVEMENT
- EAT YOUR VEGGIES
- JOURNAL
- GOAL REVIEW
- GRATITUDE
- EVENING RITUAL
- ______

TUESDAY ______

7 ______
8 ______
9 ______
10 ______
11 ______
12 ______
1 ______
2 ______
3 ______
4 ______
5 ______
6 ______
7 ______
8 ______
9 ______

daily checklist

- MORNING RITUAL
- DAILY DRESS-UP
- MINDFUL MOVEMENT
- EAT YOUR VEGGIES
- JOURNAL
- GOAL REVIEW
- GRATITUDE
- EVENING RITUAL
- ______

WEDNESDAY ______

7 ______
8 ______
9 ______
10 ______
11 ______
12 ______
1 ______
2 ______
3 ______
4 ______
5 ______
6 ______
7 ______
8 ______
9 ______

daily checklist

- MORNING RITUAL
- DAILY DRESS-UP
- MINDFUL MOVEMENT
- EAT YOUR VEGGIES
- JOURNAL
- GOAL REVIEW
- GRATITUDE
- EVENING RITUAL
- ______

THURSDAY ______

7 ______
8 ______
9 ______
10 ______
11 ______
12 ______
1 ______
2 ______
3 ______
4 ______
5 ______
6 ______
7 ______
8 ______
9 ______

daily checklist

- MORNING RITUAL
- DAILY DRESS-UP
- MINDFUL MOVEMENT
- EAT YOUR VEGGIES
- JOURNAL
- GOAL REVIEW
- GRATITUDE
- EVENING RITUAL

FRIDAY ______

7 ______
8 ______
9 ______
10 ______
11 ______
12 ______
1 ______
2 ______
3 ______
4 ______
5 ______
6 ______
7 ______
8 ______
9 ______

daily checklist

- MORNING RITUAL
- DAILY DRESS-UP
- MINDFUL MOVEMENT
- EAT YOUR VEGGIES
- JOURNAL
- GOAL REVIEW
- GRATITUDE
- EVENING RITUAL

SATURDAY ______

7 ______
8 ______
9 ______
10 ______
11 ______
12 ______
1 ______
2 ______
3 ______
4 ______
5 ______
6 ______
7 ______
8 ______
9 ______

daily checklist

- MORNING RITUAL
- DAILY DRESS-UP
- MINDFUL MOVEMENT
- EAT YOUR VEGGIES
- JOURNAL
- GOAL REVIEW
- GRATITUDE
- EVENING RITUAL

SUNDAY ______

7 ______
8 ______
9 ______
10 ______
11 ______
12 ______
1 ______
2 ______
3 ______
4 ______
5 ______
6 ______
7 ______
8 ______
9 ______

daily checklist

- MORNING RITUAL
- DAILY DRESS-UP
- MINDFUL MOVEMENT
- EAT YOUR VEGGIES
- JOURNAL
- GOAL REVIEW
- GRATITUDE
- EVENING RITUAL

INTENTION:

weekly checklist

- PLAN WEEK'S MITS
- SOAK IN THE TUB
- TAKE A DIGITAL DAY OFF
- CLEAR CLUTTER
- PEN A LOVE NOTE
- BUY/PICK FRESH FLOWERS
- TAKE AN ARTIST DATE
- SAVOR A GREEN JUICE
- ____________________

MITs

- ____________________
- ____________________
- ____________________
- ____________________
- ____________________

wellness planning

M ____________________
T ____________________
W ____________________
TH ____________________
F ____________________
S ____________________
S ____________________

GRATITUDE:

MONDAY ____________________

7 ____
8 ____
9 ____
10 ____
11 ____
12 ____
1 ____
2 ____
3 ____
4 ____
5 ____
6 ____
7 ____
8 ____
9 ____

daily checklist

- MORNING RITUAL
- DAILY DRESS-UP
- MINDFUL MOVEMENT
- EAT YOUR VEGGIES
- JOURNAL
- GOAL REVIEW
- GRATITUDE
- EVENING RITUAL
- ____________________

TUESDAY ____________________

7 ____
8 ____
9 ____
10 ____
11 ____
12 ____
1 ____
2 ____
3 ____
4 ____
5 ____
6 ____
7 ____
8 ____
9 ____

daily checklist

- MORNING RITUAL
- DAILY DRESS-UP
- MINDFUL MOVEMENT
- EAT YOUR VEGGIES
- JOURNAL
- GOAL REVIEW
- GRATITUDE
- EVENING RITUAL
- ____________________

WEDNESDAY ____________________

7 ____
8 ____
9 ____
10 ____
11 ____
12 ____
1 ____
2 ____
3 ____
4 ____
5 ____
6 ____
7 ____
8 ____
9 ____

daily checklist

- MORNING RITUAL
- DAILY DRESS-UP
- MINDFUL MOVEMENT
- EAT YOUR VEGGIES
- JOURNAL
- GOAL REVIEW
- GRATITUDE
- EVENING RITUAL
- ____________________

THURSDAY

7
8
9
10
11
12
1
2
3
4
5
6
7
8
9

daily checklist

- MORNING RITUAL
- DAILY DRESS-UP
- MINDFUL MOVEMENT
- EAT YOUR VEGGIES
- JOURNAL
- GOAL REVIEW
- GRATITUDE
- EVENING RITUAL

FRIDAY

7
8
9
10
11
12
1
2
3
4
5
6
7
8
9

daily checklist

- MORNING RITUAL
- DAILY DRESS-UP
- MINDFUL MOVEMENT
- EAT YOUR VEGGIES
- JOURNAL
- GOAL REVIEW
- GRATITUDE
- EVENING RITUAL

SATURDAY

7
8
9
10
11
12
1
2
3
4
5
6
7
8
9

daily checklist

- MORNING RITUAL
- DAILY DRESS-UP
- MINDFUL MOVEMENT
- EAT YOUR VEGGIES
- JOURNAL
- GOAL REVIEW
- GRATITUDE
- EVENING RITUAL

SUNDAY

7
8
9
10
11
12
1
2
3
4
5
6
7
8
9

daily checklist

- MORNING RITUAL
- DAILY DRESS-UP
- MINDFUL MOVEMENT
- EAT YOUR VEGGIES
- JOURNAL
- GOAL REVIEW
- GRATITUDE
- EVENING RITUAL

INTENTION:

weekly checklist

- PLAN WEEK'S MITS
- SOAK IN THE TUB
- TAKE A DIGITAL DAY OFF
- CLEAR CLUTTER
- PEN A LOVE NOTE
- BUY/PICK FRESH FLOWERS
- TAKE AN ARTIST DATE
- SAVOR A GREEN JUICE
- ______

MITs

- ______
- ______
- ______
- ______
- ______

wellness planning

M ______
T ______
W ______
TH ______
F ______
S ______
S ______

GRATITUDE:

MONDAY ______

7 ______
8 ______
9 ______
10 ______
11 ______
12 ______
1 ______
2 ______
3 ______
4 ______
5 ______
6 ______
7 ______
8 ______
9 ______

daily checklist

- MORNING RITUAL
- DAILY DRESS-UP
- MINDFUL MOVEMENT
- EAT YOUR VEGGIES
- JOURNAL
- GOAL REVIEW
- GRATITUDE
- EVENING RITUAL
- ______

TUESDAY ______

7 ______
8 ______
9 ______
10 ______
11 ______
12 ______
1 ______
2 ______
3 ______
4 ______
5 ______
6 ______
7 ______
8 ______
9 ______

daily checklist

- MORNING RITUAL
- DAILY DRESS-UP
- MINDFUL MOVEMENT
- EAT YOUR VEGGIES
- JOURNAL
- GOAL REVIEW
- GRATITUDE
- EVENING RITUAL
- ______

WEDNESDAY ______

7 ______
8 ______
9 ______
10 ______
11 ______
12 ______
1 ______
2 ______
3 ______
4 ______
5 ______
6 ______
7 ______
8 ______
9 ______

daily checklist

- MORNING RITUAL
- DAILY DRESS-UP
- MINDFUL MOVEMENT
- EAT YOUR VEGGIES
- JOURNAL
- GOAL REVIEW
- GRATITUDE
- EVENING RITUAL
- ______

THURSDAY

7
8
9
10
11
12
1
2
3
4
5
6
7
8
9

daily checklist

- MORNING RITUAL
- DAILY DRESS-UP
- MINDFUL MOVEMENT
- EAT YOUR VEGGIES
- JOURNAL
- GOAL REVIEW
- GRATITUDE
- EVENING RITUAL

FRIDAY

7
8
9
10
11
12
1
2
3
4
5
6
7
8
9

daily checklist

- MORNING RITUAL
- DAILY DRESS-UP
- MINDFUL MOVEMENT
- EAT YOUR VEGGIES
- JOURNAL
- GOAL REVIEW
- GRATITUDE
- EVENING RITUAL

SATURDAY

7
8
9
10
11
12
1
2
3
4
5
6
7
8
9

daily checklist

- MORNING RITUAL
- DAILY DRESS-UP
- MINDFUL MOVEMENT
- EAT YOUR VEGGIES
- JOURNAL
- GOAL REVIEW
- GRATITUDE
- EVENING RITUAL

SUNDAY

7
8
9
10
11
12
1
2
3
4
5
6
7
8
9

daily checklist

- MORNING RITUAL
- DAILY DRESS-UP
- MINDFUL MOVEMENT
- EAT YOUR VEGGIES
- JOURNAL
- GOAL REVIEW
- GRATITUDE
- EVENING RITUAL

INTENTION:

weekly checklist

- ❍ PLAN WEEK'S MITS
- ❍ SOAK IN THE TUB
- ❍ TAKE A DIGITAL DAY OFF
- ❍ CLEAR CLUTTER
- ❍ PEN A LOVE NOTE
- ❍ BUY/PICK FRESH FLOWERS
- ❍ TAKE AN ARTIST DATE
- ❍ SAVOR A GREEN JUICE
- ❍ ____________

MITs

- ❍ ____________
- ❍ ____________
- ❍ ____________
- ❍ ____________
- ❍ ____________

wellness planning

M ____________
T ____________
W ____________
TH ____________
F ____________
S ____________
S ____________

GRATITUDE:

MONDAY ____________

7 ____________
8 ____________
9 ____________
10 ____________
11 ____________
12 ____________
1 ____________
2 ____________
3 ____________
4 ____________
5 ____________
6 ____________
7 ____________
8 ____________
9 ____________

- ❍ ____________
- ❍ ____________
- ❍ ____________
- ❍ ____________
- ❍ ____________
- ❍ ____________
- ❍ ____________
- ❍ ____________
- ❍ ____________
- ❍ ____________

- ❍ ____________
- ❍ ____________
- ❍ ____________
- ❍ ____________
- ❍ ____________
- ❍ ____________

daily checklist

- ❍ MORNING RITUAL
- ❍ DAILY DRESS-UP
- ❍ MINDFUL MOVEMENT
- ❍ EAT YOUR VEGGIES
- ❍ JOURNAL
- ❍ GOAL REVIEW
- ❍ GRATITUDE
- ❍ EVENING RITUAL
- ❍ ____________

TUESDAY ____________

7 ____________
8 ____________
9 ____________
10 ____________
11 ____________
12 ____________
1 ____________
2 ____________
3 ____________
4 ____________
5 ____________
6 ____________
7 ____________
8 ____________
9 ____________

- ❍ ____________
- ❍ ____________
- ❍ ____________
- ❍ ____________
- ❍ ____________
- ❍ ____________
- ❍ ____________
- ❍ ____________
- ❍ ____________
- ❍ ____________

- ❍ ____________
- ❍ ____________
- ❍ ____________
- ❍ ____________
- ❍ ____________
- ❍ ____________

daily checklist

- ❍ MORNING RITUAL
- ❍ DAILY DRESS-UP
- ❍ MINDFUL MOVEMENT
- ❍ EAT YOUR VEGGIES
- ❍ JOURNAL
- ❍ GOAL REVIEW
- ❍ GRATITUDE
- ❍ EVENING RITUAL
- ❍ ____________

WEDNESDAY ____________

7 ____________
8 ____________
9 ____________
10 ____________
11 ____________
12 ____________
1 ____________
2 ____________
3 ____________
4 ____________
5 ____________
6 ____________
7 ____________
8 ____________
9 ____________

- ❍ ____________
- ❍ ____________
- ❍ ____________
- ❍ ____________
- ❍ ____________
- ❍ ____________
- ❍ ____________
- ❍ ____________
- ❍ ____________
- ❍ ____________

- ❍ ____________
- ❍ ____________
- ❍ ____________
- ❍ ____________
- ❍ ____________
- ❍ ____________

daily checklist

- ❍ MORNING RITUAL
- ❍ DAILY DRESS-UP
- ❍ MINDFUL MOVEMENT
- ❍ EAT YOUR VEGGIES
- ❍ JOURNAL
- ❍ GOAL REVIEW
- ❍ GRATITUDE
- ❍ EVENING RITUAL
- ❍ ____________

THURSDAY ____

7 ____
8 ____
9 ____
10 ____
11 ____
12 ____
1 ____
2 ____
3 ____
4 ____
5 ____
6 ____
7 ____
8 ____
9 ____

daily checklist

- MORNING RITUAL
- DAILY DRESS-UP
- MINDFUL MOVEMENT
- EAT YOUR VEGGIES
- JOURNAL
- GOAL REVIEW
- GRATITUDE
- EVENING RITUAL

FRIDAY ____

7 ____
8 ____
9 ____
10 ____
11 ____
12 ____
1 ____
2 ____
3 ____
4 ____
5 ____
6 ____
7 ____
8 ____
9 ____

daily checklist

- MORNING RITUAL
- DAILY DRESS-UP
- MINDFUL MOVEMENT
- EAT YOUR VEGGIES
- JOURNAL
- GOAL REVIEW
- GRATITUDE
- EVENING RITUAL

SATURDAY ____

7 ____
8 ____
9 ____
10 ____
11 ____
12 ____
1 ____
2 ____
3 ____
4 ____
5 ____
6 ____
7 ____
8 ____
9 ____

daily checklist

- MORNING RITUAL
- DAILY DRESS-UP
- MINDFUL MOVEMENT
- EAT YOUR VEGGIES
- JOURNAL
- GOAL REVIEW
- GRATITUDE
- EVENING RITUAL

SUNDAY ____

7 ____
8 ____
9 ____
10 ____
11 ____
12 ____
1 ____
2 ____
3 ____
4 ____
5 ____
6 ____
7 ____
8 ____
9 ____

daily checklist

- MORNING RITUAL
- DAILY DRESS-UP
- MINDFUL MOVEMENT
- EAT YOUR VEGGIES
- JOURNAL
- GOAL REVIEW
- GRATITUDE
- EVENING RITUAL

INTENTION:

weekly checklist

- PLAN WEEK'S MITS
- SOAK IN THE TUB
- TAKE A DIGITAL DAY OFF
- CLEAR CLUTTER
- PEN A LOVE NOTE
- BUY/PICK FRESH FLOWERS
- TAKE AN ARTIST DATE
- SAVOR A GREEN JUICE
- ________

MITS

wellness planning

M
T
W
TH
F
S
S

GRATITUDE:

MONDAY ________

7
8
9
10
11
12
1
2
3
4
5
6
7
8
9

daily checklist

- MORNING RITUAL
- DAILY DRESS-UP
- MINDFUL MOVEMENT
- EAT YOUR VEGGIES
- JOURNAL
- GOAL REVIEW
- GRATITUDE
- EVENING RITUAL
- ________

TUESDAY ________

7
8
9
10
11
12
1
2
3
4
5
6
7
8
9

daily checklist

- MORNING RITUAL
- DAILY DRESS-UP
- MINDFUL MOVEMENT
- EAT YOUR VEGGIES
- JOURNAL
- GOAL REVIEW
- GRATITUDE
- EVENING RITUAL
- ________

WEDNESDAY ________

7
8
9
10
11
12
1
2
3
4
5
6
7
8
9

daily checklist

- MORNING RITUAL
- DAILY DRESS-UP
- MINDFUL MOVEMENT
- EAT YOUR VEGGIES
- JOURNAL
- GOAL REVIEW
- GRATITUDE
- EVENING RITUAL
- ________

THURSDAY

7
8
9
10
11
12
1
2
3
4
5
6
7
8
9

daily checklist

- MORNING RITUAL
- DAILY DRESS-UP
- MINDFUL MOVEMENT
- EAT YOUR VEGGIES
- JOURNAL
- GOAL REVIEW
- GRATITUDE
- EVENING RITUAL

FRIDAY

7
8
9
10
11
12
1
2
3
4
5
6
7
8
9

daily checklist

- MORNING RITUAL
- DAILY DRESS-UP
- MINDFUL MOVEMENT
- EAT YOUR VEGGIES
- JOURNAL
- GOAL REVIEW
- GRATITUDE
- EVENING RITUAL

SATURDAY

7
8
9
10
11
12
1
2
3
4
5
6
7
8
9

daily checklist

- MORNING RITUAL
- DAILY DRESS-UP
- MINDFUL MOVEMENT
- EAT YOUR VEGGIES
- JOURNAL
- GOAL REVIEW
- GRATITUDE
- EVENING RITUAL

SUNDAY

7
8
9
10
11
12
1
2
3
4
5
6
7
8
9

daily checklist

- MORNING RITUAL
- DAILY DRESS-UP
- MINDFUL MOVEMENT
- EAT YOUR VEGGIES
- JOURNAL
- GOAL REVIEW
- GRATITUDE
- EVENING RITUAL

year's review

a letter to my future self

ATTACH AN ENVELOPE WITH YOUR LETTER FROM P. 20 TO REVIEW AT YEAR'S END.

inspiration pages

USE THESE PAGES TO DOODLE, LIST, COLLAGE, OR WRITE WHAT'S INSPIRING YOU.

love note

Thank you for your gracious support of this Daybook. *This planning system was crafted with lots of love, and I hope it's been a source of inspiration for designing and organizing your days with intention.*

To connect with like-hearted planners, stop by our private Facebook group and introduce yourself. Watch for planning resources and download your bonuses over on my website. Receive ongoing inspiration on everyday tranquility via the *Tranquility du Jour* blog, podcast, and newsletter.

Your purchase helps support petite female-owned businesses, pig sanctuaries and pug rescues through Pigs & Pugs Project, and the planting of 500 trees. What we do has a compassionate ripple effect, so thank you again! You are beautiful.

#TDJDAYBOOK

KIMBERLYWILSON.COM

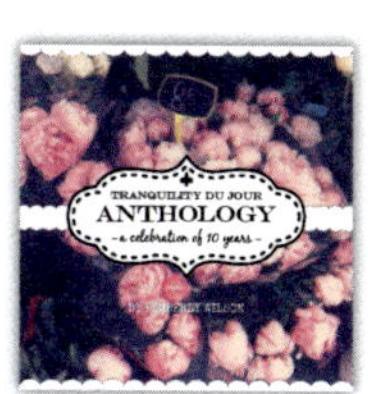

LET YOUR
LIGHT SHINE.

BRIGHTLY
AND
BOLDLY.

Made in the USA
Middletown, DE
04 June 2019